Transforming information literacy instruction using learner-centered teaching

Joan R. Kaplowitz

facet publishing

Published by Facet Publishing
7 Ridgmount Street, London WC1E 7AE
www.facetpublishing.co.uk

Facet Publishing is wholly owned by CILIP: the Chartered Institute of
Library and Information Professionals.

First published in the USA by
Neal-Schuman Publishers, Inc., 2012.
This UK edition 2012.

British Library Cataloguing in Publication Data
A catalogue record for this book is available
from the British Library.

ISBN 978-1-85604-835-4

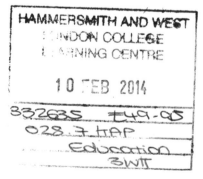
Printed and bound in the United States of America.

Dedication

I would like to dedicate this book to all my friends and colleagues who patiently listened to me go on and on about my learner-centered teaching notions and who urged me to write this book so that I could share my thoughts with a broader audience as well as to all my students and workshop participants who helped me field-test my ideas about how to apply learner-centered teaching to information literacy instruction.

This book is also dedicated to Hillary and Greg, who always seem to think Mom can do anything she sets her mind to, and to all my feline friends—past and present—who accompanied me on this writing journey. Barnabus, Josette, and Zen—I miss you every day. Aidan, Kieran, and Ronan—thanks for taking over as my furry cheering (purring?) section.

And finally, I dedicate this book to all my previous readers. I hope this latest one gives you a new perspective on information literacy instruction and that you find it useful in your own practice.

Contents

v

Part III: Applying Learner-Centered Teaching in Practice

List of Illustrations

TABLES

FIGURES

Foreword

Let the main object of this, our didactic, be as follows: To seek and to find a method of instruction, by which teachers may teach less, but learners may learn more.

—Comenius, *The Great Didactic*, 1649

Transforming Information Literacy Instruction Using Learner-Centered Teaching challenges readers to consider how they can commit to Comenius's philosophy. Identifying three central principles of learner-centered teaching (LCT) in the preface as "collaboration, participation, and [a] shared responsibility for learning between teachers and learners and among learners themselves," Joan Kaplowitz presents logical ways in which librarians can work to transform their teaching. The book provides readers with critical information on LCT theory, examples of strategies that can be applied in different modes of instruction, and case study vignettes authored by practitioners that exemplify LCT best practices.

Kaplowitz's *Transforming Information Literacy Instruction Using Learner-Centered Teaching* provides a much-needed voice of reason at a critical point in time for information literacy instruction (ILI) programming and libraries. Attention is shifting away from a focus on teaching methods and the value of information literacy programming within librarianship. Many within library and higher education administrative circles are more eager to focus on evolving technologies (e-book readers, Web 2.0, discovery systems, and mobile devices) at the expense of also nurturing ILI programming. Understandably, libraries need to position themselves for maximum relevancy in the coming decades. However, within higher education the status of the "librarian as teacher" has never faced more critical challenges. Librarians are now not only teaching within traditional face-to-face environments but also grappling with how to offer new and effective instructional approaches within the burgeoning frontiers of online, hybrid, and embedded modes of instruction.

We face a clear and present danger in devaluing the need for the professional development and pedagogical improvement of the librarian as teacher at a time when we must progress more than ever to remain vital in the emerging digital instructional landscape. The need for LCT approaches is a critical one. How we reinvigorate our collective instructional mission in the remainder of this decade will greatly impact the future of libraries and the value placed on librarians.

This book dynamically motivates and empowers instruction librarians to embrace an LCT perspective that provides a pivotal foundation for the improvement of both traditional face-to-face instruction and the teaching that takes place via embedded, online, or hybrid learning environments. Instruction librarians will not remain central to campus life if we are not able to effectively move away from a traditional lecture style that relies on the "sage on the stage" approach. While this has been mentioned before within the library literature, this book is the only monograph I know of to take such a specialized focus on improving ILI and generalized teaching through an LCT perspective. Chapter 8 of this book begins with a quote from Winston Churchill—"Things do not get better by being left alone"—and in my view this is a central message of this book that readers need to take to heart. ILI instruction will not improve—no form of instruction will—if there is not change and particularly change that puts the learner/student at the center of attention. Our profession desperately needs change agents to transform our approach to library instruction, and, not surprisingly, Joan Kaplowitz has once again emerged as a trusted voice with valuable information to share with peers.

When it comes to studying critical connections between information literacy instruction and learning theory within the field of librarianship, there are few who I trust more than Joan Kaplowitz. I was first introduced to the transformative nature of Joan's teaching style during my graduate school training at the University of California, Los Angeles, in 1998. Joan was a guest lecturer in my information literacy course that was taught by her colleague and well-known coauthor, Esther Grassian. Joan has a Doctorate in Psychology, and, after listening to her for just an hour, I knew that I was extremely fortunate to be her student. Not only could she adroitly explain why learning theory mattered when trying to engage students, she also wanted to know how we, her students for just one day, liked to learn and why we wanted to teach. It was clear that Joan was open to being a mentor and colleague to anyone who was interested enough to join her in her lifetime journey of working hard to become a better teacher. Joan has gone on to reach so many through her writings, presentations, and role as faculty member in the Association of College and Research Libraries Immersion Program. She is a dynamic teacher who takes risks and embraces change. Anyone who has ever heard Joan speak knows that she believes that it is imperative that one "share the responsibility of learning with your learners." She definitely continues to practice what she preaches—and this book is yet another example of why so many within our field continue to view Joan as a mentor and leader.

Lynn D. Lampert
Chair, Reference and Instructional Services
Coordinator of Information Literacy
California State University, Northridge

Preface

How many times have you taught what you thought was a very successful information literacy instruction (ILI) session filled with relevant examples, well-constructed exercises, and all the information that your learners should need to address their information needs, only to encounter these learners at a later date and find that they seem to have gained next to nothing from your time with them? If you are anything like me, this prompts you to return to the drawing board and begin to tinker and tweak your materials in the seemingly unending quest to improve your endeavors.

After many years of searching for a better way of working with my learners, I came upon the concept of learner-centered teaching (LCT), which I immediately felt had enormous potential for those of us who are involved in ILI. *Transforming Information Literacy Instruction Using Learner-Centered Teaching* shares my discoveries in this area with you.

The pages that follow cover the evolution of LCT, explore its historical roots, and present the research evidence from education, psychology, and the neurosciences that supports the principles associated with it. Building on that foundation, the book then goes on to show how LCT can be applied to ILI, offers the reasons why doing so can improve the effectiveness of ILI endeavors, and provides examples of how ILI librarians can transform their practice.

The book is divided into four parts. Part I, "Finding Out about Learner-Centered Teaching," offers background information about LCT. Chapter 1 covers what is meant by the term LCT and introduces the three principles of this philosophy—Collaboration, Participation, and shared Responsibility for learning among all participants, teachers, and learners alike, which is referred to in the book as the CPR perspective for teaching. Chapter 2 looks at the characteristics of LCT and discusses how being learner-centered helps ILI librarians listen to, engage, and inspire their learners. Chapter 3 examines the historical and research-based roots of LCT and offers further support for the effectiveness of this teaching philosophy.

The chapters in Part II, "Planning for Learner-Centered Teaching," look at teaching and assessment methodology through the LCT lens. Chapter 4 examines a variety of instructional methods from an LCT perspective and includes practical examples of how to incorporate these methods into ILI. Chapter 5 deals with assessment issues and offers suggestions to help ILI librarians ensure that the methods used to measure the effectiveness of their instructional endeavors also have a learner-centered point of view.

Part III, "Applying Learner-Centered Teaching in Practice," offers a practical look at how LCT principles can be implemented in face-to-face (Chapter 6) and online (Chapter 7) formats. Both chapters include the advantages and drawbacks of using each mode of delivery and show how applying LCT principles can maximize the advantages while compensating for the drawbacks of each type of instructional format. Chapter 8 discusses how to combine the two formats using a blended or hybrid delivery mode and describes a case study in which an entirely face-to-face course was transformed into one that uses a blended format. The good, the not so good, and the (sometimes) ugly aspects of the transformational process are addressed as well as lessons learned and plans for the future. The section ends with Chapter 9 wherein real-life librarians from all types of libraries share their experiences and LCT ideas in a series of vignettes.

Finally, Part IV, "Summing It All Up," offers suggestions for how to take everything covered in the book and begin to use it to transform the reader's own ILI practice. Chapter 10 sums up all the preceding material as well as discusses how the reader can begin to transition into using a more LCT approach. Some thoughts on the future and the continued impact of technology are also included in this final chapter.

Transforming Information Literacy Instruction Using Learner-Centered Teaching is dedicated to the idea that the principles of LCT can be applied in all types of ILI and in any kind of library (academic, public, school, and special). It is intended to be useful to anyone interested in ILI, whether they are students in a formal graduate library science program or working professionals who wish to improve and/or update their ILI teaching skills.

All good teachers know that learning to teach is a journey and not a destination. We are all in search of a "better way" to engage and inspire our learners. And we are never completely satisfied with our instructional endeavors—always suspecting that a better way to go is lurking just out of our reach. If we are very lucky, we catch a glimpse of that "better way" during a conference, while attending a workshop, as we watch our colleagues teach, and as we scan relevant literature. Sometimes one of these experiences can completely transform us. I had just such an experience when I came upon Maryellen Weimer's 2003 *Change* article on what she referred to as "learner-centered teaching." It was one of those "aha" moments when suddenly everything made complete sense. I felt that this was the approach I had been moving toward for many years but could not completely articulate on my own. Ms. Weimer's words (and others like her) inspired me to explore what LCT really meant and to see in what ways these ideas could be applied to ILI.

I learned that when moving to an LCT approach the most important step to take is the first one—that of turning the focus around and thinking about everything from the learner's perspective. Learner-centered teachers do not talk about what they are going to teach. They address what their learners will be learning. A learner-centered teacher's job is to create opportunities for people to learn. Learner-centered teachers are no longer desperate to "cover" as many topics as they can during their instructional sessions. Instead their task becomes addressing material in ways that engage learners, allow learners to apply what they learned, and help learners retain that material long after they leave us. Learner-centered teachers do not lead, they facilitate. They do not talk at learners, but rather with them. Learner-centered teachers guide learners as they find solutions to their specific information needs.

The principles of LCT fit in perfectly with the goals of ILI—especially in terms of creating lifelong learners. It is my hope that you will find the discussion of LCT included in this book as inspiring as I did and may even have your own "aha" experience as you read how LCT can favorably impact ILI practice. Whether you decide to completely transform your instructional approach, or prefer to start a bit smaller by just incorporating some LCT ideas into your current endeavors, I hope that *Transforming Information Literacy Instruction Using Learner-Centered Teaching* offers you the support, encouragement, and confidence to continue on your journey to becoming more effective information literacy instructors.

Acknowledgments

Lots of people helped me birth this book. First, I would like to thank the 16 information literacy instruction professionals who so generously and enthusiastically shared their own learner-centered teaching stories in Chapter 9. Their work continues to inspire me and reinforces my belief that learner-centered teaching really works.

Thanks to my daughter and collaborator Hillary, who coauthored two of the chapters in this book, and whose expertise and good common sense kept me on track and relatively sane as I struggled to get my ideas on paper.

Writing is a solitary and often lonely process. So I greatly appreciated the support and assistance I received from Sandy Wood, editor extraordinaire. Sandy was my lifeline during the writing, editing, and revision process and was unbelievably prompt in all her replies to my frantic and sometimes panicked messages. I never felt isolated and alone knowing that Sandy was out there, just an e-mail away.

And finally, thanks to Charles Harmon, Neal-Schuman's Vice President and Director of Publishing, who not only thought yet another book on information literacy instruction was a good idea but felt it would be an exciting new prospect as well.

Part I

Finding Out about Learner-Centered Teaching

Chapter 1

What Is Learner-Centered Teaching?

A journey of a thousand miles begins with a single step.

—Confucius

THE ADVENTURE BEGINS

Congratulations! By picking up this book you are exhibiting the two most important traits for becoming a learner-centered teacher—the willingness to change and a dedication to your continued growth as a teacher. You are about to embark on what I hope will be an exciting and inspirational journey—one that will cause you to view your information literacy instruction (ILI) endeavors in a new and energized way.

My journey began with an epiphany. I had been in the ILI business for many years and was doing research for a book I was writing when I came upon an article titled "Focus on Learning. Transform Teaching" (Weimer, 2003). This article changed my life and caused me to take a long, hard look at my own teaching practices. As I read the article, I felt like I was coming home. Not only did I recognize the ideas the author was promoting as things I did in my own practice, but her words seemed to reflect exactly how I felt about teaching and learning.

It seemed to me that the ideas behind learner-centered teaching (LCT) addressed a growing frustration I had developed with ILI in general and my own teaching endeavors in particular. No matter how well I prepared my sessions, how well-organized and interesting I tried to make them, my learners never really seemed "to get" what I told them. I filled my classes with great examples and useful and appropriate handouts with tips, techniques, and strategies that certainly "covered" everything a learner would need to know to successfully complete the immediate task at hand and to transfer that knowledge to further research endeavors. Yet when I encountered these very same learners (who had seemed so attentive in my classes) at the reference desk, via e-mail questions, during chat sessions, consultations, or office hours, they would ask questions that indicated

3

they had not learned what I had been trying to teach. Then I read the Weimer article and had one of those great "aha" moments. The problem was that I was telling them what I thought they needed to know rather than letting them experience it for themselves. I had fallen into the "tyranny of coverage" trap and had committed the ultimate "teaching hubris" mistake—if I tell them, they will know. As it turns out, this is not really the case. LCT proposes that learning happens when we talk with our learners, not just at them, and when we invite our learners to join us in an active exploration of the ideas and concepts we wish them to attain.

The Weimer article awakened a hunger in me to find out more about these exciting ideas. I wanted to learn about it so that I could transform my own practice, become a more effective teacher, and ground my practice in the educational and psychological theory and research that supports LCT. This book is a result of my explorations up to this point.

WHAT'S SO SPECIAL ABOUT LCT?

So—what exactly is LCT, and how does it differ from other teaching approaches? Steeped in years of educational and psychological research on how people learn, LCT offers us a new way of looking at our learners, our methods, and ourselves as teachers. It invites us to transform our interactions with our learners so that we are truly helping them to become self-sufficient, self-directed, effective, self-confident lifelong learners. LCT is not a set of rules, techniques, or methods. It is not a list of finite characteristics on a checklist. LCT is a set of beliefs—a way of thinking about teaching itself with special emphasis on how we interact with our learners. It requires an attitude adjustment in the way we view our learners. Rather than a "them versus us" approach, we come to regard our learners as partners in the educational enterprise. In the LCT environment learners and teachers are all in it together.

The principles of LCT offer guidelines for our practice that help us listen to, engage, and inspire our learners. These guidelines encourage us to get to know our learners and their specific learning needs and to be flexible, adaptable, and respectful in our interactions with them. Learner-centered teachers create a warm, supportive, engaging, and motivating learning environment that encourages people to become confident, skillful, and self-directed lifelong learners (Grassian and Kaplowitz, 2009).

LCT is a lens through which we can view all our teaching practices—from planning and development to assessment. It is reflected in the vocabulary we use when describing our instructional efforts. See Table 1.1 to learn more about the language of LCT.

Learner-centered teachers do not talk about what they are going to teach. They discuss what they want their learners to learn. Learner-centered teachers

Table 1.1. Talking the Talk: The Language of LCT	
Traditional Teachers Use Words Like	**LC Teachers Use Words Like**
Teaching	Learning
Cover	Investigate/explore
Inform	Facilitate
Present/deliver	Experience/interact
Facts	Ideas
Memorize	Relate/understand
Replicate	Construct/apply
Compete	Cooperate/collaborate
Grades	Improvement

do not present material. They offer learners ways to interact with that material. Learner-centered teachers do not accept the tyranny of coverage. They adhere to the "less is more" tenet of teaching and include only what can be reasonably addressed in the time frame available. Learner-centered teachers do not offer prepackaged ideas and solutions. They offer learners the freedom to construct their own knowledge and take ownership of the information they are acquiring. In short, learner-centered teachers agree with William Butler Yeats' view of education.

> Education is not filling a bucket, but lighting a fire.
>
> —William Butler Yeats

LEARNER-CENTERED TEACHING: CPR FOR YOUR PRACTICE

On the surface, LCT with its emphasis on learner involvement seems to be just another active learning methodology. However, to create a truly learner-centered educational experience goes beyond merely including exercises and activities in our instructional offerings. Although incorporating active learning techniques is a big part of LCT, it is not the whole picture. LCT cannot be described simply in terms of methods used. Rather, it is a teaching philosophy that permeates every aspect of instruction. The three principles of this philosophy are **C**ollaboration, **P**articipation, and shared **R**esponsibility for learning among all participants— teachers and learners alike. Let's call this the **CPR** perspective. To move to LCT requires reexamining a course or class from this viewpoint—analyzing every instructional aspect (modes of delivery, types of exercises and assignments used, grading methods, and the overall structure of the instruction) with the goal of increasing the learners' role in the process. Learners must be given opportunities to take control of and have the responsibility for their own and their fellow learners' achievements through the use of collaborative projects, peer-to-peer teaching, and multiway discussions—between teacher and learners, and among learners themselves. They are expected to be active participants in the learning process and to collaborate with each other as they engage with the material. Teachers must, therefore, structure their classes and courses so that learners are given appropriate opportunities to collaborate, participate, and take responsibility—in other words, teach from the CPR perspective (Grassian and Kaplowitz, 2009; Kaplowitz, 2008). LCT inspires us to tap into our creativity as teachers in order to design authentic learning experiences that are relevant to our learners. LCT asks us to let go and let learning happen!

SUPPORT FOR LCT

LCT rests on a long and compelling history of theory and research. Explore the writings of educators and psychologists such as John Dewey, Lev Vygotsky, Abraham Maslow, Jerome Bruner, Jean Piaget, B.F. Skinner, Carl Rogers, and the like, and you will see elements of what is now called LCT (Eggen and Kauchak, 2010; Slavin, 2011). All three major psychological theories of learning seem to support the LCT approach (Grassian and Kaplowitz, 2009; Kaplowitz, 2008). The active participation or "doing" aspect appeals to behaviorists as does the immediate feedback and reinforcement opportunities that arise as teachers see and respond to learning as it is happening. Cognitive/constructivists applaud the fact that learners are expected to use what they are learning to help them build their own mental models and organize the material in a way that makes personal sense, thus enhancing the likelihood of retaining and retrieving the material whenever they might need it again. Humanists support the notions of learners taking personal responsibility for learning, the development of communities of learners, learners having some control over the learning process, the use of collaborative learning environments, the opportunities for a variety of voices to be heard, and the fact that learners are given the chance to work on issues and problems that have personal, real-world meaning. Humanists also like the self-efficacy aspects that seem built into the LCT approach, as learners see they are accomplishing something of value and are being given the chance to try their hands at applying important and useful skills, knowledge, and abilities. Constructivists and humanists alike support the "learning as a social experience" aspects of LCT practices (Bransford et al., 2006; Freilberg and Driscoll, 2005; Marshall, 1998; McCombs and Miller,

2007; Smart and Csapo, 2007). See Chapter 3 for a more detailed account of the theory and research behind LCT practices.

Support also comes from memory and retention research—most notably cognitive overload theory. Learning does not really happen until new material is transferred from short-term to long-term memory storage. Too much information leads to cognitive overload. New information cannot be absorbed, because the learner is still trying to move the previous information into long-term memory. It's like trying to pour water into an already full glass. No additional water can be added until some of it is moved into another receptacle. The activities that are so much a part of LCT not only provide learners with the opportunity to practice and apply what they have learned, but practice breaks also serve as a way to reduce cognitive overload. Stopping for an activity gives learners time to make the transfer from short- to long-term memory. Furthermore, getting to apply what they learned further solidifies the material in their long-term memory storage (Clark and Taylor, 1994; Grassian and Kaplowitz, 2010; Mayer and Moreno, 2003; Veldof, 2006).

The 1990s saw an increased interest in the LCT approach. The American Psychological Association (APA), under the leadership of its then president Barbara L. McCombs, undertook a project to develop a set of learner-centered principles that were grounded in theory-based research and could be applied by practitioners to their own teaching efforts. The goal of this project was to develop principles that would be of practical use to teachers in the field. The result was *Learner-Centered Psychological Principles: A Framework for School Reform and Redesign* (American Psychological Association Work Group of the Board of Educational Affairs, 1997). The *Principles,* much like the Association of College and Research Libraries' (ACRL) *Information Literacy Competency Standards for Higher Education* (ACRL, 2000), provide a basis for practice, but need to be interpreted and applied to teaching practices. The *Principles* do not recommend specific techniques. The 14 *Principles* in the document serve as a guideline for teaching. Think of them as a filter through which we view our teaching practices in order to transform the way we teach. The elements of these *Principles* and how they contributed to our understanding of LCT practices will be covered in Chapters 2 and 3.

SHIFTING THE BALANCE OF POWER

So, with all this support for the learner-centered approach to teaching, why don't we see more evidence of its influence in our education systems? The "talking head" lecture still dominates higher education (Saulnier et al., 2008). Even the K–12 environment, though more open to the ideas of active learning and learner involvement, still has not endorsed the idea completely. In part that is because LCT requires a shift of power in the classroom. It invites the learner into the process and gives individual learners more control over and responsibility for his or her own learning. Learning happens in a community setting in which everyone (learners and teachers alike) is expected to participate actively and to work together as they engage with the material in order to attain specific learning goals (Grassian and Kaplowitz, 2009; McCombs and Miller, 2007; Weimer, 2002).

The learner-centered approach transforms teaching from the banking model in which teachers deposit information into the waiting receptacles of the learners' brains (Freire, 2002; Nelken, 2009) to one where teachers facilitate and guide learners. Teachers must give up the role of "sage on the stage" to become the "guide on the side" (King, 1993). Teachers offer support and guidance by listening and responding to their learners' needs as learning progresses. LCT asks learners to do the work of learning, to become actively involved in the material to be learned, and to then create their own understanding of that material (Gagnon and Collay, 2001; Landry et al., 2008; Rovai, 2004). As such it shifts the balance of power from teacher to learner. Learners are seen as active partners who are as accountable as the teacher for the attainment of learning outcomes (Bain, 2004; Felder and Brent, 1996; Weimer, 2002).

This shift from "sage on the stage" to "guide on the side" can feel disconcerting to both teacher and learner alike. It is very comforting to prepare a lecture that contains everything we think the learner should know about a topic and then to just pour all that information into the learners' waiting ears and brains. We know that we have covered all the necessary material and can go home with a feeling of accomplishment. But although we may have "taught" the material, there is more and more evidence to support the idea that our learners have not in fact learned much of anything. But to abandon the implied control of the lecture method of teaching and move to the more open and free-form LCT approach seems overwhelming. Because much LCT depends on activities, group work, discussions, collaborative projects, and the like, the format of these types of educational environments is more fluid and less structured than the teacher-dependent presentation format in a lecture setting. This is both good news and bad news for the teacher. On the plus side, working with each group of learners will provide a unique experience. LCT is not regimented. Although the topic may be the same for each group with which we work, the ways in which each group interacts with the material will depend on who is in the group and what skills, knowledge, interests, and background each learner brings to the mix. In a very real way, attention to diversity is actually built into the LCT approach. With its focus on the needs and experiences of the individual learner, and its tendency to incorporate a mix of methods, LCT can appeal to learners with many different learning styles and to those who come from a wide variety of cultures, ethnic groups, lifestyles, and perspectives.

On the negative side is the idea that the teacher is no longer completely in control of the agenda and as a result may find there is insufficient time to cover all the planned-for material. However, the impression that the learner-centered teacher is giving up control of the situation is an erroneous one. For LCT to work, teachers need to be even more organized and systematic than ever. As learner-centered teachers, we first need to decide on the content to which we want our learners exposed and develop expected learning outcomes (ELOs) for this content. Then we have to create ways in which the learners will interact with this material. We must make decisions about how much can be accomplished in a given time frame. Does everything have to happen in the classroom itself, or can some of it happen before or after the session? If we are in a face-to-face (F2F) setting, we will need to monitor the time spent on each activity to make sure they are completed within the time allotted for them. We must act as a facilitator during discussions (both F2F and online) to ensure that everyone is being heard and that all viewpoints are being respected. And we must keep a close eye on activities and group work so that we can offer suggestions and support as needed. So, in fact, we have an even bigger role in controlling the flow of the instruction than we have in the traditional "teacher as presenter" lecture mode.

Those who are reluctant to go the LCT route also point to a conflict between needing to teach to certain standards and follow specific curriculum guidelines and the pressure of preparing their learners for standardized tests as reasons behind sticking to the tried and true traditional methods of teaching. However, those who have adopted LCT practices have shown that their learners do as well as and in some cases better than those who have been taught using traditional formats. That is because LCT is more closely aligned with the way people actually learn and so is a more effective way to reach our learners (Alexander and Murphy, 1998; Bransford et al., 2000, 2006; National Research Council, 2005; Nilson, 2003; Weinberger and McCombs, 2001). Learner-centered teachers believe that it is better to have their learners successfully acquire a small number of new ideas and skills than to have them overwhelmed and frustrated by a multitude of topics that are more than any one person can be expected to grasp during the instructional encounter.

Although LCT has proven to be more effective, engaging, motivating, and fun for learners, our own learners may be shocked by our request that they take a more active role in the instruction. Learners may even resent it a bit. After all, we are the experts who have all the answers. Why are we making them search for those answers when we could just tell them "the truth"? Don't be surprised to get some "push back" from learners as a result. It is helpful to explain the principles behind LCT before beginning instruction and to share the reasons behind why they are being asked to participate in a particular type of activity (Bain, 2004; Minstrell and Stimpson, 1996; Powell, 1988; Weimer, 2002).

Those of us who are involved in ILI have an even harder task, because we are often guests in other people's classrooms. If the person we are working with does not teach in a learner-centered fashion, his or her students will be even more surprised when we ask them to do something other than just sit back and listen. On the other hand, ILI librarians are often less constrained than their academic collaborators. Unless we are teaching a full-term, for-credit class, we do not formally grade our learners. We do not have to conform to curriculum guidelines or "teach to the test" in our course-integrated or our one-shot endeavors. And we tend to have a bit more latitude even in our for-credit courses regarding the way we structure our classes. So it may be easier for us to experiment and move to different types of teaching approaches. In doing so, we can also set a positive example for our learners and for our teaching collaborators in the K–20 environment.

So if both teachers and learners alike feel a bit uncomfortable about LCT practices, why adopt them? The most fundamental reason is that we teach because we want our learners to learn. LCT has a whole host of benefits for our learners. Because learners are being given more responsibility for and ownership in the process, they are more likely to learn and retain the material being presented (Bain, 2004; McCombs, 2003; Weimer, 2002, 2003). LCT can also increase learner motivation by allowing students to work with materials in a meaningful way and then include that new information into their own personal worldview. Retention improves as learners obtain a better understanding of the material and how it applies to their own lives (Bain, 2004; Vella, 2000; Weimer, 2003).

LCT encourages a deep rather than a surface understanding of the material being studied. It has been found to be more effective at achieving higher level cognitive objectives such as analysis, synthesis, and evaluation. Learners are encouraged to go beyond the basics of rote memorization and the reproduction or regurgitation of that memorized material. They are asked, instead, to think about the material, to connect new knowledge to that which is already known, and to become critical thinkers and problem solvers capable of producing, creating, and constructing new knowledge (Biggs, 1999; Gagnon and Collay, 2001; McCombs and Miller, 2007; Weimer, 2002). In short, there is ample evidence to suggest that real, long-lasting learning happens in an LCT environment. Additional supporting evidence for the effectiveness of LCT can be found in Chapter 3.

LCT AND ILI

Most of you who have picked up this book are librarians who have ILI as part of your job responsibilities. So you may be wondering how LCT relates to your own instructional endeavors. It is interesting to note that APA's *Learner-Centered Psychological Principles* (American Psychological Association Work Group of the

Board of Educational Affairs, 1997) and the ALA's work on defining and promoting information literacy (ALA, 1998; ALA. Presidential Committee on Information Literacy, 1989) occurred during roughly the same ten-year span. Underlying both organizations' agendas was the idea of improving people's abilities to become self-directed, self-motivated, lifelong learners. Thus there is a natural connection between LCT and ILI. LCT offers ILI librarians the means to create instructional endeavors that empower learners to become information-literate individuals who can succeed in a complex, diverse, and rapidly changing information society (Beyers, 2009; Darling-Hammond, 1996; Halpern and Hakel, 2002; Reed and Stravreva, 2006). LCT approaches help learners develop the skills, knowledge, and abilities that define an information-literate individual—someone who is able to recognize an information need and can locate, evaluate, and use information effectively and ethically (ALA, 1998; ALA. Presidential Committee on Information Literacy, 1989).

FINAL REMARKS

The rest of this book will show how using LCT principles can transform ILI practices. It will offer tips and examples from my own practice and from that of some of my colleagues who have also adopted these LCT ideas. Hopefully, as you read more about LCT, you, too, will be inspired to incorporate these ideas and practices into your own teaching.

Can those of us who teach IL become learner-centered teachers? Of course we can. Should we make this effort? If we truly wish to effectively reach and teach our learners, how can we not at least try? LCT works. It engages our learners, involves them in the learning process, and motivates them to learn during our instructional endeavors. Furthermore, it provides them with the skills, knowledge, and abilities to continue to learn in the future. And it is fun for teacher and learner alike. Read on, and see if you don't agree that becoming a learner-centered teacher is an idea worth exploring.

REFLECTIONS

1. Think about something you teach regularly. Examine your practice from the LCT perspective. Can you identify elements in your teaching in which you apply the "CPR" point of view? That is:
   - Do you offer your learners opportunities to **collaborate** with each other and with you as they approach the material? Give an example of how you do so.
   - Are your learners asked to actively **participate** during the instructional endeavor? In what ways do they do so?

- Finally, do you offer your learners the opportunity to take control of and take **responsibility** for their own and their fellow learners' experiences? How do they exhibit that control and responsibility?

2. Now that you have identified ways in which you are already applying CPR to your teaching, can you think of additional ways you can offer your learners opportunities to collaborate, participate, and take responsibility? List two or three changes you might make to your teaching practices that would increase the CPR quotient in your teaching.

EXPLORATIONS

American Psychological Association Work Group of the Board of Educational Affairs. 1997. *Learner-Centered Psychological Principles: A Framework for School Reform and Redesign.* Washington, DC: American Psychological Association.

This foundational document was the culmination of a ten-year project to integrate research and theory from psychology and education. The resultant 14 principles are divided into four parts (Cognitive and Metacognitive Factors, Developmental and Social Factors, Individual Differences Factors, and Motivational and Affective Factors). This document also was intended to define LCT from a research-validated perspective.

Bransford, John D., et al. 2006. "Learning Theories and Education: Toward a Decade of Synergy." In *Handbook of Educational Psychology*, edited by Patricia A. Alexander and Phillip H. Winne, 209–244. Mahwah, NJ: Lawrence Erlbaum.

This chapter offers a good overview of the topic from an historical perspective and provides insight into current ideas as well.

King, Alison. 1993. "From Sage on the Stage to Guide on the Side." *College Teaching* 41, no. 1: 30–35.

Read this article to find out more about the thinking behind this popular expression.

McCombs, Barbara L., and Lynda Miller. 2007. *Learner-Centered Classroom Practices and Assessments: Maximizing Student Motivation, Learning, and Achievement.* Thousand Oaks, CA: Corwin Press.

Coauthored by the APA president who initiated work that resulted in APA's Principles, this book provides an update on current research and practice in LCT.

Weimer, Mary Ellen. 2003. "Focus on Learning. Transform Teaching." *Change* 35, no. 5: 49–54.

If you were going to read only one thing on this topic, this would be it. Reading this article inspired me to begin my exploration of LCT.

REFERENCES

ACRL. 2000. *Information Literacy Competency Standards for Higher Education.* American Library Association. http://www.ala.org/ala/mgrps/divs/acrl/standards/information literacycompetency.cfm.

ALA. 1998. *A Progress Report on Information Literacy: An Update on the American Library Association Presidential Committee on Information Literacy: Final Report.* American Library Association. http:www.ala.org/acrl/nili/nili.html.

ALA. Presidential Committee on Information Literacy. 1989. *Final Report.* Chicago: American Library Association.

Alexander, Patricia A., and P. Karen Murphy. 1998. "The Research Base for APA's Learner-Centered Psychological Principles." In *How Students Learn: Reforming Schools through Learner-Centered Education,* edited by Nadine M. Lambert and Barbara L. McCombs, 1–22. Washington, DC: American Psychological Association.

American Psychological Association Work Group of the Board of Educational Affairs. 1997. *Learner-Centered Psychological Principles: A Framework for School Reform and Redesign.* Washington, DC: American Psychological Association.

Bain, Ken. 2004. *What the Best College Teachers Do.* Cambridge, MA: Harvard University Press.

Beyers, Ronald. 2009. "A Five Dimensional Model for Educating the Net Generation." *Educational Technology and Society* 12, no. 4: 218–227.

Biggs, John B. 1999. *Teaching for Quality Learning at the University.* Buckingham, Great Britain: Open University Press.

Bransford, John D., Ann L. Brown, Rodney R. Cocking, and National Research Council, eds. 2000. *How People Learn: Brain, Mind, Experience and School.* Washington, DC: National Academies Press.

Bransford, John D., et al. 2006. "Learning Theories and Education: Toward a Decade of Synergy." In *Handbook of Educational Psychology,* edited by Patricia A. Alexander and Phillip H. Winne, 209–244. Mahwah, NJ: Lawrence Erlbaum.

Clark, Ruth C., and David Taylor. 1994. "The Cause and Cure of Worker Overload." *Training* 31, no. 7: 40–43.

Darling-Hammond, Linda. 1996. "The Right to Learn and the Advancement of Teaching: Research, Policy, and Practice for Democratic Education." *Educational Researcher* 25, no. 6: 5–17.

Eggen, Paul, and Don Kauchak. 2010. *Educational Psychology: Windows on Classrooms.* Upper Saddle River, NJ: Merrill.

Felder, Richard M., and Rebecca Brent. 1996. "Navigating the Bumpy Road to Student-Centered Instruction." *College Teaching* 44, no. 2: 43–47.

Freilberg, H. Jerome, and Amy Driscoll. 2005. *Universal Teaching Strategies.* Boston: Allyn and Bacon.

Freire, Paulo. 2002. *Pedagogy of the Oppressed.* New York: Continuum.

Gagnon, G.W., and M. Collay. 2001. *Designing for Learning: Six Elements in Constructivist Classrooms.* Thousand Oaks, CA: Corwin Press.

Grassian, Esther, and Joan Kaplowitz. 2009. *Information Literacy Instruction: Theory and Practice.* 2nd ed. New York: Neal-Schuman.

———. 2010. "Information Literacy Instruction." In *Encyclopedia of Library and Information Science*, edited by M.J. Bates and M. Maack. Oxford, UK: Taylor & Francis.

Halpern, Diane E., and Milton D. Hakel. 2002. "Applying the Science of Learning to University Teaching and Beyond." *New Directions for Teaching and Learning* 2002, no. 89: 3–7.

Kaplowitz, Joan. 2008. "The Psychology of Learning: Connecting Theory to Practice." In *Information Literacy Instruction Handbook*, edited by C.N. Cox and E.B. Lindsay. Chicago: ALA.

King, Alison. 1993. "From Sage on the Stage to Guide on the Side." *College Teaching* 41, no. 1: 30–35.

Landry, Jeffrey P., Bruce M. Saulnier, Teresa A. Wagner, and Herbert E. Longenecker Jr. 2008. "Why Is the Learner-Centered Paradigm So Profoundly Important for Information Systems Education?" *Journal of Information Studies Education* 19, no. 2: 175–179.

Marshall, Hermine. 1998. "Teaching Educational Psychology: Learning-Centered and Constuctivist Perspectives." In *How Students Learn: Reforming Schools through Learner-Centered Education*, edited by Nadine M. Lambert and Barbara L. McCombs, 449–473. Washington, DC: American Psychological Association.

Mayer, Richard E., and Roxanne Moreno. 2003. "Nine Ways to Reduce Cognitive Load in Multimedia Learning." *Educational Psychologist* 38, no. 1: 43–52.

McCombs, Barbara L. 2003. "A Framework for the Redesign of K–12 Education in the Context of Current Educational Reform." *Theory into Practice* 42, no. 2: 93–101.

McCombs, Barbara L., and Lynda Miller. 2007. *Learner-Centered Classroom Practices and Assessments: Maximizing Student Motivation, Learning, and Achievement*. Thousand Oaks, CA: Corwin Press.

Minstrell, Jim, and Virginia Stimpson. 1996. "A Classroom Environment for Learning: Guiding Students' Reconstruction of Understanding and Reasoning." In *Contributions of Instructional Innovations to Understanding Learning*, edited by Leona Schauble and Robert Glaser, 175–202. Mahwah, NJ: Lawrence Erlbaum.

National Research Council. 2005. *How Students Learn: History, Math and Science in the Classroom*. Washington, DC: National Academies Press.

Nelken, Melissa I. 2009. "Negotiating Classroom Practices: Lessons from Adult Learning." *Negotiation Journal* 25, no. 2: 181–194.

Nilson, Linda B. 2003. *Teaching at Its Best : A Research-Based Resource for College Instructors*. Bolton, MA: Anker.

Powell, J.P. 1988. "Reducing Teacher Control." In *Developing Autonomy in Student Learning*, edited by David Boud, 104–118. London: Kogan Page.

Reed, Shannon L., and Kirilka Stravreva. 2006. "Layering Knowledge: Information Literacy as Critical Thinking." *Teaching Literature, Language, Composition and Culture* 6, no. 3: 435–452.

Rovai, Alfred P. 2004. "A Constructivist Approach to College Learning." *Internet and Higher Education* 7, no. 2: 79–93.

Saulnier, Bruce M., Jeffrey P. Landry, Herbert E. Longenecker Jr., and Teresa A. Wagner. 2008. "From Teaching to Learning: Learner-Centered Teaching and Assessment in Information Systems Education." *Journal of Information Studies Education* 19, no. 2: 169–173.

Slavin, Robert E. 2011. *Educational Psychology: Theory and Practice.* 10th ed. Boston: Allyn and Bacon.

Smart, Karl L., and Nancy Csapo. 2007. "Learning by Doing: Engaging Students through Learner-Centered Activities." *Business Communication Quarterly* 70, no. 4: 451–457.

Veldof, Jerilyn. 2006. *Creating the One-Shot Library Workshop: A Step by Step Guide.* Chicago: American Library Association.

Vella, Jane. 2000. *Learning to Listen. Learning to Teach.* 2nd ed. San Francisco: Josssy-Bass.

Weimer, Mary Ellen. 2002. *Learner-Centered Teaching: Five Key Changes to Practice.* San Francisco: Jossey-Bass.

———. 2003. "Focus on Learning. Transform Teaching." *Change* 35, no. 5: 49–54.

Weinberger, Elizabeth, and Barbara. L. McCombs. 2001. "The Impact of Learner-Centered Practices on the Academic and Non-Academic Outcomes of Upper Elementary and Middle School Students." Paper presented at American Educational Research Association Conference, Seattle, WA, April 10–12.

Chapter 2

How Will You Know Learner-Centered Teaching When You See It?

A leader is best when people barely know he exists. When his work is done, his aim fulfilled, they will say: we did it ourselves.

—Lao Tzu

I'LL KNOW IT WHEN I SEE IT

I hope that Chapter 1 has whetted your appetite about learner-centered teaching (LCT) and that you are eager to find out more. You are starting to create a picture of LCT in your mind, but it is in the form of broad strokes—not specific details. So you may be asking yourself, "What makes teaching learner-centered?" In other words, you may be wondering, "How will I know it when I see it?" or, more to the point, "What do I do in my teaching practice to make it learner-centered?"

To fill in the details, let's rephrase our questions in terms of the basic principles of LCT—Collaboration, Participation, and shared Responsibility (CPR). We can start by examining our teaching practices and asking ourselves, "How can we create an atmosphere that supports collaboration between learners and teachers and among learners themselves; one in which active participation is the norm; and where learners are expected to take responsibility for their own and their fellow learners' learning?"

Simply put, we become learner-centered teachers by following these three guidelines. We are learner-centered when we:

- **Listen** to our learners both prior to working with them and also during the actual instructional interactions.
- **Engage** our learners by allowing them to interact with the content in meaningful, relevant, and useful ways.

- **Inspire** our learners to become lifelong learners by sharing our passion for the content and by expressing our heartfelt and honest belief in the potential of each and every one of them to become self-reliant, capable, self-confident learners and ultimately successful members of society.

Many people have written about LCT and have described it in a variety of ways. Let's take a look at the various characteristics that these writers use to describe the concept and the ways in which they feel LCT differs from the traditional, teacher/content-centered approach. In doing so, we may begin to see how a LCT practice helps us "listen to," "engage," and "inspire" our learners.

COMPONENTS OF LCT

The advocates of LCT characterize the approach in a range of different, yet related ways. Many align the idea to active learning and to the constructivist philosophy of teaching. Some refer to principles associated with the humanist theories of learning. Others talk about the importance of social aspects of learning and the building of communities (Eggen and Kauchak, 2010). But all agree on one thing. LCT differs from the traditional approach that has dominated our educational systems for many, many years. What are those differences? For the most part, the distinction lies in how the role of the teacher and the role of the learner are viewed. It boils down to a notion of power or who is seen as being "in charge" of the learning process (Weimer, 2002). Traditional teaching puts control in the hands of the teacher and views him or her as the dispenser of information and knowledge. In the learner-centered approach, power, control, and responsibility for learning is shared by everyone involved—teacher and learners alike. Learners actively construct or create their own knowledge. They are not just passive recipients drinking at some fountain of wisdom pouring forth from the teacher and/or the text (Bain, 2004; Grassian and Kaplowitz, 2009; Huba and Freed, 2000; McCombs and Miller, 2007). Table 2.1 gives an overview of how LCT differs from the traditional more teacher-centered approach.

Overall the characteristics associated with LCT represent a shift in perspective about how learning happens. This shift manifests itself in everything learner-centered teachers do. It is exemplified by the ways they regard their learners and is evident in every interaction they have with them. Learner-centered teachers listen to learners in order to understand and be respectful of their needs. These teachers use this information to find ways to engage their learners and invite them to actively contribute to and participate in the learning process. And they inspire their learners to "own their own learning"—to take responsibility for it and to develop the abilities, strategies, and skills that will empower them to

Table 2.1. Traditional versus LC Teaching		
Characteristic	**Traditional Teaching**	**LC Teaching**
How knowledge is exchanged	One-way—from teacher to learner	Jointly constructed by teacher and learners
How teacher is viewed	As expert—one who shares his or her knowledge with learners	As facilitator—one who creates opportunities for learners to have meaningful interactions with the material to be learned
How learner is viewed	Passive vessel to be filled by knowledge	Active constructor, discoverer, and creator of knowledge
How learning is viewed	As acquiring information	As constructing understanding
Where power/responsibility for learning resides	In hands of the teacher	Shared by teacher and learners
Whose voice is heard most during instruction	Teacher's voice dominates	Learners' voices tend to be heard more than that of teacher
How learners experience new material	By reading about it and/or from listening to experts	By interacting directly with material individually or in collaboration with other learners
What learners are expected to do with new material	Memorize and repeat it exactly as read/heard	Relate it to previous material learned and use it to construct new knowledge
How learning is assessed	By learners producing or selecting right answer	By learners' working on authentic problems/cases/ situations that allow for multiple approaches and solutions
Who assesses learning	Teacher has sole responsibility for assessment	Self- and peer assessment opportunities included along with teacher assessment approaches

become lifelong learners (Grassian and Kaplowitz, 2009). Let's take a closer look at how learner-centered teachers accomplish these goals.

LISTEN TO YOUR LEARNERS

When you think about teaching, you probably focus on the ways in which you plan to share information with your learners. After all, you are the expert on the material and are ready, willing, and able to expose your learners to all that expertise. While you are indeed the authority on the material, you must also become knowledgeable about your learners. LCT asks you to find out as much as you can about your learner population. It also calls for open, respectful, and responsive interchanges with your learners. Your dedication to the learner-centered approach starts with the ways in which you talk with and listen to your learners.

Part of listening is having a firm understanding of your learners and their needs. Knowing your audience is one of the most fundamental tenets of teaching. Without this base, how can you design your instruction in an appropriate and relevant fashion? So, listening starts with good, solid research. But it goes beyond that. It is also reflected in the ways in which you interact with your learners before, during, and even after the instructional interaction. Do you invite questions? Do you acknowledge and respect learners' comments? Are you flexible enough to make "on-the-spot" instructional course corrections if your learners seem to be having difficulty with the material or if they seem to need something other than what you intended to share with them? Do you contact them prior to instruction to introduce yourself and find out more about their current information needs? Do you offer ways that your learners can continue to interact with the material and/or contact you once instruction is completed? If you can answer yes to some of these questions, then you are exhibiting ways in which you already "listen" to your learners and are well on the way to becoming a learner-centered teacher.

LCT values the contributions of everyone involved, teacher and learners alike. If we are indeed "all pulling together" toward a common goal, then we must be ready to hear what our learners have to say (Fink, 2003; Grassian and Kaplowitz, 2009; Vella, 2000). The ways in which we listen to our learners can take many forms. However, they do tend to fall into the following categories:

- Performing regular needs assessments—prior to and during instruction
- Creating a welcoming and supportive environment
- Offering positive and constructive feedback throughout learning
- Nurturing the creation of learning communities

Let's take a look at each of these ideas in more detail.

Performing Needs Assessments

Performing regular needs assessments is vital to the health of any instructional endeavors (Dick, Carey, and Carey, 2005; Freilberg and Driscoll, 2005). It enables us to know what is important to our learners and to customize our instruction to best meet their needs. Although it may not always be possible to undertake an in-depth needs assessment for each group with whom we are going to interact, doing some background research on our community of learners can provide some general information that may be applicable in specific situations.

To be complete, these background or general needs assessments should consider the institution's culture, climate, and political structure, as well as the needs of the individual learners (Grassian and Kaplowitz, 2005; MacDonald, 2008). It is also a great way to introduce ourselves to our community, help identify those people who share our commitment to developing information-literate individuals, and make contact with potential future collaborators. These contacts may prove invaluable as we develop courses, classes, and programs down the road.

Check with appropriate institutional and local offices and agencies to gather demographic information. Student services and registrars offices can provide vast amounts of valuable and relevant data in higher education environments. City offices and library boards can provide comparable information for the public library. School boards and boards of education should be contacted in the K–12 setting. Human resources offices may be willing to share general information about those working in a special library situation. Be creative. Contact whoever might be able to help. Look at groups that deal with special segments of your population, such as those that offer support for people with disabilities or older/reentry learners. Check with organizations that are dedicated to the interests and needs of specific cultural or special interest groups to find out how instruction can be made more relevant to their members. And don't forget to reach out to the learners themselves via surveys, interviews, and impromptu conversations. Library staff can also provide excellent background information based on their day-to-day interactions with your learners.

When we undertake a needs assessment we are showing that we really care about making our instructional endeavors relevant and useful to our learners. There is no better way to find out what matters to our learners and to identify how best to support their needs with our instructional offerings (Vella, 2000). Use the data from these assessments to create goals and learning outcomes that target learners' specific interests and information literacy needs. By doing so we show our learners that we have heard them, have paid attention to them, and are viewing them as partners in the planning process (Grassian and Kaplowitz, 2009).

Listening does not end with the completion of the needs assessment. Effective teachers find ways to listen to their learners during the instructional experience itself. If circumstances or logistics prevent you from doing any kind of advanced needs assessment for a specific group with whom you are working, you can do some quick surveying during the first few minutes of the class. Find out if participants have written research-based papers before. How often do they come into the library? Why do they come into the library? One really good way to break the ice and find out more about a group is to ask them to describe any assignment/project they may be working on (in the K–20 setting) or what they are trying to research (in public and special library environments). This will help you to confirm that what you have prepared is on target. But be ready to have to switch gears on the spot if your information does not match what they tell you. You can also ask them how they feel about this particular assignment (or library-based research in general). They may be surprised to learn that everyone has some level of anxiety when approaching this kind of work and relieved to discover that it is a natural part of the process and not a reflection on their own abilities (Kuhlthau, 1988, 1993). Sharing some of your own experiences, problems you had, and anxieties you felt when you were new to the research process can also help learners see that their feelings are natural and that you can relate to those feelings, having felt them yourself (Palmer, 1998). Getting those concerns out in the open can help smooth the way and offers you an excellent entry into the material. You are there to help them learn how to make the process a little less painful and hopefully reduce their anxiety levels as well.

Creating a Welcoming and Supportive Environment

Listening continues as you and your learners move through the material. If you are working in a face-to-face (F2F) situation, you should be alert to the "feel" of the room. Jacob Kounin (1970) refers to this as monitoring the group's "with-it-ness." Do your learners seem interested, engaged, and motivated, or are they staring off into space or, worse still, snoring on their desks? Are people responding to your questions and actively exchanging ideas with each other? It is pretty easy to gauge if they are still with you or if you have lost them in the dust. If learners seem to be restless or disinterested, change gears and do something different. If they get that "glazed over" expression, perhaps you have gone too fast and need to regroup and rephrase the material already addressed. Asking the learners to summarize what has just happened is a good way to wake those sleepers up and get everyone's attention back on track. It also serves as a way to assess how well (or not) your learners have grasped the material at hand and whether or not you can move on. If people seem confused, you might wish to add a few more examples or ask them what still seems unclear. Your learners may also lose interest if you have dwelled on a topic for a bit too long. Maybe you have reached the "too much of a good thing" point of your instruction and it is time to move on. A good "temperature taking" approach at any time in the instruction is to ask, "What questions do you have for me now?" This not only offers the opportunity to clear up any misconceptions or issues the learners may have but also sets a tone of shared inquiry and once again indicates your interest in listening to your learners (Cruickshank, Jenkins, and Metcalf, 2009; Freilberg and Driscoll, 2005; Grassian and Kaplowitz, 2009; Vella, 2000). Obviously this temperature taking or other means of listening can easily be incorporated in any F2F instructional situation. But it is equally important in an online instructional setting. Chapters 5 (F2F) and 6 (online) will offer more examples of how to "listen" in these formats.

Offering Positive and Constructive Feedback

Activities, multiway discussions, and open and honest dialogue between teacher and learners and among learners themselves are at the heart of LCT. Before learners are willing to participate in these activities (which may be very different from those they experience in other instructional settings) you must make sure they are at ease and trust that their participation will be valued and honored.

The ways in which you facilitate these interactions can make or break the situation. You set the tone by how you work with your learners and the expectations you set for them when you ask them to exchange ideas and collaborate with each other. One sure way to lose learners' trust is to ask a question or initiate a discussion and then not wait for responses from your learners. That tells your learners that you are not really interested in their views, especially if you just go on and expound on your own ideas on the subject. To really show you are inviting them to join you in exploring the topic, you must give them time to think, to formulate their responses, and to build up the courage to speak up. Waiting for as little as ten seconds for responses can encourage more active participation. Plus it shows that you are really interested in and anxious to hear what they have to say (Brookfield, 1990; Grassian and Kaplowitz, 2009; McKeachie and Svinicki, 2006).

Building trust does not stop there. You can also show your respect for your learners by how you respond to their comments and the work they do on the activities and exercises you set for them. Remember that you are trying to promote an atmosphere of shared learning. Even when your learners may be heading in the wrong direction, your comments about their work should be positive and supportive (McKeachie and Svinicki, 2006). Honor their attempts and offer suggestions about how they could improve. Never criticize or demean your learners. Say, "That is an interesting idea, but we may want to look at it from some different angles." Then go on to ask others in the group what they might suggest to improve the original comment or activity/exercise result. Whatever feedback you provide, make sure you are phrasing it in terms of ways to improve learning. Every effort is valuable and every contribution can be useful—even if that contribution is just a jumping-off point for further discussion and examination of the topic at hand.

Nurturing the Creation of Learning Communities

All the ways in which we interact with our learners—through needs assessments, instructional interactions, and the comments and feedback we provide—tell our learners that we truly believe in the idea that we all win if we work together in a mutual, collaborative, and respectful manner. We do not set ourselves apart from or above our learners. While we may have a certain level of expertise on the subject and wish to share that knowledge, we also know that everyone has something to bring to the table, and we all gain from that sharing of viewpoints. We all have something to learn, even the person who is standing at the front of the room. That is why we refer to ourselves as facilitators, coordinators, co-constructors of knowledge, and partners in the larger learning community formed by everyone in the group. We show our respect for others by modeling this type of behavior (walking the talk, so to speak), and we set the expectation that everyone in the group will follow our lead and show respect for and value the contributions of everyone involved. It may be helpful to set some mutually agreed upon ground rules and norms for group discussions and activities to further encourage this learning community outlook.

Community building and norm setting are especially important if you are working with learners who are accustomed to interacting with their teachers in the more traditional, transmittal mode (Grassian and Kaplowitz, 2009; Powell, 1988; Tollefson and Osborn, 2008). See Chapters 4, 5, and 6 for more tips on how to set this collaborative and respectful tone when using various instructional methods in both the F2F and the online environments.

Clearly it is easy to promote the idea of learning communities when we have ongoing relationships with our learners in term-long courses. We can take time at the beginning of the term to set this tone and talk about the merits and advantages of this sort of collaborative approach. We can even preset the learners' expectations by the language we use in various course materials, our syllabus, and our course webpage if we have one. Simply using inclusive words such as "we" and "us" sets the stage for the idea that working together is the expected norm (Mundhenk, 2004).

But what can we do if we have limited contact with our learners? How can we build the idea of learning communities if we are only meeting with our learners once or twice as part of someone else's course? The one-shot and stand-alone workshops are still very prevalent in all types of library environments. Although it might be a bit more challenging under these circumstances, we can still encourage the collaborative learning mind-set by the tone we set for the instruction, how we structure the learners' interactions with the material, and the ways in which we communicate with learners throughout our contact with them. We may not be explicitly discussing the concept, but our every action during instruction supports the development of a collaborative learning community atmosphere.

When we listen to our learners we are inviting them to join us in the learning process. We are demonstrating the inclusive rather than the transmittal format of teaching. Teachers and learners become partners and collaborators. This serves to further engage learners and to give them a sense of ownership in and responsibility for their learning. It also instills a sense of shared responsibility for the learning of everyone in the group. Listening, therefore, sets the stage for the two other components of LCT—engagement and inspiration (Grassian and Kaplowitz, 2009; McCombs, 2003).

ENGAGE YOUR LEARNERS

Moving from traditional teaching to the LCT approach means giving up our "sage on the stage" teaching role. We are no longer solely responsible for transmitting information to our learners. Our role in LCT is to create opportunities for our learners to interact with the material to be learned so that they can construct their own meaning. It is not surprising, therefore, that active and collaborative learning techniques play a large part in LCT. Having our learners actively involved with the material has many benefits. It is much harder for learners to ignore what is going on when they have to do something themselves. While brief presentations may be useful if we are trying to set the stage for the material or wish to summarize, synthesize, or pull together information from a lot of different sources, research shows that people lose interest in and are unable to process information after 10 to 15 minutes of a lecture-type presentation (Bligh, 2000; Cruickshank, Jenkins, and Metcalf, 2009; Freilberg and Driscoll, 2005; Jacobson, 2008). Activities provide a change of pace, allow the learners to practice and apply the material being addressed, and give them time to process the information.

So, having learners "do" instead of having them just "listen and watch" increases interest in the material, helps improve motivation, and increases the likelihood of retention and transfer to new situations. Using relevant examples in these activities is another way to appeal to our learners. In short, activities help us capture our learners' attention and keep them engaged throughout our work with them. For more on how to utilize the range of methods available to you, see Chapter 4.

Just as listening can take a variety of forms, engaging our learners shows up in a number of different ways. We encourage engagement through the format of our instructional endeavors—both in the ways in which we ask our learners to work with the material to be learned and by the opportunities provided to exchange ideas in a collaborative and cooperative setting. We engage our learners by:

- creating appropriate, relevant, and thought-provoking ways for learners to interact with the material to be learned, and

- offering opportunities for learners to collaborate and to co-construct knowledge.

Here's how we go about making sure our instruction is engaging.

Creating Opportunities for Learners to Interact with the Material to Be Learned

The traditional approach to teaching generally starts with the teacher deciding what topics need to be covered and then outlining the points he or she plans to include during a lecture. Although some demonstrations and questioning might be included, the emphasis is on one-way communication—from teacher to learners. The learner-centered teacher still needs to decide on content but looks at that content from the learners' perspective. That is, the learner-centered teacher starts with determining appropriate expected learning outcomes (ELOs) for his or her learners—what the learners will know and be able to do following instruction. The learner-centered teacher is less interested in what he or she is going to say and more interested in how instruction can be structured so that learners are interacting with the material in such a way that enables them to reach the ELOs (Bain, 2004; Battersby and Learning Outcomes Network, 1999; Grassian and Kaplowitz, 2009; Weimer, 2002).

Good "listening" or data gathering from our needs assessments helps us determine the most appropriate and relevant ELOs for our learners. Once we have those in place, we can begin to explore the various ways that the learners can interact with the material so that they can attain the ELOs. Activities can also provide some informal assessment data as we observe learners exhibiting the degree to which they have attained the ELOs. We need to take a look at each individual outcome and review our teaching "bag of tricks" to see which of the various methods might be a suitable way for the learners to attain that outcome. If we want them to be able to define, articulate, or describe a concept, we might wish to use some kind of simple brainstorming or concept mapping exercise. If we are interested in having them interpret facts, or compare and contrast different concepts or resources, we might have them work in pairs or small groups where learners can exchange their ideas, or we could ask groups of learners to take different sides of a topic and present their arguments in a debate-like setting. If we want to see if learners can apply what they have learned in a new situation, we might have them work alone or collaboratively in small groups on some kind of case study or problem. Asking a series of thought-provoking questions can be a great way to find out if the learners have been able to synthesize the material addressed and to discover what conclusions they have drawn. Chapter 4 discusses all these methods and offers suggestions on how to use them to enhance the learner-centered quality of instruction. Chapter 5 covers the concept of assessment and shows how ELOs, instructional activities, and assessments are interrelated.

Once we have decided on what types of discussions, questioning exchanges, activities, exercises, and collaborative group tasks we will be including for each of the outcomes, we have pretty much developed our instruction. All we need now is a good attention-getting opening, an overview of what's to come that also sets the tone for the collaborative learning environment we intend to promote, an effective and upbeat ending that helps learners to summarize for themselves what they have just experienced, and some brief talking points to tie each of the segments together. Rather than starting with how to present the content, we have focused on what learners will be doing during the instruction that will help them reach the ELOs we have set (Grassian and Kaplowitz, 2009; McAdoo and Manwaring, 2009).

Offering Opportunities for Learners to Collaborate and to Co-construct Knowledge

As can be seen from the previous section, learners can be offered many different ways to interact with the material to be learned. One common theme in all these interactions, however, is that learners are rarely working in isolation from each other. Although there may be moments when we encourage private thinking, reflection, and the individual construction of knowledge, a basic premise of LCT is that learning is a social endeavor. We learn best when we work with others, exchange ideas, examine different perspectives, collaborate with the members of our learning community, and use the learning experience to construct new insights into the material. So, we not only promote the idea of a learning community, we craft our instruction to encourage such collaborations. We include various large and small group activities throughout our instruction and try to ensure that all voices are heard and respected. For more on collaborative teaching methods, see Chapter 4.

INSPIRE YOUR LEARNERS

Listening to and engaging our learners are both vital components of LCT. But to be true learner-centered teachers we must also inspire them to continue to learn long after their experiences with us and our material have come to an end. We do this by showing how much we care about the material and about the learners themselves. We make sure that our words and our actions demonstrate that we believe in them and their potential for success. The LCT credo is that if we expect the best from our learners then that is what we will get. We inspire our learners by:

- exhibiting our passion for the subject;
- highlighting the relevance of the material to our learners;
- providing learners with choices about how they interact with the material and how they exhibit learning;

- demonstrating our belief in our learners' capabilities and potential for learning; and
- promoting a self-reflective, self-directed, metacognitive approach to learning.

Let's examine each of these points in turn.

Exhibiting Our Passion for the Subject

As information literacy librarians, we are dedicated to empowering our learners. We passionately believe in the importance of information literacy in today's complex world. Being information literate is truly a survival skill—one that is vital to everyone's success in anything he or she chooses to do. So why are we afraid to let that passion show? Passion leads to excitement, and excitement is infectious. If we are fairly perfunctory about our material, then our learners will be as well. If we don't show we care, why should they?

So let your enthusiasm for information literacy in general and for the specific techniques and resources you are sharing with them show. Offer examples about how being information literate can improve their lives. Introduce new ideas, concepts, and resources by telling them what these things can do for them. If you have a favorite resource, let them know it is your favorite and why that is so. Stories about how you used some method, technique, or resource to deal with your own information needs are great ways to make it all real to your learners. It also helps you to connect to them on a more personal level (Bain, 2004; Brookfield, 1990; Grassian and Kaplowitz, 2009; Weimer, 2002).

Highlighting the Relevance of the Material to Your Learners

No matter how excited we might be by the material, our learners may still be unimpressed. Although the importance of the information may seem obvious to us, our learners may not be quite so sure. They may think it is only important if we are librarians. Or they may feel that being information literate is useful only to complete assignments in a school situation. Of course, if we are working in the K–20 setting and our learners do have an assignment, that is an excellent way to catch their interest. The information literacy instruction (ILI) session is going to save them time and trouble and should result in better grades on their assignments. Most learners will find this ample motivation to pay attention to what we are offering. However, it is also up to us to help our learners see that being information literate has more far-reaching implications. So, a big part of ILI is "selling our product." That is, we have to show our learners that what we are teaching relates to them both in the short run (for whatever has brought them to the current ILI) and over the long haul throughout their lives. Including relevant and meaningful examples builds interest and helps them to connect the material to their own lives. Needs assessment data should be able to provide some ideas about what types of examples would prove relevant to learners—especially in regard to their current information needs. Another way to build interest is to ask learners what sorts of information they looked for in the past week or so. Compile these information quest topics into a list, and then ask learners for ideas about how they would go about finding this information. This can lead to a lively discussion of the pros and cons of different approaches and also provides a way to make suggestions about both the resources they may have used and others that will be shared with them during instruction.

When working with learners, make sure to emphasize that everyone searches for information just about every day of their lives. Everyone needs reliable, trustworthy, accurate, and timely information to decide on what movies to watch, which political candidates to vote for, and what cell phone plan would work best. We use information to help us find out what's going on in the world, check on current weather and traffic information, explore educational and career opportunities, locate areas in which to live, discover the best ways to invest our money, locate consumer health information, and find the most appealing (and economically priced) vacation spots. And of course we also need quality information in our educational pursuits in order to complete our various projects and assignments. Identifying what is important to our learners can be used as a way of catching and keeping their attention.

Providing Learners with Choices about How They Interact with the Material and How They Exhibit Learning

Keep in mind that one of the basic premises of LCT is giving learners some control over their own learning. So allowing learners some say in what they will be doing during ILI not only builds interest but also gives them more responsibility over the learning process. Choice can be incorporated into both short-term (one- or two-shot instructional classes) and more extended (term-long) encounters. Supply learners with a list of possible topics, and ask them to rank them in order of importance. Include only as many of the top-ranking topics that are feasible in the time frame. Offer alternative ways for learners to find out about the topics that won't be addressed during instruction, such as individual consultations, appropriate websites, or even print handouts (Bain, 2004; Cruickshank, Jenkins, and Metcalf, 2009; McCombs and Miller, 2007).

When teaching in an online mode, incorporate flexibility into the navigation of the site so that learners can work with the material in whatever order makes sense to them. Consider providing ways for them to skip over material they feel they already know. Start them off with some sort of diagnostic tool that enables learners to self-assess their skill level. Once they have determined their level, learners could then be pointed to the appropriate parts of the online material that will help them fill in their information literacy gaps.

Whether teaching F2F or online, offer the learners some options regarding the topics they might be using as they interact with the material. Provide a list of topics from which they can select, allow them to search whatever seems interesting to them, or use a combination of both. Consider learners' levels of sophistication and experience as you decide upon how much choice to allow them. More naïve learners may not be able to come up with topics on their own and would appreciate suggestions, whereas more sophisticated learners will be delighted to get the chance to work on their own projects during the ILI session.

In some cases we might be able to offer some options on how learners demonstrate attainment of the ELOs for the instruction as well. Depending on how much contact time we have with our learners and the degree to which we are involved in formal assessment of their performance, we might give them some choice in how they exhibit their accomplishments. Some learners might wish to write a paper, whereas others prefer a more verbal presentation. Still others might enjoy presenting their material in some sort of online format. Obviously this is easier to do in more formal, long-term courses, but there are a variety of collaborative learning activities that can be done in short-term sessions that allow learners to select the role in the group that most suits them—leader, recorder, reporter, and so forth. See Chapter 4 for more on this topic.

Demonstrating Our Belief in Our Learners' Capabilities and Potential for Learning

We want our learners not only to gain some expertise in the ILI topics we are sharing with them but also to leave the experience more self-reliant and with an increased sense of confidence in their abilities. In psychological jargon, the belief that one can and will succeed is called "self-efficacy" (Bandura, 1977, 1982; Mundhenk, 2004). (See Chapter 3 for more on this idea.) We encourage self-efficacy by creating a positive, comfortable, warm, safe, and supportive learning environment. The whole idea of learning communities is based on the conviction that everyone is not only welcome to contribute, but they are expected to do so. So we make sure that we are talking with, not at, our learners. We applaud all efforts. Our comments are geared toward promoting learning, not pointing out mistakes. And we expect our learners to do the same and to treat each other with respect and consideration. Learning communities not only honor diversity, they celebrate it. The more perspectives and ideas in the mix, the better we like it. Diversity of opinions strengthens and enhances the learning process for everyone in our learning community (Grassian and Kaplowitz, 2009; Tollefson and Osborn, 2008; Vella, 2000).

Finally, we can promote self-efficacy and demonstrate our belief in our learners through a very simple adjustment in our own thinking about how we view our learners. Do you think to yourself that everyone can and will learn the material given enough time and support? Or do you expect that there are people who will never get it no matter what you do? Our beliefs about our learners will be reflected in the ways in which we interact with them. If we indicate we don't believe in them, they will become frustrated, disinterested, and unmotivated. On the other hand, if we are encouraging and supportive, they will feel good about themselves and their efforts. They will remain motivated and on task, thus increasing the likelihood that they will actually succeed (Cruickshank, Jenkins, and Metcalf, 2009; Grassian and Kaplowitz, 2009; Kaplowitz, 2008; McCombs and Miller, 2007).

Promoting a Self-Reflective, Self-Directed, Metacognitive Approach to Learning

There is one last topic we need to address if we want a complete picture of the LCT environment—that of metacognition. Remember that one of the goals of ILI is to develop lifelong learners. For that to happen, learners must not only interact with the material to be learned but also reflect on how they learned it (Beyer, 1992; Bransford et al., 2000; Davis, 2009; Schneider and MacFarlane, 2003). They need time to stop and consider what worked and what did not work for them as they interacted with the material. And if something did not work, they must be able to figure out a way to approach the material from another direction that will be more successful for them.

Learners skilled in metacognition are able to recognize the best ways in which they learn and to manage their learning endeavors accordingly. This further supports the idea of giving people some choice in their educational experiences. However, because choice is not always possible, learners must develop ways to compensate for less successful learning encounters. For example, if an individual is someone who learns by doing, but is in a presentation, lecture-heavy type of instructional experience, he or she needs to develop ways to actively interact with the material. This might occur during the lecture itself in the form of structured note taking, or the learner might develop active ways to review the material after the fact. Study groups that get together after lectures to discuss the material and try to apply what was presented would be another way to address the needs of the "learn by doing" person. Or the learner might try to summarize the material without reference to his or her notes and then compare the results. Many "learn by doing" people have experienced the more passive, transmittal forms of instruction in their formal education. The more successful of them have developed ways to "relearn" the material in a manner that is more suited to their active learning preference.

Learner-centered teachers try to encourage the development of metacognitive skills in their learners. They often model the process by something called the "think aloud" method in which they share their problem-solving methodology with their learners. They also include opportunities for self-reflection in their instructional endeavors. Taking "reflection" breaks during instruction has many benefits. It allows learners to catch up on their note taking, fill in gaps, identify further questions, and ensure that the notes make sense. Learners can use the reflection period to begin to process the information and organize it in a personally meaningful fashion. Reflection also allows for time to move the material into long-term memory storage, thus increasing likelihood of transferring newly acquired knowledge to novel situations (Bransford et al., 2000; Eggen and Kauchak, 2010; Grassian and Kaplowitz, 2009; Innes, 2004).

There are many techniques that encourage learners to think about both the content and the learning experience. Stop and ask the learners to summarize the material individually, with a partner, in small group discussions, or with the full group at intervals during the instruction. Keeping research journals encourages learners to discuss the strategies they used to gather information and reflect on how successful these strategies were in their information-gathering process. Learners might also include what steps they took to correct and/or modify less-than-successful approaches (Grassian and Kaplowitz, 2009; McGinness and Brien, 2007; Rankin, 1988). Classroom assessment techniques (CATS), such as the One Minute Paper, encourage metacognitive reflection and can be included in any individual class session (Angelo and Cross, 1993). For more on CATS and other reflection techniques, see Chapter 4. While incorporating reflection opportunities may, on the surface, seem to take away from instruction time, they actually enhance the experience. Allowing learners time to reflect ensures that they will gain even more from the ILI and will be further on the road to becoming lifelong learners.

FINAL REMARKS

So, how will you know an LCT environment when you see it? You will know it because the instructor exhibits a deep understanding of and knowledge about his or her learners and their particular information needs. You will know it because the learners are engaged and actively interacting with the material to be learned. And you will know it because learners will leave the experience with an enhanced sense of confidence about their information literacy abilities and will be inspired to continue to use these abilities in every aspect of their lives. Using LCT, you will have helped learners become information literate and develop life-long learning skills, and you can congratulate yourself on a job well done.

REFLECTIONS

1. Table 2.2 presents the characteristics of traditional versus LC teaching methods that were listed in Table 2.1. Think about your own teaching

Table 2.2. Teaching Characteristics Self-Assessment							
Characteristic	Traditional Teaching	1	2	3	4	5	Learner-Centered Teaching
How knowledge is exchanged	One-way-from teacher to learner						Jointly constructed by teacher and learner
How teacher is viewed	As expert-one who shares his or her knowledge with learners						Facilitator-one who creates opportunities for learners to have meaningful interactions with the material to be learned
How learner is viewed	Passive vessel to be filled by knowledge						Active constructor, discoverer, and creator of knowledge
How learning is viewed	As acquiring information						As constructing understanding
Where power/ responsibility for learning resides	In hands of the teacher						Shared by teacher and learners
Whose voice is heard most during instruction	Teacher's voice dominates						Learners' voices tend to be heard more than that of teacher
How learners experience new material	Read about it and/or listen to experts						Interact directly with material individually or in collaboration with other learners
How learning is assessed	Emphasis on producing or selecting right answer						Performance or problem-based projects with multiple approaches and solutions possible
Who assesses learning	Teacher has sole responsibility for assessment						Self- and peer assessment opportunities included along with teacher assessment approaches

practices. Put a check mark in the column that best reflects where your practice falls in the continuum from traditional to learner-centered.

2. For each characteristic that you marked with either a 4 or 5, give an example from your own teaching of how you exhibit learner-centered approaches.

3. For each characteristic that you marked with a 1, 2, or 3, can you think of ways in which you could redesign your practice so that it might be more learner-centered?

4. You might wish to revisit this exercise from time to time to see if your view of yourself as a teacher has changed.

EXPLORATIONS

Bain, Ken. 2004. *What the Best College Teachers Do.* Cambridge, MA: Harvard University Press.

> This book provides an excellent overview of best practices for LCT.

Huba, Mary E., and Jann E. Freed. 2000. *Learner-Centered Assessment on College Campuses.* Boston: Allyn and Bacon.

> Huba and Freed's book is considered by many as a classic resource on moving your assessment practices toward a more learner-centered approach.

McCombs, Barbara. L. 2003. *Defining Tools for Teacher Reflection: The Assessment of Learner-Centered Practices (ALCP).* ERIC Centre for Curriculum, Transfer and Technology. ED478622.

> Written by the former APA president who initiated the development of the Association's Learner-Centered Teaching Principles, this book includes checklists to help you determine how learner-centered your teaching practices really are.

Vella, Jane. 2000. *Learning to Listen. Learning to Teach.* 2nd ed. San Francisco: Jossey-Bass.

> Vella provides an interesting take on teaching by looking at it from the perspective of listening to your learners.

Weimer, Mary Ellen. 2002. *Learner-Centered Teaching: Five Key Changes to Practice.* San Francisco: Jossey-Bass.

> This book offers an in-depth treatment of the author's ideas about LCT and includes discussions on preparation, planning, interacting with learners, and assessment.

REFERENCES

Angelo, Thomas A., and K. Patricia Cross. 1993. *Classroom Assessment Techniques: A Handbook for College Teachers.* 2nd ed. The Jossey-Bass Higher & Adult Education Series. San Francisco: Jossey-Bass.

Bain, Ken. 2004. *What the Best College Teachers Do.* Cambridge, MA: Harvard University Press.

Bandura, Albert. 1977. "Self-Efficacy: Toward a Unifying Theory of Behavioral Change." *Psychogical Review* 84, no. 2: 191–215.

———. 1982. "Self-Efficacy Mechanism in Human Agency." *American Psychologist* 37, no. 1: 122–147.

Battersby, Mark, and Learning Outcomes Network. 1999. *So What's a Learning Outcome Anyway?* ERIC Centre for Curriculum, Transfer and Technology. ED430611.

Beyer, Barry K. 1992. "Teaching Thinking: An Integrated Approach." In *Teaching for Thinking*, edited by James W. Keefe and Herbert J. Walberg, 93–109. Reston, VA: National Association of Secondary School Principals.

Bligh, Donald A. 2000. *What's the Use of Lectures?* San Francisco: Jossey-Bass.

Bransford, John D., Ann L. Brown, Rodney R. Cocking, and National Research Council, eds. 2000. *How People Learn: Brain, Mind, Experience and School.* Washington, DC: National Academy Press.

Brookfield, Stephen D. 1990. *The Skillful Teacher: On Technique, Trust and Responsiveness in the Classroom.* San Francisco: Jossey-Bass.

Cruickshank, Donald R., Deborah Bainer Jenkins, and Kim K. Metcalf. 2009. *The Act of Teaching.* 5th ed. Boston: McGraw-Hill.

Davis, Barbara Gross. 2009. *Tools for Teaching.* 2nd ed. San Francisco: Jossey-Bass.

Dick, Walter W., Lou Carey, and James O. Carey. 2005. *The Systematic Design of Instruction.* 6th ed. Boston: Pearson/Allyn and Bacon.

Eggen, Paul, and Don Kauchak. 2010. *Educational Psychology: Windows on Classrooms.* Upper Saddle River, NJ: Merrill.

Fink, L. Dee. 2003. *Creating Significant Learning Experiences: An Integrated Approach.* San Francisco: Jossey-Bass.

Freilberg, H. Jerome, and Amy Driscoll. 2005. *Universal Teaching Strategies.* Boston: Allyn and Bacon.

Grassian, Esther, and Joan Kaplowitz. 2005. *Learning to Lead and Manage Information Literacy Instruction.* New York: Neal-Schuman.

———. 2009. *Information Literacy Instruction: Theory and Practice.* 2nd ed. New York: Neal-Schuman.

Huba, Mary E., and Jann E. Freed. 2000. *Learner-Centered Assessment on College Campuses.* Boston: Allyn and Bacon.

Innes, Robert B. 2004. *Reconstructing Undergraduate Education.* Mahwah, NJ: Lawrence Erlbaum.

Jacobson, Trudi E. 2008. "Motivation." In *Information Literacy Instruction Handbook*, edited by Chistopher N. Cox and Elizabeth B. Lindsay, 73–83. Chicago: ALA. ACRL.

Kaplowitz, Joan. 2008. "The Psychology of Learning: Connecting Theory to Practice." In *Information Literacy Instruction Handbook*, edited by Christopher N. Cox and Elizabeth B. Lindsay, 26–49. Chicago: ALA. ACRL.

Kounin, Jacob S. 1970. *Discipline and Group Management in Classrooms.* New York: Holt, Rinehart and Winston.

Kuhlthau, Carol Collier. 1988. "Developing a Model of the Library Search Process: Cognitive and Affective Aspects." *RQ* 28, no. 3: 232–242.

———. 1993. *Seeking Meaning: A Process Approach to Library and Information Services, Information Management, Policy, and Services.* Norwood, NJ: Ablex.

MacDonald, Mary C. 2008. Program Management. In *Information Literacy Instruction Handbook*, edited by Christopher N. Cox and Elizabeth B. Lindsay, 113–137. Chicago: ALA. ACRL.

McAdoo, Bobbi, and Melissa Manwaring. 2009. "Teaching for Implementation: Designing Negotiation Curricula to Maximize Long-Term Learning." *Negotiation Journal* 25, no. 2: 195–215.

McCombs, Barbara. L. 2003. *Defining Tools for Teacher Reflection: The Assessment of Learner-Centered Practices (ALCP).* ERIC Centre for Curriculum, Transfer and Technology. ED478622.

McCombs, Barbara L., and Lynda Miller. 2007. *Learner-Centered Classroom Practices and Assessments: Maximizing Student Motivation, Learning, and Achievement.* Thousand Oaks, CA: Corwin Press.

McGinness, Claire, and Michelle Brien. 2007. "Using Reflective Journals to Assess the Research Process." *Reference Services Review* 35, no. 1: 21–40.

McKeachie, Wilbert J., and Marilla Svinicki. 2006. *McKeachie's Teaching Tips.* 12th ed. Boston: Houghton-Mifflin.

Mundhenk, Leigh. 2004. "Toward an Understanding of What It Means to Be Student-Centered: A New Teacher's Journey." *Journal of Management Education* 28, no. 4: 447–462.

Palmer, Parker J. 1998. *The Courage to Teach: Exploring the Inner Landscape of a Teacher's Life.* 1st ed. San Francisco: Jossey-Bass.

Powell, J.P. 1988. "Reducing Teacher Control." In *Developing Autonomy in Student Learning,* edited by David Boud, 109–188. London: Kogan Page.

Rankin, Virginia. 1988. "One Route to Critical Thinking." *School Library Journal* 34, no. 1: 28–31.

Schneider, Andrea K., and Julie MacFarlane. 2003. "Having Students Take Responsibility for the Process of Learning." *Conflict Resolution Quarterly* 20, no. 4: 455–462.

Tollefson, Kaia, and Monica K. Osborn. 2008. *Cultivating the Learner-Centered Classroom: From Theory to Practice.* Thousand Oaks, CA: Corwin Press.

Vella, Jane. 2000. *Learning to Listen. Learning to Teach.* 2nd ed. San Francisco: Jossey-Bass.

Weimer, Mary Ellen. 2002. *Learner-Centered Teaching: Five Key Changes to Practice.* San Francisco: Jossey-Bass.

Chapter 3

Where Did Learner-Centered Teaching Come From?

If I have seen farther it is by standing on the shoulders of giants.

—Sir Isaac Newton

THE EVOLUTION OF AN IDEA

After reading Chapters 1 and 2, a picture of what learner-centered teaching (LCT) is and how you would recognize an LCT environment when you see one should be forming in your mind. But you might be wondering where the idea of LCT originated. Although the term started to be used by educators and psychologists in the 1990s, a look back at the history of educational psychology shows that the principles of LCT have been around for a very long time. As with any field or discipline, current practice is built on what went before. Although theorists and researchers such as Dewey, Pavlov, Freire, Skinner, Piaget, Bruner, Rogers, Maslow, Bandura, Vygotsky, and the like may not have used the term, an examination of their writings reveals elements that support LCT teaching principles. Those who promote the ideas that underlie LCT have drawn upon and expanded the works of these giants in the field. This chapter will describe how "those who have gone before" contributed to and inspired current LCT practices. It will also direct the reader to the research literature from education, psychology, and the neurosciences that offer support for these practices.

It is also interesting to note that the evolution of LCT principles parallels that of the establishment of information literacy as a concept in the library profession. Ideas related to both concepts have been around for a long time, but both began to get some serious attention in the mid- to late 1990s. LCT can trace its origins back to John Dewey's work from the early 1900s (Dewey, 1916, 1938), and elements of LCT can be seen in all major theories of learning spanning the 1920s to the 1980s. The components of LCT were pulled together in the late 1990s in the APA's

Learner-Centered Psychological Principles (American Psychological Association Work Group of the Board of Educational Affairs, 1997) and began to influence teaching practices at that time.

On the information sciences side, the term "information literacy" was first used in 1974 (Zurkowski, 1974) but did not come into common use until 1989 when the American Library Association's (ALA) Presidential Committee on Information Literacy published its final report (ALA. Presidential Committee on Information Literacy, 1989). However, just as LCT did not appear out of nowhere, elements of information literacy can be traced back to the ways librarians worked with their users from the 1970s through the 1980s. So, both the terms LCT and information literacy became part of the vocabulary of their respective fields in the same ten-year span—from 1989 to 1998. And both support the goal of creating learners who are self-reliant, self-directed, lifelong learners. The connection between both concepts is strong and further supports the idea that LCT is a good approach for those of us who engage in information literacy instruction (ILI).

JOHN DEWEY AND THE PROGRESSIVE EDUCATION MOVEMENT

Before we search for the origins of LCT in the various psychological learning theories, we need to pause and examine one of the most influential educators of the twentieth century—John Dewey. Dewey not only spearheaded the educational reform movement in the first quarter of the twentieth century, he also helped set up laboratory schools to test out his ideas. Dewey and his colleagues planted many seeds of what would later be referred to as LCT as they attempted to change the way learners and teachers interacted in the school setting (Dewey, 1916, 1938; Marlow and Page, 2005; Schutz, 2001).

Dewey and his followers argued that ideas couldn't be transferred directly from one person to another—an idea later expanded upon by Paulo Freire. Both Dewey and Freire argued against what Freire referred to as the "transmittal or banking model" of teaching in which learners are viewed as empty vessels just waiting for "teachers as experts" to fill their minds with truth. Education from this perspective is seen as working on rather than with the learner (Freire, 1970, 1974). For real learning to occur, learners need to be viewed as participants rather than spectators, and teachers as those who facilitate the learning process. Acquiring and developing knowledge, from this perspective, requires active involvement on the part of the learner through relevant, thought-provoking projects that simulate real-life issues—an idea that later grew into the authentic or problem-based learning approach to teaching. Learners' needs and interests should be taken into account so that instructors can develop projects and create learning experiences that build upon previous experiences and that connect to and have personal meaning for their learners. The idea that knowledge and meaning is socially constructed through cooperative inquiry in which people solve problems together also has its roots in Dewey's work. Finally, Dewey felt that school and learning should be positive experiences that inspire people to continue learning throughout their lives—a definite tie to information literacy as well as to LCT (Innes, 2004; Marlow and Page, 2005; Schutz, 2001).

While Dewey (and later Freire) was promoting ways to reform education and schools, psychologists were taking a closer look at how people learn. Although the majority of Dewey's work overlapped with that of early twentieth-century theorists and researchers who would come to be called behaviorists, his ideas have remained relevant to the present day despite the evolution of ideas regarding learning that have appeared in the psychological literature over the years. Psychologists from both the cognitive and humanist perspectives included many elements of Dewey's work in their theoretical approaches. Freire's work in the 1970s seems especially relevant to the cognitive ideas of knowledge construction and collaborative learning, as well as to the humanists' views on a more mutually supportive relationship between teachers and learners. Now let's turn our attention to what all these psychological learning theories have to say about how people learn and the impact of that work on LCT.

HOW PSYCHOLOGICAL LEARNING THEORIES CONTRIBUTE TO LCT

Although there is a vast amount of literature and research on how people learn, psychological learning theories are generally considered to fall into three major groups—behaviorist, cognitive/constructivist, and humanist (Elliott et al., 2000; Slavin, 2011). These groups also can be referred to as, respectively, the "doing," "thinking," and "feeling" theorists (Grassian and Kaplowitz, 2009; Kaplowitz, 2008). Keep in mind that none of these theories is completely right or totally wrong. Each is built on the theories that came before it—incorporating some elements, expanding or revising others, and adding new ideas as well. Let's take a look at the elements of LCT that can be traced to these "doing," "thinking," and "feeling" theories of learning.

Doing, or the Behaviorist's View of Learning

Generally considered the oldest of the three ideas, the behaviorist approach has its origins in the works of Pavlov, Thorndike, Tolman, Watson, and B.F. Skinner. The behaviorist movement began, in part, as an attempt to move toward a more scientific study of human behavior. The publication of Darwin's *Origin of the Species* and *The Expression of Emotions in Man and Animals* (in 1859 and 1872, respectively) opened the door for more laboratory-based experimentation on animals, the findings of which could be extrapolated to human behavior. The Russian physiologist Ivan Petrovich Pavlov's (1927) work on the salivation reflex in dogs inspired behaviorists such as Thorndike (1913) and Tolman (1932) to explore how stimulus–response associations were developed and strengthened through reinforcement. John Watson expanded the ideas to include the conditioning of human emotional responses (Watson and Rayner, 1920), and B.F. Skinner, in his over 50 years of active research, developed links between theoretical research and actual classroom practices (Skinner, 1938, 1968, 1974, 1983). Skinner's work on the value of active participation, immediate feedback, reinforcement, mastery learning, chunking, modeling, teaching to individual differences, and allowing learners to move at their own paces were especially influential and can certainly be seen as elements of LCT. The techniques of computer-assisted instruction and online tutorials also have their origins in this "doing" theoretical orientation (Cruickshank, Jenkins, and Metcalf, 2009; Eggen and Kauchak, 2010; Slavin, 2011).

Thinking, or the Cognitive View of Learning

Cognitive psychologists developed their theories as a reaction to the behaviorists' view of learning, which cognitive psychologists felt was too limited in scope. While the behaviorists concentrated on trial and error and the reinforcement of observable behavior, the cognitive psychologists looked at changes in behavior that occur without this trial and error practice. For example, insight, or the "aha" phenomenon, in which a learner suddenly seems to come up with the solution to a problem just by thinking about it, is difficult for behaviorists to explain (Köhler and Winter, 1925). With its roots in the field of perception, cognitive psychology viewed learning as it relates to patterns (Wertheimer, 1912). Theorists from this school of thought believed that learning happens when situations or experiences come in conflict with a person's worldview or mental models. This conflict creates a tension that the learner must work to resolve in order to form new mental models.

Piaget, one of the most influential of the early cognitive psychologists, concentrated on changes in thinking that occur over time via maturation (Piaget and Inhelder, 1969; Inhelder and Piaget, 1958; Piaget, 1953). The idea of readiness, that learning cannot occur until the child is old enough to learn it, is very much rooted in Piagetian ideas. Later cognitive psychologists adopted a more experiential notion about how mental models develop and change. Known as constructivists, these theorists concentrate on the idea that learners actively build, create, or construct new mental models through their interactions with their environment. For these constructivists, learning is dependent on the types of opportunities or experiences offered to the learner. Learning, therefore, is a process in which learners construct meaning rather than merely take in ideas and memorize them. The constructivist movement greatly influenced education and resulted in the promotion of more active or participatory learning approaches to teaching, such as Bruner's Discovery Method (Bruner, 1961)—thus further paving the way for LCT ideas (Eggen and Kauchak, 2010; Elliott et al., 2000; Kaplowitz, 2008; Slavin, 2011).

The constructivist perspective also promotes learning through social interactions that allow learners to test their understanding against those of others. So we can trace the principle of learning through collaboration back to these theorists, most notably to Vygotsky (Vygotsky and Cole, 1978), who believes that social construction of knowledge occurs when people come together and collaborate in learning communities to formulate and test out ideas based on shared experiences (Bransford et al., 2006; Eggen and Kauchak, 2010; Elliott et al., 2000).

So the cognitive/constructivists theories provide support for the LCT principles of collaboration and participation. This "thinking" theoretical orientation encourages us to get our learners to interact actively with content so that they can build their own mental models, organize the material in a way that makes sense to them, and then retrieve it more readily when needed at a later time. Furthermore, this theoretical orientation, with its emphasis on the social construction of knowledge, endorses collaborative learning and group work as an effective way for people to learn.

Feeling, or the Humanist View of Learning

This brings us to the third philosophical orientation, the humanist approach to learning. Just as the previous two theoretical viewpoints were products of their time, the humanists looked at learning from the more free-spirited, "do your own thing" viewpoint of the 1960s. While building on and incorporating some of the ideas of the "doing" and "thinking" schools of thought, the humanists looked at learning from a different perspective, that of the affective or feeling side of the equation. Humanists stressed the importance of teaching to the whole person and recognized that how people feel about themselves and what they are learning is as important as what they think about the material (Grassian and Kaplowitz, 2009; Kaplowitz, 2008).

Not surprisingly, humanists such as Bandura, Maslow, and Rogers were interested in what motivates people to learn and how learning situations can contribute to (or detract from) the learners' feelings of self-esteem and self-efficacy (Bandura, 1977a, 1977b; Maslow, 1970; Rogers, 1969). Creating a safe, welcoming, and supportive learning environment is of paramount importance to those who promote the humanist approach to teaching. Grading on a curve does not exist in the humanist classroom. Each learner is valued for his or her own contributions. Humanist teachers expect the best from their learners and believe that everyone can learn given the right opportunities and support.

Cooperation, rather than competition, is encouraged. Every voice is given an equal chance to be heard, and all views are respected. Honoring diversity is a natural outgrowth of this approach to education. Furthermore, taking responsibility for one's own learning and helping and supporting one's fellow learners are major characteristics of the humanist perspective. So this "feeling" orientation contributed a great deal to the learner-centered ideas of shared responsibility and collaborative learning. For the humanists, the value of collaboration is the opportunity to work with, hear from, and learn about people who view the world from a wide variety of perspectives. In doing so, each learner's worldview expands, not just about the cognitive content being reviewed but also about how others think and feel about what they are learning.

COMMON THREADS—COLLABORATION, PARTICIPATION, RESPONSIBILITY

Clearly LCT can claim each of the three theories of learning as part of its heritage. Although each approach developed from different perspectives, a closer look at the principles associated with each of the theories uncovers some interesting commonalities that offer support for the three main components of LCT—Collaboration, Participation, and shared Responsibility (CPR).

Both the cognitive/constructivists and the humanists support the idea of collaboration as a crucial component of learning. Knowledge, to the cognitive/constructivists, is not constructed in a vacuum. Although we each develop our own mental models, we must test out our ideas in our communities before we decide if they are truly valid. Humanists want us to work in communities so our knowledge grows from an understanding of a diversity of perspectives and viewpoints (Grassian and Kaplowitz, 2009). LCT approaches that incorporate collaborative learning techniques, group work, and the creation of learning communities all have their origins in these theoretical ideas. Furthermore, collaboration implies that learners are actively involved with the material, which leads us to the second component of LCT—participation.

The idea of active participation is supported by all three theoretical viewpoints. However, the reasons for this participatory approach to learning differ slightly. For the behaviorists, learners need to be actively engaged in a trial and error type of situation so that they can "accidentally" stumble upon the best solution to the problem at hand, giving the instructor the opportunity to offer immediate feedback and reinforce this correct response. The cognitive/constructivists view active participation as key to the learners' abilities to discover new ways of knowing and to construct or reconstruct mental models. Both the cognitive/constructivists and the humanists want learners to actively participate not only with the material but also with each other in keeping with both theories' ideas about the importance of social learning.

Active participation also implies that learners have the necessary skills and abilities to interact with the material. All three theories address this crucial aspect of learning. The behaviorist's principles of readiness, mastery, and chunking of material examine the ways in which learners are supported as they move through the material. These ideas are consistent with cognitive/constructivist views that new learning builds on what is already known. Humanists also agree that it is important to understand what learners already know before attempting to introduce them to anything new. Allowing learners to move through material at their own pace and the importance of providing learners with constructive feedback on their progress through this material is supported by all three theories as well (Grassian and Kaplowitz, 2009). All of these common threads have influenced how learner-centered instructors create ways for their learners to engage with the content to be learned.

Now let's look at the third characteristic of LCT—responsibility. One implication of having learners work collaboratively is that they are doing so in order to help each other learn the material. While cognitive/constructivists might emphasize the "whole is greater than the sum of its parts" benefit of working with others in order to create or re-create mental models, humanists promote collaboration for its more social, mutually supportive aspects. But both would agree that working together in groups implies some sort of shared responsibility for learning. Furthermore, the learner-centered focus on learners taking more responsibility for their own learning is an outgrowth of the principles of metacognition and relevance, both of which are supported by the cognitive/constructivists and the humanists (Grassian and Kaplowitz, 2009). Table 3.1 provides an overview of how all these theoretical perspectives have contributed to our understanding of teaching and learning.

CPR FROM THE TEACHER'S PERSPECTIVE: LISTEN, ENGAGE, INSPIRE

The move to LCT is clearly a natural outgrowth of the ideas and principles introduced by these great educators and psychologists. As we move to this more inclusive philosophy of teaching, we must look for ways to create instructional situations that allow our learners to collaborate, participate, and take responsibility for their own and others' learning. In order to do so, we must listen to our learners and both engage and inspire them.

Collaboration, participation, and shared responsibility are not just attributes we desire in our learners. They are also component parts of our LCT approach.

Table 3.1. Connecting Theory to Practice: Who Said It?					
Principles	Dewey	Freire	Behaviorist	Cognitive/ Constructivist	Humanist
Active participation	X	X	X	X	X
Positive reinforcement			X	X	X
Feedback	X		X	X	X
Moving at own pace			X	X	X
Readiness			X	X	X
Mastery			X	X	
Modeling			X	X	
Discovery learning				X	
Teacher as facilitator	X	X		X	X
Relevance/personal meaning	X			X	X
New knowledge built on prior knowledge	X		X	X	X
Collaborative learning	X	X		X	X
Self-efficacy/belief in learner's abilities					X
Personal responsibility					X
Metacognition				X	X
Reflection				X	X

We must take a collaborative approach in our work with our learners—creating a safe, welcoming, and supportive learning climate in which we are all working together for the common goal of improving everyone's knowledge, skills, and abilities. Learners and teachers alike can benefit from these mutually supportive interactions. Learner-centered instructors often comment about how much they, themselves, have learned from working with their learners. To be truly learner-centered, we must be active participants in the process, both in our roles as facilitators and as content experts who offer constructive feedback that helps learners attain their learning outcomes. And we have a responsibility to attend to the needs of our learners and respond to those needs as appropriate. Knowing as much as we can about our learners' backgrounds, previous learning experiences, and individual instructional and information needs is a vital part of LCT. We need to know what they know and what matters to them in order to create the most relevant and useful instructional situation.

We also exhibit a learner-centered orientation through our interactions with our learners. We do so by inviting questions, comments, and discussion; by honoring all voices; and by encouraging everyone to do the same. Furthermore, we strive to provide timely and informative feedback that helps the learners gain an even better grasp of the material. And, finally, we invite learners into the learning process as much as possible by giving them choices about how they wish to interact with the material, as well as some options about how their progress will be assessed. Allowing learners some choice in the topics for their assignments and perhaps even those addressed during the instruction itself illustrates our learner-centered philosophy. In short, we do whatever we can to listen to our learners, both prior to and during instruction, create engaging learning opportunities that allow them to interact with the material, and empower and inspire them to continue their learning long after the instructional situation is over (Grassian and Kaplowitz, 2009).

The remainder of this book will show how to use these theories in order to move to a more learner-centered approach to teaching. The following chapters will offer suggestions on how to listen to, engage, and inspire learners. And they will discuss how to apply these ideas in a variety of settings, such as face-to-face, online, and blended or hybrid approaches. But before we move on to exploring how to apply theory to practice, let's take a look at the research findings in education, psychology, and the neurosciences that have offered even more support for LCT approaches.

LCT: THE RESEARCH BASE

Knowing the theoretical origins of the ideas that led to the LCT approach is an important step in transforming our teaching practices. But for many years there seemed to be a lack of connection between the theoretical and the practical. As we have already seen, vast quantities of material have been written about the various theories and the principles associated with each. An equally rich and varied research literature existed that dealt with best practices in the actual teaching environment. However, it was unclear how the best practices research intersected with theoretical principles. This led the American Psychological Association (APA) under the leadership of Barbara L. McCombs to embark on the project that ultimately resulted in the publication of *Learner-Centered Psychological Principles* (American Psychological Association Work Group of the Board of Educational Affairs, 1997).

This publication not only defined the concept of LCT; it also distilled years of research on teaching and learning into the 14 principles felt to constitute the LCT approach. Meant as a practical guide to teaching, these principles moved LCT from the theoretical to the actual and serve as a benchmark against which teachers can measure the ways in which they interact with their learners. The 14 principles are categorized into four research-validated domains important to learning—metacognitive and cognitive factors; affective and motivational factors; developmental and social factors; and individual difference factors—and are intended to serve as a framework for designing learner-centered practices at all levels of schooling. Instructors who use these principles in their teaching practices include learners in decisions regarding how and what is being learned, as well as the ways in which that learning will be assessed. They respect and accommodate individual differences in their learners and value the various perspectives each learner brings to the learning situation. Furthermore, learner-centered teachers treat learners as co-creators and partners in both the teaching and the learning process (American Psychological Association Work Group of the Board of Educational Affairs, 1997). In other words, APA's principles really set the stage for teaching practices based on collaboration, participation, and shared responsibility.

Support from Research on Teaching and Learning

Further support for LCT practices comes from the various National Research Council reports that appeared in the five or six years following the publication of APA's *Principles*. Taken together, *How People Learn: Brain, Mind, Experience and School, How People Learn, Bridging Research and Practice*, and *How Students Learn: History, Math and Science in the Classroom* expanded what we know about the science behind LCT (Bransford et al., 1999, 2000, 2006; National Research Council, 2005) and served as foundational documents for the research examining the effectiveness of LCT that continues to appear in the literature to this day.

Let's take a look at a sample of some of this research. Cornelius-White in his 2007 meta-analysis of research on learner-centered teacher–learner relations concluded that learning is enhanced in contexts where learners are in supportive relationships with their teachers, have a sense of ownership and control over their own learning, and are allowed to learn from each other in a safe and trusting environment (Cornelius-White, 2007). Meece and her colleagues examined the impact of using LCT practices on middle school and young adolescent learners. Their findings indicated that learners who had experienced LCT reported more positive forms of motivation and greater academic engagement when they perceived their teachers as using learner-centered practices. Practices that involve creating learning activities around themes that are meaningful to learners, promoting critical and higher-order thinking skills, providing complex and challenging learning activities, and providing opportunities for learners to choose their own projects, work at their own pace, and collaborate with their peers during the learning process were viewed as especially important. These learner-centered teachers were seen as caring about their learners and as ones who honor learners' voices and adapt instruction to individual needs (Meece,

2003; Meece, Herman, and McCombs, 2003; Schunk, Pintrich, and Meece, 2008). McCombs (2003a, 2003b) confirmed that these findings were applicable across all grade (K–12) and all age levels.

Dean and Kuhn (2007) looked at discovery, active participation, and practice, with or without direct instruction, and concluded that direct instruction alone is not sufficient to sustain learning over time. Practice that allowed learners some elements of self-discovery was necessary for learning to transfer to new situations. Best transfer occurred when learners were given multiple opportunities to practice with different problems.

Blatchford et al. (2006) explored the impact of collaborative group work. Their results showed more active, sustained engagement, more connectedness, and more higher-order thinking and reasoning in collaborative groups than in their learners who did not work in this group setting. Evidence also exists indicating that learners who study under various forms of peer interaction (such as discussions rather than lectures) have more positive attitudes toward the subject matter and increased motivation to learn and are better satisfied with the experience than those who have been offered less opportunities to interact with their fellow learners and their teachers. Group work has also been shown to promote learning from diversity because it encourages input from a variety of perspectives (Barkley, Cross, and Major, 2004). Furthermore, research has demonstrated that people who learn in collaborative settings perform better than those in competitive or individualistic ones in terms of reasoning and how well they transfer learning from one situation to another. In addition, these learners were shown to have higher levels of self-understanding, commitment, and performance and a sense of belonging (LePage, Darling-Hammond, and Akar, 2005; Slavin, 1990).

Support from Research on Memory

Support for LCT can also be found in an examination of how memory works and the concept of cognitive overload. First, we must understand the various types of memory—sensory memory that briefly stores stimuli from the environment until it can be processed, short-term or working memory where people process and try to make sense of this input, and long-term memory where information is stored for future retrieval (Cruickshank, Jenkins, and Metcalf, 2009; Eggen and Kauchak, 2010; Jensen, 1998). We cannot really say we learned anything until that information has moved from short- to long-term memory storage. The problem with short-term memory is that it has a limited capacity (Miller, 1956; Pressley and Harris, 2006). So, once it is full, we cannot process any new information until space is made. It's like trying to add water to an already full glass. Nothing can be added until some of it is moved to another receptacle (Grassian and Kaplowitz, 2009). Asking learners to deal with too much information at once can lead to something referred to as "cognitive overload." If learners are not given time to process what is in their short-term memory and move it to long-term storage, new information just overrides what is already in the short-term memory space. LCT, with its emphasis on active learning, practice, and reflection, breaks up the information flow into more manageable chunks and encourages learners to thoroughly process new information through discussion, collaborative activities, and practice. Learners are encouraged to engage in practice that asks them to try and apply what they have learned to new situations. All this helps to reduce cognitive overload by giving learners the chance to move newly learned material into long-term memory. Furthermore, getting to apply what they learned further solidified the material in that long-term storage (Clark and Taylor, 1994; Denman, 2005; Mayer and Moreno, 2003; Veldof, 2006).

Support from Research on Deep versus Surface Learning

LCT also draws support from the literature and research on deep versus surface learning. Studies have shown that learner-centered approaches are better at encouraging the attainment of higher cognitive skills such as analysis, synthesis, and evaluation than more passive learning situations. As a result, learner-centered approaches contribute to the development of lifelong learning skills, attitudes, and behaviors—yet another reason why LCT is such a good choice of ILI.

LCT results in deep rather than surface learning. Surface learners retain the information for only a short period of time. But, in LCT teaching environments, learners are not just passively absorbing facts and information. They are asked to connect the new information to what they already know and to use those connections to restructure their thinking. So, instead of just being asked to replicate what was presented (by the teacher or in the text), learners are challenged to become critical thinkers and problem solvers who are able to construct and produce information. They are able to go beyond just reproducing or regurgitating information, gain a deep understanding of the material, and thus become knowledge creators in their own right (Grassian and Kaplowitz, 2009; King, 1993; Marlow and Page, 2005; Weimer, 2003).

Support from Neuroscience Research

Educational and psychological research clearly offers a great deal of support for LCT teaching. Now let's look at the evidence presented from the more biological research arena. Advances in neural imaging and biochemistry have enabled researchers to examine what actually happens in the brain during learning. Imaging techniques have allowed scientists to localize areas of the brain that underlie cognitive functioning. With this advanced imaging, researchers can watch areas of the brain "light up" under various learning conditions (Berninger and Richards, 2002; Bransford et al., 2005). Here's what this body of research tells us about LCT.

First, this research shows that the brain is not a static organ but rather one designed to change in response to experience. Rather than being fixed, the brain is dynamically changing and restructuring throughout life (Garland and Howard, 2009; Jenkins et al., 1990; Mundkur, 2005; Nudo, Jenkins, and Merzenich, 1996). Although the number of neurons in the brain does not change over time, the brain actually increases in mass as we develop. How can that be? The reason lies in how neurons communicate with each other. They do so by sending out branches called "dendrites" and "axons" that serve as a way for neurons to transfer information between them (Leamnson, 2000). At birth each neuron has about 7,500 connections. These connections increase during the first two years of life until they are twice that of the adult brain. This is followed by a pruning period in which the connections that are used most are retained, while other less used ones are discarded. Newly formed connections are weak and labile. If nothing further happens with that connection, it stops functioning. The connections between cells that are active together are strengthened and preserved. The more times a connection is activated, the stronger that connection becomes. In other words, "use it or lose it." With sufficient use, the connections stabilize and can then be thought of as permanent—something that will last throughout our lives (Di Filippo et al., 2009; Garland and Howard, 2009; Leamnson, 2000; Mundkur, 2005). The origin of this idea can be traced back to work done more than 50 years ago by the renowned researcher Donald Hebb (1949). Hebb postulated that neurons form networks if they are stimulated in close temporal proximity. Neuroscientists summarize this idea by saying neurons that fire together, wire together (Begley, 2007; Doidge, 2007; Mundkur, 2005). So the organization of the adult brain, particularly that of the cerebral cortex area, can be and is substantially changed and reorganized as a result of practice and experience (Garland and Howard, 2009; Kelly, Foxe, and Garavan, 2006). New connections between various parts of the brain can be formed, and those already in place can be strengthened based on how we interact with the world around us.

Clearly LCT practices that incorporate active participation in learning seem entirely in line with what we know about how the brain grows and changes through experience. There is also some support that suggests social experiences influence the development of new neural connections (Garland and Howard, 2009; Jensen, 1998)—thus confirming the importance of collaborative learning and group work as part of that active participation. However, as we all know, simply getting learners involved through practice and in collaborative group work is not enough for learning to occur. We must capture their attention and somehow get them emotionally involved in the material. Which brings us to the concept of relevance.

Research on the contributions of the limbic system to the learning experience supports the idea that relevance is an important mechanism to get and keep our learners' attention. Sometimes called the "emotional" or "ancient" brain, the limbic system is linked to many other areas, most notably the frontal lobes of the neocortex. Part of the neocortex's role is that of organizing brain activity. This is the region that keeps track of input, weighs it, calculates its importance, and ultimately prioritizes it. In other words, the frontal lobes help the brain pick out what deserves our attention from the vast amount of information that is impinging on us at all times. So the frontal lobes help us concentrate on what's important and to disregard distractions. In order to do that, the frontal lobes need input from the limbic system. It is the limbic system that adds the emotional overtone to the incoming information, which greatly affects how we feel about that information. This limbic system–frontal lobe connection seems to support the idea that learning is enhanced or speeded up as a result of some level of emotional involvement with the content. Hands-on activity facilitates learning only when the frontal (or thinking) part of the brain is communicating with the limbic (or feeling) modules. Getting the limbic system involved through emotional engagement with the material is an effective way to set off signals that focus attention on that material. Even from the neurological standpoint, learners need to be involved with and engaged in material during learning (Jensen, 1998; Kovalik and Olsen, 1998; Leamnson, 2000).

While it is interesting to "watch" the brain during learning through techniques like functional magnetic resonance imaging, it is also enlightening to examine changes at the biochemical levels. There are a variety of neural transmitters, peptides, and hormones that are constantly circulating throughout the body. It is through the distribution and movement of these chemicals that information is transmitted from neuron to neuron. Of special interest are the peptides, which constitute the largest of these information-carrying molecules. Peptides are produced in every cell of the body, and every known peptide has receptors in the brain, thus providing a way for the body to communicate with the brain and affect its responses to input. Furthermore, the limbic system contains an amazing amount of these neuropeptides, which leads researchers to speculate that these molecules play a major role in telling the brain what is worth attending to and how we should feel about it. This research lends even further support for the idea that emotions drive attention and attention drives learning. Rewarding and encouraging our learners, and helping them feel good about themselves and what they are learning, further stimulates the emotional centers of the brain, not only increasing motivation but also causing the learning to imprint even more strongly (Jensen, 1998; Kovalik and Olsen, 1998; Mundkur, 2005).

As the learning experience progresses, different parts of the brain get involved. While the limbic system is important for getting the learners' attention and involvement, the hippocampus seems to be where short-term memory is processed. Long-term storage requires cortical involvement as well. Once a memory is permanently stored in areas commonly referred to as the "subcortical" or "striatum" area, the more surface neocortex regions are freed up to process newer input. Finally, it has been shown that the more complex cognitive abilities seem to require a larger involvement of the brain, especially in the cortical regions, and that practice strengthens the connections between these different areas (Aragona and Carelli, 2006; Di Filippo et al., 2009; Kelly, Foxe, and Garavan, 2006).

Returning to the concept of cognitive overload for a moment, we can also see support for incorporating a variety of activities into our teaching practices as a way to break up the instruction and allow learners not only to practice and engage with the material but also to provide time for this short- to long-term transfer. Furthermore, there appears to be evidence that our ability to stay alert and attentive fluctuates in cycles. So we actually cannot be expected to continually engage with new information (Jensen, 1998; Lavie, 1982; Rossi and Nimmons, 1991). If we are not given these break periods, we will take them anyway—thus the commonly experienced phenomenon of learners' "spacing out" or getting that glazed-over expression in their eyes. It is not because learners are rude or don't care. Their brains have just gone into overload, and they simply are no longer physically capable of learning anything else at that moment. Even giving learners a short stretch break or having them move around the room to form new learning groups may help get them back in the learning mode.

FINAL REMARKS

So, what have we learned from this journey through the annals of theory and research associated with how people learn? We have seen that our LCT practices grew out of a sound theoretical base and that their effectiveness has been tested and confirmed by educators and psychologists alike over the years—both in the field and in the laboratory. Furthermore, we have learned that an examination on the more neurological and molecular level also offers support for LCT. While many of us may relate to LCT concepts at a purely gut level, feeling intuitively that they are the best way in which to relate to our learners, it is comforting to know that these ideas have been vetted and proved to be effective over the years. A firm understanding of the theory and research that supports LCT gives us confidence that we are moving in the right direction as we transform ourselves into learner-centered teachers. And it gives us the needed ammunition to help us convince our colleagues, administrators, learners, and other members of our community that LCT is an idea whose time has come.

REFLECTIONS

1. Think about the overall characteristics of each of the three main theories (doing, thinking, feeling) that were discussed in this chapter. If you had to

pick one theory to describe the type of teacher you wish to be, would you be a behaviorist, cognitive/constructivist, or a humanist? What is it about that theory that influenced your decision?

2. Now consider a more mix-and-match approach. What elements of the various theories appeal to you? Can you think of ways in which these elements can be combined and then applied to actual teaching practices? What type of exercises, activities, and/or teaching techniques would best illustrate the elements you wish to incorporate in your teaching practices?

3. Next think about your own learning experiences. Have you personally encountered any of these theory-inspired teaching practices? If so, do you think they contributed to your learning? Why or why not?

4. Finally, think about the teaching practices you identified in number 3 as best contributing to your learning. Which of these practices would you like to incorporate in your own instructional endeavors? Also consider those that seemed to have gotten in the way of your learning. How would you modify those practices to make them more effective?

EXPLORATIONS

American Psychological Association Work Group of the Board of Educational Affairs. 1997. *Learner-Centered Psychological Principles: A Framework for School Reform and Redesign.* Washington, DC: American Psychological Association.

This document is commonly thought of as foundational to the LCT movement. It gives a snapshot of what LCT is all about in just a few short pages. Well worth a look.

Bransford, John D., et al. 2000. *How People Learn: Brain, Mind, Experience, and School.* Washington, DC: National Academies Press.

In this work, Bransford and his colleagues pull together and summarize a vast quantity of research literature on learning and behavior.

———. 2006. "Learning Theories and Education: Toward a Decade of Synergy." In *Handbook of Educational Psychology*, edited by Patricia A. Alexander and Phillip H. Winne, 209–244. Mahwah, NJ: Lawrence Erlbaum.

Bransford and his colleagues review the most influential theories of learning and show how they have influenced teaching practices.

Eggen, Paul, and Don Kauchak. 2010. *Educational Psychology: Windows on Classrooms.* Upper Saddle River, NJ: Merrill.

Refer to this 2010 textbook for an overview of psychological and education theories in teaching and learning and a look at current teaching practices.

Elliott, Stephen N., Thomas R. Kratochwill, Joan Littlefield Cook, and John F. Travers. 2000. *Educational Psychology: Effective Teaching, Effective Learning.* 3rd ed. Boston: McGraw-Hill.

> Elliott and his colleagues' outstanding textbook provides a thorough overview of teaching and learning research and practice. Though a bit older than Eggen and Kauchak's textbook, it offers excellent insight and suggestions.

Kaplowitz, Joan. 2008. "The Psychology of Learning: Connecting Theory to Practice." In *Information Literacy Instruction Handbook*, edited by Christopher N. Cox and Elizabeth B. Lindsay, 26–49. Chicago: ALA. ACRL.

> This chapter offers a brief overview to how what we know about learning theories can be applied to practice.

McCombs, Barbara L., and Lynda Miller. 2007. *Learner-Centered Classroom Practices and Assessments: Maximizing Student Motivation, Learning, and Achievement.* Thousand Oaks, CA: Corwin Press.

> Coauthored by the former president of the American Psychological Association, who helped create the 1997 Learner-Centered Psychological Principles, this book offers a lot of practical advice about putting those principles into practice. Although geared to K–12 teachers, much of the material can be applied to teaching in any environment.

Slavin, Robert E. 2011. *Educational Psychology: Theory into Practice.* 10th ed. Upper Saddle River, NJ: Prentice Hall.

> This is another excellent textbook in the field. As indicated by its title, Slavin not only introduces the ideas that underlie the various learning theories, he also shows how those theories can be applied to teaching practices.

REFERENCES

ALA. Presidential Committee on Information Literacy. 1989. *Final Report.* Chicago: American Library Association.

American Psychological Association Work Group of the Board of Educational Affairs. 1997. *Learner-Centered Psychological Principles: A Framework for School Reform and Redesign.* Washington, DC: American Psychological Association.

Aragona, Brandon J., and Regina M. Carelli. 2006. "Dynamic Neuroplasticity and the Automation of Motivated Behavior." *Learning and Memory* 13, no. 5: 558–559.

Bandura, Albert. 1977a. "Self-Efficacy: Toward a Unifying Theory of Behavioral Change." *Psychological Review* 84, no. 2: 191–215.

———. 1977b. *Social Learning Theory.* Englewood Cliffs, NJ: Prentice-Hall.

Barkley, Elizabeth F., K. Patricia Cross, and Claire Howell Major. 2004. *Collaborative Learning Techniques: A Handbook for College Faculty.* San Francisco: Jossey-Bass.

Begley, Sharon. 2007. *Train Your Mind. Change Your Brain.* New York: Ballantine.

Berninger, Virginia W., and Todd L. Richards. 2002. *Brain Literacy for Educators and Psychologists.* San Diego, CA: Academic Press.

Blatchford, Peter, Ed Baines, Christine Robie-Davis, Paul Bassett, and Anne Chowne. 2006. "The Effect of a New Approach to Group Work on Pupil–Pupil and Teacher–Pupil Interactions." *Journal of Educational Psychology* 98, no. 4: 750–765.

Bransford, John D., Ann L. Brown, Rodney R. Cocking, and National Research Council. 1999. *How People Learn: Bridging Research and Practice.* Washington, DC: National Academies Press.

———, eds. 2000. *How People Learn: Brain, Mind, Experience and School.* Washington, DC: National Academies Press.

Bransford, John D., Sharon Derry, David Berliner, Karen Hammerness, and Kelly Lynn Becket. 2005. "Theories of Learning and Their Role in Teaching." In *Preparing Teachers for a Changing World: What Teachers Should Learn and Be Able to Do*, edited by Linda Darling-Hammond and John D. Bransford, 40–87. San Francisco: Jossey-Bass.

Bransford, John D., Reed Stevens, Dan Schwartz, Andy Meltzoff, Roy Pea, Jeremey Roscelle, et al. 2006. "Learning Theories and Education: Toward a Decade of Synergy." In *Handbook of Educational Psychology*, edited by Patricia A. Alexander and Philip H. Winne, 209–244. Mahwah, NJ: Lawrence Erlbaum.

Bruner, Jerome. 1961. "The Act of Discovery." *Harvard Educational Review* 31, no. 1: 21–32.

Clark, Ruth C., and David Taylor. 1994. "The Cause and Cure of Worker Overload." *Training* 31, no. 7: 40–43.

Cornelius-White, Jeffrey. 2007. "Learner-Centered Teacher Student Relationships Are Effective: A Meta-Analysis." *Review of Educational Research* 77, no. 1: 113–143.

Cruickshank, Donald R., Deborah Bainer Jenkins, and Kim K. Metcalf. 2009. *The Act of Teaching.* 5th ed. Boston: McGraw-Hill.

Darwin, Charles. 1859. *On the Origin of the Species by Means of Natural Selection.* London: J. Murray.

———. 1872. *Expression of the Emotions in Man and Animals.* London: J. Murray.

Dean, David Jr., and Deana Kuhn. 2007. "Direct Instruction VS Discovery: The Long View." *Science Education* 91, no. 3: 384–397.

Denman, Mariate. 2005. "How to Create Memorable Lectures." *Speaking of Teaching* 14, no. 1: 1–5.

Dewey, John. 1916. *Democracy and Education.* New York: MacMillan.

———. 1938. *Experience and Education.* New York: MacMillian.

Di Filippo, Massimiliano, et al. 2009. "Short-Term and Long-Term Plasticity at Corticostriated Synapses: Implications for Learning and Memory." *Behavioural Brain Research* 199, no. 1: 108–118.

Doidge, Norman. 2007. *The Brain That Changes Itself.* New York: Viking.

Eggen, Paul, and Don Kauchak. 2010. *Educational Psychology: Windows on Classrooms.* Upper Saddle River, NJ: Merrill.

Elliott, Stephen N., Thomas R. Kratochwill, Joan Littlefield Cook, and John F. Travers. 2000. *Educational Psychology: Effective Teaching, Effective Learning.* 3rd ed. Boston: McGraw-Hill.

Freire, Paulo. 1970. *Pedagogy of the Oppressed.* New York: Continuum.

———. 1974. *Education for Critical Consciousness.* London: Sheed Ward.

Garland, Eric L., and Matthew Owen Howard. 2009. "Neuroplasticity, Psychosocial Genomics and the Biopsychosocial Paradigm in the 21st Century." *Health and Social Work* 34, no. 3: 191–199.

Grassian, Esther, and Joan Kaplowitz. 2009. *Information Literacy Instruction: Theory and Practice.* 2nd ed. New York: Neal-Schuman.

Hebb, Donald. 1949. *The Organization of Behavior.* New York: Wiley.

Inhelder, Bärbel, and Jean Piaget. 1958. *The Growth of Logical Thinking from Childhood to Adolescence: An Essay on the Construction of Formal Operational Structures.* London: Routledge & Kegan Paul.

Innes, Robert B. 2004. *Reconstructing Undergraduate Education.* Mahwah, NJ: Lawrence Erlbaum.

Jenkins, William M., et al. 1990. "Functional Reorganization of Primary Somatosensory Cortex in Adult Owl Monkeys after Behaviorally Controlled Tactile Stimulation." *Journal of Neurophysiology* 63, no. 1: 82–104.

Jensen, Eric. 1998. *Teaching with the Brain in Mind.* Alexandria, VA: Association for Supervision and Curriculum Development.

Kaplowitz, Joan. 2008. "The Psychology of Learning: Connecting Theory to Practice." In *Information Literacy Instruction Handbook,* edited by Christopher N. Cox and Elizabeth B. Lindsay, 26–49. Chicago: ALA. ACRL.

Kelly, Clare, John J. Foxe, and Hugh Garavan. 2006. "Patterns of Neuronal Human Brain Plasticity after Practice and Their Implications for Neurorehabilitation." *Archives of Physical Medicine and Rehabilitation* 87, no. 12, Suppl 2: S20–S29.

King, Alison. 1993. "From Sage on the Stage to Guide on the Side." *College Teaching* 41, no. 1: 30–35.

Köhler, Wolfgang, and Ella Winter. 1925. *The Mentality of Apes.* London: K. Paul Trench Trubner & Co.

Kovalik, Susan, and Karen D. Olsen. 1998. "The Physiology of Learning: Just What Does Go on in There?" *Schools in the Middle* 7, no. 4: 32–37.

Lavie, Peretz. 1982. "Ultradian Rhythms in Human Sleep and Wakefulness." In *Biological Rhythms, Sleep and Performance,* edited by Wilse B. Webb, 239–271. New York: John Wiley and Sons.

Leamnson, Robert. 2000. "Learning as Biological Brain Change." *Change* 32, no. 6: 34–40.

LePage, Pamela, Linda Darling-Hammond, and Hanife Akar. 2005. "Classroom Management." In *Preparing Teachers for a Changing World: What Teachers Should Learn and Be Able to Do,* edited by Linda Darling-Hammond and John D. Bransford, 327–357. San Francisco: Jossey-Bass.

Marlow, Bruce A., and Marilyn L. Page. 2005. *Creating the Constructivist Classroom.* Thousand Oaks, CA: Corwin Press.

Maslow, Abraham H. 1970. *Motivation and Personality.* 2nd ed. New York: Harper & Row.

Mayer, Richard E., and Roxanne Moreno. 2003. "Nine Ways to Reduce Cognitive Load in Multimedia Learning." *Educational Psychologist* 38, no. 1: 43–52.

McCombs, Barbara. L. 2003a. "A Framework for the Redesign of K–12 Education in the Context of Current Educational Reform." *Theory into Practice* 42, no. 2: 93–101.

———. 2003b. *Defining Tools for Teacher Reflection: The Assessment of Learner-Centered Practices (ALCP)*. ERIC Centre for Curriculum, Transfer and Technology. ED478622.

Meece, Judith L. 2003. "Applying Learner-Centered Principles to Middle School Education." *Theory into Practice* 42, no. 2: 109–116.

Meece, Judith L., Phillip Herman, and Barbara L. McCombs. 2003. "Relations of Learner-Centered Teaching Practices to Adolescents' Achievement Goals." *International Journal of Educational Research* 39, no. 3: 457–475.

Miller, George A. 1956. "The Magic Number Seven, Plus or Minus Two: Some Limits on Our Capacity for Processing Information." *Psychological Review* 63, no. 2: 81–97.

Mundkur, Nandini. 2005. "Neuroplasticity in Children." *Indian Journal of Pediatrics* 72, no. 10: 855–857.

National Research Council. 2005. *How Students Learn: History, Math and Science in the Classroom*. Washington, DC: National Academies Press.

Nudo, Randolf J., William M. Jenkins, and Michael M. Merzenich. 1996. "Use Dependent Alterations of Movement Representations in Primary Motor Cortex of Adult Squirrel Monkeys." *Journal of Neuroscience* 16, no. 2: 785–807.

Pavlov, Ivan Petrovich. 1927. *Conditioned Reflexes*. New York: Dover.

Piaget, Jean. 1953. *The Origin of Intelligence in the Child*. London: Routledge & Kegan Paul.

Piaget, Jean, and Bärbel Inhelder. 1969. *The Psychology of the Child*. London: Routledge & Kegan Paul.

Pressley, Michael, and Karen R. Harris. 2006. "Cognitive Strategies Instruction: From Basic Research to Classroom Instruction." In *Handbook of Educational Psychology*, edited by Patricia A. Alexander and Philip H. Winne, 265–286. Mahwah, NJ: Lawrence Erlbaum.

Rogers, Carl R. 1969. *Freedom to Learn: A View of What Education Might Become*. Columbus, OH: C.E. Merrill.

Rossi, Ernest Lawrence, and David Nimmons. 1991. *The 20-Minute Break: Reduce Stress, Maximize Performance, and Improve Health and Emotional Well-Being Using the New Science of Ultradian Rhythms*. Los Angeles: J.P. Tarcher.

Schunk, Dale H., Paul R. Pintrich, and Judith L. Meece. 2008. *Motivation in Education: Theory, Research and Applications*. 3rd ed. Upper Saddle River, NJ: Merrill/Pearson.

Schutz, Aaron. 2001. "John Dewey's Conundrum: Can Democratic Schools Empower?" *Teachers College Record* 103, no. 2: 267–302.

Skinner, B.F. 1938. *The Behavior of Organisms*. New York: Macmillan.

———. 1968. *The Technology of Teaching*. New York: Appleton-Century-Crofts.

———. 1974. *About Behaviorism*. New York: Knopf.

———. 1983. *A Matter of Consequences*. New York: Knopf.

Slavin, Robert E. 1990. *Cooperative Learning: Theory, Research and Practice*. Englewood Cliffs, NJ: Prentice Hall.

———. 2011. *Educational Psychology: Theory into Practice*. 10th ed. Upper Saddle River, NJ: Prentice Hall.

Thorndike, Edward L. 1913. *Educational Psychology*. New York: Teachers College, Columbia University.

Tolman, Edward Chace. 1932. *Purposive Behavior in Animals and Men*. New York: The Century Co.

Veldof, Jerilyn. 2006. *Creating the One-Shot Library Workshop: A Step by Step Guide.* Chicago: American Library Association.

Vygotsky, Lev S., and Michael Cole. 1978. *Mind in Society: The Development of Higher Psychological Processes.* Cambridge: Harvard University Press.

Watson, John B., and Rosalie Rayner. 1920. "Conditioned Emotional Reactions." *Journal of Experimental Psychology* 3: 1–14.

Weimer, Mary Ellen. 2003. "Focus on Learning. Transform Teaching." *Change* 35, no. 5: 49–54.

Wertheimer, Max. 1912. "Experimental Studies of the Perception of Movement." *Zeitschrift fur Psychologie* 61: 161–265.

Zurkowski, Paul G. 1974. *The Information Service Environment: Relationships and Priorities.* Washington, DC: National Commission on Libraries and Information Science.

Part II

Planning for Learner-Centered Teaching

Chapter 4

What Will Learners Do?— Learner-Centered Teaching Methods

Variety's the very spice of life that gives it all its flavor.

—William Cowper

Now that you have a pretty good idea of how to describe the principles of learner-centered teaching (LCT), what LCT looks like, and where LCT came from, you may be asking yourself, *What's next?* How do I take all this information and translate it into ways that will transform my own teaching practice into a learner-centered one? And how will I know that I have been successful in my attempts to do so? To answer these questions, we need to look at the possible instructional and assessment methods available to us. This chapter, and the one immediately following it, will do just that.

In this chapter we will examine a variety of instructional methods from an LCT perspective with an eye toward helping you incorporate LCT approaches into your own instructional repertoire. The following chapter will turn the LCT lens on the topic of assessment in order to ensure that the ways in which you determine if learning has occurred as a result of your instructional endeavors also have a learner-centered point of view.

HOW DO I TEACH? LET ME COUNT THE WAYS

There are lots of teaching methodologies to choose from when planning instructional endeavors. Some may be more familiar to you than others. The more teacher-centered methods, such as the traditional lecture approach, are referred to as "direct instructional techniques." Others are described as "indirect" and grew out of the desire to transform instruction into a more active, learner-centered experience (Cruickshank, Jenkins, and Metcalf, 2009; Freilberg and Driscoll,

2005; Slavin, 2011). Let's examine each of the methods in turn, starting at the direct end of the spectrum and moving toward the indirect. No one method is the best or the only way to teach. Each has its advantages and its drawbacks. Selecting a particular method depends on many things—the content we are addressing, the characteristics and needs of our audience, the expected learning outcomes for the instruction, logistical constraints (space, time, available equipment, etc.), and so on. The more we know about each of the methods available to us, the better we can select the ones best suited to our particular instructional situation.

THE MANY FLAVORS OF LEARNING

Before exploring these methods, let's take a moment to look at learning from the learners' perspective. Just as there are many different ways to teach, there are also many different ways to learn. Any collection of learners is going to vary in how individual members like to interact with the material to be learned. In other words, learners are going to have a variety of learning styles. Because of this fact, most pedagogical experts recommend use of a variety of instructional methods and techniques in order to maximize the potential of reaching most, if not all, learners.

There is an enormous amount of literature on the subject of learning styles—much more than can be addressed in this book. So let's concentrate on just two ways that learning styles are described. The first, and probably most familiar, is referred to as "perceptual modality" learning styles—or the idea that people prefer to learn through listening (auditory learners), seeing (visual learners), or doing (kinesthetic learners). While this is certainly a useful way to view learning styles, it does not necessarily represent a complete picture of how learners differ.

Another way of looking at learning styles was developed by Peter Honey and Alan Mumford. In their paradigm, learners fall into four categories—Activists, Pragmatists, Theorists, and Reflectors (Honey and Mumford, 1995). Unlike other learning style paradigms, such as Kolb's more widely known Experiential Learning model (Kolb, 1984), Honey and Mumford use a fairly jargon-free language to describe the four styles. Their Learning Styles Questionnaire (LSQ) uses terms such as activists, pragmatists, theorists, and reflectors, making it fairly easy to figure out what type of person each style represents. Other learning style inventories use far more complicated and harder to understand language. Furthermore, the LSQ seems easier to take and to score than other learning style inventories. And, finally, the LSQ gives the learner scores in all four categories. So, although the learner tends to show greater tendencies for one of the four styles, the scores show where the learner falls in all of them—thus offering a clearer and richer picture of his or her style (Grassian and Kaplowitz, 2009;

| Table 4.1. Learning Styles Characteristics ||
Style	Learner Characteristics
Activist	• Will try anything once • Likes fire-fighting—short-term crises • Thrives on new challenges • Becomes bored during implementation • Involves himself or herself with other people
Pragmatist	• Looks for new ideas/techniques to apply to current situation • Experiments with applications • Views problems/opportunities as challenges • Likes clear purpose for tasks • Likes to accomplish clearly defined tasks
Theorist	• Keen on assumptions, theories, models, principles, and systems thinking • Prizes rationality and logic • Tends to be detached and analytical • Unhappy with subjective/ambiguous experiences • Fits tasks into rational schemes
Reflector	• Reviews experiences from different perspectives • Collects and analyzes data before coming to conclusions • Considers all implications before action • Cautious—takes back seat in meetings • Likes to observe others in action

Kaplowitz, 2008). Table 4.1 presents some of the characteristics associated with each of the four styles described by the LSQ.

It should be obvious, even from this brief overview of learning styles, that no one method could possibly suit everyone's learning needs. In learning, as in so many other aspects of life, one size does not fit all. However, some methods are more appealing than others to individual learners (Grassian and Kaplowitz, 2009; McCombs and Miller, 2007). Let's keep these learning style variations in mind as we explore our methodological options in order to see which ones might appeal to different types of learners.

The following is just a selection of possible instructional options. Many more can be found in any good textbook and/or on websites such as Instructional Strategies Online (Saskatoon Public Schools, 2010), which are dedicated to the exploration of teaching methods. Other suggestions are listed in the Reflections section at the end of this chapter. Whenever possible, relevant source material has been cited—especially when discussing any issues relating to the method. Hopefully this introduction to the possibilities for teaching will excite you and inspire you to further explorations throughout your information literacy instruction (ILI) career.

THE LECTURE METHOD

We have all experienced the traditional, teacher-centered lecture or "sage on the stage" style of teaching (King, 1993) at some time or another in our years as learners. To some of us, this style is the perfect way to learn. We like having the material presented in an organized fashion. We are interested in the theoretical underpinnings of the topic and enjoy hearing an expert share his or her knowledge with it. But for others, just sitting and listening to someone tell them about the material is not enough. Some need visual representations of the information. Others want to work with it directly. This passive, sedentary, receptive learner role is not for everyone.

While proponents of the method insist that it is the only way to present large amounts of information in a set period of time, it is unclear whether learners gain much from this bombardment of admittedly valuable information—especially if it takes place over the hour or more that is typically associated with the lecture method. Rather than profiting from the experience, learners often suffer from cognitive overload and are unable to process the quantity of information being presented (Bligh, 2000; Clark and Taylor, 1994). As a result, they become frustrated and anxious, fearing they will never succeed in learning the material (Cruickshank, Jenkins, and Metcalf, 2009; Jensen, 1998; McKeachie and Svinicki, 2006; Veldof, 2006)—certainly not the effect we had in mind for our instructional endeavor. Table 4.2 provides an overview of the advantages and drawbacks of the lecture method.

Literature on the nature of memory supports the idea that the traditional lecture method may actually be counterproductive to learning. To understand why that is so, we must take a short digression into the research surrounding the memory process itself. In 1956, George Miller published his classic paper on memory, describing what he referred to as "short-term" and "long-term" memory. Sensory input is stored in our short-term memory. But short-term memory has a limited capacity. Once it is full, nothing new can be absorbed unless something is removed. So, new information is constantly overriding the information already in our short-term memory storage. It's like trying to pour more water into an already full glass. Nothing can go in until space is made for it (Grassian and Kaplowitz, 2009). Unless information is moved from short- to long-term memory storage (which has been theorized to have unlimited capacity), it may be lost forever. Just like the glass of water example, if we try to push too much information into our learners' heads in a short period of time, they may not be able to take in anything new (due to cognitive overload), and some of

Table 4.2. The Lecture Method	
Advantages	**Drawbacks**
Can address large amounts of information in short periods of time.	Learner in passive role.
Suitable for large groups.	Does not effectively attract and maintain attention.
Good for presenting an overview and for complex information.	Does not allow teachers to check for understanding.
Can offer organized structure for the information.	Can cause cognitive overload if too much information is presented and result in learner's inability to process into long-term memory.
Helps learners integrate information from a variety of sources that might be difficult for learners to find on their own.	Does not encourage critical thinking and analysis.
Can expose learners to multiple points of view.	Can be difficult for some learners to transfer information from lectures to other situations and apply it in real-life settings.
Can present the most up-to-date information, expanding on what is available in the written material.	Encourages memorization and more surface approach to learning.
Most appealing to auditory learners and to theorists.	Less appealing to visual and kinesthetic learners and to activists, pragmatists, and reflectors.

that valuable information will get lost in the shuffle (Clark and Taylor, 1994; Denman, 2005; Mayer and Moreno, 2003).

On the other hand, lectures have the advantage of allowing the instructor to summarize, synthesize, and pull together large amounts of information from various different sources and can illustrate the intellectual process involved in doing so. Lectures are intended to help learners acquire organized bodies of knowledge. The lecture can also serve as a model for how experts think and view the content of their field. Lectures obviously have a clear and important place in teaching. They appeal to certain types of learners, and they serve a legitimate purpose (Cruickshank, Jenkins, and Metcalf, 2009; Eggen and Kauchak, 2010; Freilberg and Driscoll, 2005). So, what is the best way to use the lecture method? The solution is to use the lecture appropriately and judiciously, trying to make lectures as engaging and stimulating as possible (Brookfield, 1990; McKeachie and Svinicki, 2006). For one thing, it is important to limit the amount of time spent in this direct instructional format. The lecture method has been shown to dwindle in effectiveness after about 10 to 15 minutes in adults—possibly less in children (Bligh, 2000; Brookfield, 1990). Breaking up the lecture into smaller chunks, and interspersing other methods between the chunks, can go a long way to increasing the effectiveness of this method. It can boost energy levels and helps learners feel more involved in the material (Cooper and Robinson, 2000). Pausing for questions, or some brief activity for as little as two to five minutes may be all that is necessary (Rowe, 1976, 1980; Di Vesta and Smith, 1978; Ruhl, Hughes, and Schloss, 1987). Interspersing other, more indirect types of activities (interactive questioning, discussions, and/or small group activities) may be even more effective as long as the types of activities selected are appropriate to the material being addressed. Giving learners time to review their notes (alone or with a partner) or other types of reflection activities that challenge the learner to summarize the material addressed in the lecture can also help to enhance the lecture experience, allowing learners to process the information, put it in their own frame of reference, and move it from short- to long-term memory storage. Here are some simple ways to create a more dynamic lecture experience while still maintaining a more teacher-centered, direct instruction approach (Harwood, 1996; Stead, 2005).

Punctuated Lectures

In this approach, also referred to as Listen, Stop, Reflect, Write, and Give Feedback, the lecture is broken up into 10- to 15-minute segments. After each of these segments, learners are asked to reflect on their experiences during that segment—particularly if the material and the way they listened to it helped or hindered their understanding of the information. Learners then write down their comments and share them with the teacher in oral or written feedback. This technique promotes active listening and self-reflection skills, which lead to a deeper learning experience (Angelo and Cross, 1993; Maier and Panitz, 1996).

Lecture-Systematic Questioning

This approach calls for the instructor to intersperse periods of focused, teacher-directed questions at specific points in the lecture. The material to be addressed is broken up into four parts: Introduction/Review; Presentation of Information; Comprehension Monitoring; and Integration. During the Introduction/Review segment the instructor puts the information to be addressed into context, ties it to the interests and needs of the learners, and reviews previously presented material as appropriate. This is the attention-getting portion of the lecture, helping to orient the learners to what is to come and motivating them to listen. The information itself is presented in the second segment. These presentation segments should be kept as short as possible to prevent overloading the learners' short-term memory. The Comprehension Monitoring segment follows, in which the instructor asks a series of questions as a check for understanding. This puts the learners into a more active role, allowing the instructor to check on learners' perceptions of the material and to correct any errors in those perceptions. The instructor then moves on to Integration and asks additional questions that help the learners integrate this new information into their prior knowledge. The sequence is then repeated for the next chunk of information being addressed (Eggen and Kauchak, 2010). One of the advantages of this approach is that the instructor does not move on to new material until he or she has determined that the current material has been correctly understood or, in behaviorist terminology, mastered.

Guided Note Taking

In this approach, also known as the Empty Outline (Angelo and Cross, 1993), the instructor prepares a handout that offers the learners a conceptual framework for the material, thus guiding them through the content being presented. Space is provided so that the learners can capture key ideas and relationships in their own words, as well as personal comments on the material. This exercise has the advantage of modeling the organization of the material, highlighting important concepts being addressed, and alerting learners to where they should be focusing their attention (Ausubel, 1960; Eggen and Kauchak, 2010; Marzano, Pickering, and Pollock, 2001).

Summarizing

Another way to check for understanding is to ask learners to summarize the material just presented. Summarizing requires learners to prepare a concise description of the material just presented (Eggen and Kauchak, 2010; Marzano, Pickering, and Pollock, 2001). After giving the learners time to write down their thoughts, a few learners are asked to share their thoughts. Alternatively, learners can exchange their summaries with a partner and spend a few minutes discussing what was written. As learners compare and contrast their ideas, they can deepen their understanding of the material. Pairs can be asked to turn in a single, joint summary that combines and synthesizes comments from both learners for review and feedback or to report back orally to the full group.

Concept Mapping

Concept maps are graphical representations of complex concepts and, if appropriate, the relationships among them. Asking learners to generate these maps is a wonderful way to involve learners in the creation of a big-picture view of the material to be addressed (Boxtel et al., 2002; Mezeske, 2007; Romance and Vitale, 1999; Saskatoon Public Schools, 2010). A typical concept map, also known as a "spider diagram," places a key concept in the middle with other related words and phrases radiating out from the center (Fox and Morrison, 2005; Marzano, Pickering, and Pollock, 2001).

How Concept Mapping Works

A concept mapping exercise starts by asking learners to generate a list of words or phrases related to the central concept. When working with the entire group of learners, ask them to call out their ideas or ask for volunteers to respond. Another approach is to ask learners to write down their ideas and turn them in. Recruit some of the learners to be recorders who write these ideas on the board, or do this recording yourself. Next ask learners to group the ideas into categories—perhaps through some kind of polling or voting (via electronic devices or by raising their hands) or just by calling on individual learners for their comments. To add even more interactivity, have learners record their ideas on Post-it notes, which can be placed on the board or a wall and can be moved around during the discussion (Fox and Morrison, 2005).

Concept Mapping—Individually or in Groups

Concept mapping works with any number of learners. It can be done individually, in pairs, in small groups, or with the entire class exchanging ideas in a sort of brainstorming mode as described earlier (Fox and Morrison, 2005). See the next section on informal small group discussions to find out how small groups can be created even in the largest of lecture halls. If learners are working on their concept maps in pairs or small groups, ask as many pairs or groups as the time permits to share their ideas during the reporting segment of the exercise. Groups can report back in a number of ways. In part this depends on the number of learners in the class, the physical layout of the room, and the time allotted for the exercise. Just a few groups could be asked to share their ideas verbally, or each pair/group could be supplied with large sheets of paper so they could post their completed maps on the walls around the room. In any case, common themes will probably surface as different maps are shared. These themes can then be used to develop a map that represents all the ideas from the class.

Cognitive and Affective Aspects of Concept Mapping

Concept map exercises are best when used at the beginning of a topic, as they are intended to help the learners build an overall idea of how the information being addressed is organized. When learners do this for themselves rather than merely being presented with the organization, they are more likely to grasp the concepts involved and to put them into a frame of reference that makes sense to them. The concept mapping exercise provides insight into learners' thinking about and understanding of the material being addressed and can serve as a jumping-off point for further discussions (Boxtel et al., 2002; Romance and Vitale, 1999). Furthermore, it gets learners actively involved with the material from the very beginning, captures their attention, and creates a positive mind-set for learning more about the topic.

Use this technique to get at some of the negative feelings that people often associate with having to do "library" research. Start by asking learners to jot down how they feel when they are told they have to do an assignment that requires gathering, analyzing, and synthesizing a body of information on a topic. Then collect these ideas in a variety of ways—depending on the size of the group. When working with 15 to 25 people, ask them to jot their ideas down on 4 × 6–inch Post-it sheets. Then ask them to put these notes on a board or on the wall, grouping them with ideas that seem related to their own. Next, have everyone review the ideas and regroup as necessary. The end result is a bunch of concepts all related to the feelings associated with having to do research—some negative (anxious, overwhelmed, nervous, insecure) and some positive (excited, energized, eager to learn). This exercise can form the basis for a discussion on how the information literacy skills, strategies, and concepts that will be the focus of the session can help to maximize the positive and minimize the negative feelings associated with information-gathering research. Furthermore, getting these feelings out in the open and showing that others share in these feelings helps learners feel more comfortable about embarking on their information-seeking adventures.

Informal Small Group Discussions

Learners are presented with a question or a problem to think about and discuss with one or two neighbors. In most cases these small groups are then asked to report their findings to the whole class. These activities are generally used to punctuate the lecture at key points along the way and generally take only a few minutes of class time. However, they offer a great deal of "bang" for the time investment. These discussions give learners a chance to become actively engaged with the material and to hear about other learners' perspectives on the topic. Small group discussions allow learners to check their understanding with that of their peers and review and refocus on the material just presented. Instructors should walk around and listen to these conversations as a way to monitor comprehension (Cooper and Robinson, 2000; Davis, 2009; Nelken, 2009) and to correct misconceptions on the spot. Time should be spent after this activity to review any material that seems to have been misunderstood.

Any size group can be broken up into smaller subgroups for these types of activities. The simplest technique is to just have learners turn to the person who is next to them. When teaching in a large lecture hall, break the class into groups of four to six by asking learners in the odd-numbered rows to turn around and work with the those directly behind them. If the room has movable furniture, set the room up in advance in a pod formation, with four to six learners gathered around small tables. It is probably best for groups to be no less than three and no more than seven—enough to generate a variety of ideas but not so large that people do not have a chance to participate in the activity (Innes, 2004).

The Appeal and Danger of the Lecture Method

We all suffer from the "tyranny of coverage" syndrome—especially those of us who have limited contact time with our learners. When we are going to have only an hour or two to provide our ILI, it is tempting to try to jam in as much as we possibly can. That is the great appeal, and the terrible temptation, of the lecture approach. However, successful instruction is not measured by how much we present. It is measured by how much our learners take away with them. It is far better to teach a few things well than many things poorly or not at all (Grassian and Kaplowitz, 2009; Ramsden, 1988; Veldof, 2006). So, interspersing our lecture-like presentations with some of the above-described activities will result in a deeper, more fruitful experience for our learners.

The lecture is a valuable part of every teacher's instructional arsenal. If used appropriately and thoughtfully in combination with other types of learning experiences, the lecture can contribute to learners' overall understanding of the information being shared with them and can promote deep learning, critical thinking, and higher cognitive skills, such as analysis, synthesis, and evaluation (Bain, 2004; Duffy, 1995; Weimer, 2002). As we move on to some other instructional techniques, keep the "mix and match" idea in mind. Any of the following methods can be used effectively in combination with the lecture and can help create a more engaging and relevant instructional experience for everyone involved.

MODELING/DEMONSTRATION

Modeling or demonstration is often used in conjunction with the lecture method. Coupled with "thinking aloud," or verbalizing the steps being taken, this is a good way for instructors to model how to perform some complicated activity or demonstrate how to use some online resource (Eggen and Kauchak, 2010). Or instructors might use video clips in which someone else introduces the ideas, activities, or resources (Cruickshank, Jenkins, and Metcalf, 2009; Freilberg and Driscoll, 2005; Saskatoon Public Schools, 2010). While this method is a good way to vary the presentation format, moving it from verbal to visual, it still suffers many of the drawbacks of the lecture method. Learners are cast in a passive, observer role. Furthermore, if too much information is included in the demonstration, there is still the risk of cognitive overload. While this style may appeal to visual learners and those who like to see how things work in a big picture, real-world sort of way, it has limited appeal to those who like to learn by doing. Furthermore, little time is available for reflection as the instructor moves through the material.

Incorporating modeling or demonstrations does offer a change of pace from the verbal heavy nature of the lecture. The key, as with the lecture itself, is to not overdo it. Short demonstrations, interspersed appropriately within the lecture, can liven up the situation. A change of pace often helps to wake people up and recaptures flagging attention. Plus this more visual, big-picture approach does help to widen the appeal to additional groups of learners. Table 4.3 presents an overview of the advantages and drawbacks of the modeling/demonstration method.

QUESTIONING

Questioning is a more inclusive and active approach than either the lecture or the modeling/demonstration techniques. For the first time, the learners' voices are heard as they are invited to join the conversation. Questioning serves many purposes. It can stimulate thinking, offer a change of pace, and help learners put the information into their own words. It also offers instructors a glimpse into the learners' minds and helps them check for comprehension and correct any misconceptions that may show up in the learners' responses (Eggen and Kauchak, 2010; Marzano, Pickering, and Pollock, 2001; Saskatoon Public Schools, 2010).

Effective questioning is an art. Questions must be framed in a way that encourages in-depth responses. They should be open ended—not those that can

Table 4.3. The Modeling/Demonstration Method	
Advantages	**Drawbacks**
Shows learners the right approach or strategy.	Learners are in a passive, observer role.
Highlights what learners should be focusing on.	It does not encourage critical thinking or analysis.
Adds a visual dimension to the presentation.	It may not hold learners' attention, especially if lights must be dimmed or turned off during the demonstration.
Good way to "walk" learners through a complex process/strategy.	Modeling complex processes or strategies can result in cognitive overload and learners' inability to process into long-term memory.
Appeals to visual learners.	Auditory learners may find the visual element distracting as they try to focus on the narration; it does not appeal to kinesthetic learners.
Some appeal for pragmatist learners, who like seeing things in action, and theorists, who like the glimpse at the big picture modeling/demonstration can offer.	It does not appeal to activist or reflective learners.

be answered by a "yes" or "no." Furthermore, it is crucial that the instructor wait a sufficient amount of time (10 to 30 seconds) for learners to respond (Davis, 2009; McKeachie and Svinicki, 2006; Minstrell and Stimpson, 1996). The biggest mistake instructors make is to panic when there is no immediate response after asking a question and provide their own answer to the question before their learners have the chance to participate. This is like throwing water on the questioning fire. Learners will stop even trying to answer the questions, confident that the instructor will supply the answer for them (Cruickshank, Jenkins, and Metcalf, 2009; Eggen and Kauchak, 2010; Freilberg and Driscoll, 2005; Grassian and Kaplowitz, 2009).

Questioning can also increase interactions among the learners themselves. Instructors should act as facilitators during the questioning activity and encourage learners to follow up on their fellow learners' responses or to even come up with questions of their own to direct at their classmates. The questioning method is a way to capture learners' attention, arouse their curiosity about the topic, review and reinforce points already addressed, encourage reflection, and promote critical thinking and active learning (Bain, 2004; Cruickshank, Jenkins, and Metcalf, 2009; Davis, 2009).

Although questioning is definitely a good way to get learners involved and engaged, some people may dislike the command performance element of the method. This is especially true when using "cold calling," directing a question to a specific learner. While many instructors feel that cold calling ensures that learners are paying attention and are coming to class prepared and up-to-date on the assignments, it can also contribute to learners' anxiety levels in class. One has to wonder whether learners are really engaged or are just worried that they are going to be called upon to perform. Cold calling can be effectively used when learners have all done some kind of assignment (in class or as homework) and are being asked to share their experiences with the rest of the group. Because everyone has done the same work, they should all have something to say. Even in this sort of situation, avoid the appearance of "picking" on specific learners by drawing names out of a bag. One advantage of incorporating some kind of online component to a class it that assignments can be posted to the course site and shared among learners in that manner. See Chapter 7 for more on LCT in the online format.

The other time cold calling might be appropriate is toward the end of a discussion. Often, only the most outgoing learners willingly engage in the conversation. If a few learners have kept out of the discussion, ask for comments from only those people who have not said anything as yet—semi–cold calling because no specific person is being singled out. Another approach is to call on some of the more quiet learners by name and ask them directly if they have anything else to add. In either case, make it clear that these quieter learners still have the option to decline from contributing to the conversation.

In all cases, our attitude and behavior during a questioning period will make or break the technique. Our questions must be clear, addressing important and relevant aspects of the material. We can show by the tone in our voices, our body language, and our general demeanor that we really are interested in our learners' responses and value their input. Our responses to learners' comments must be thoughtful, respectful, and encouraging. If what they say is incorrect, use that as a teachable moment. Acknowledge the contribution, thank them for their effort, and then gently and kindly point out where they may have gone wrong. We can then turn the original question back to the class for more responses or provide the answer ourselves and move on to the next question. Our rule of thumb for questioning, as for all our interactions in an LCT environment, is to be supportive, welcoming, and caring in our exchanges with learners (Bain, 2004; Grassian and Kaplowitz, 2009; Weimer, 2002, 2003).

The type of questioning just described is a bit different from the query that is often used during instruction to determine if learners are confused or overwhelmed by the material just addressed. This, too, is a good way to break up a session, check for comprehension, and invite participation. However, it is not meant to tap into higher-order thinking. It is more to make sure it is appropriate to move on to the next piece of information. Be very careful how these "temperature-taking" questions are framed. Remember that the idea is to stimulate conversation, not just nods of the head. So, rather than asking, "Do you have any questions?" ask "What questions do you have for me now?" This not only avoids the less than helpful "no" response or silent shakes of the head, it lets learners know that it is okay to have questions, that we expect them to have some, and that we want to hear what they have to say (Grassian and Kaplowitz, 2009). Our attitude toward learners' questions is also critical here. Be welcoming and encourage these questions. Listen carefully to them, and treat the queries with respect. Always take learners' questions seriously; show an interest in their thoughts and a willingness to provide answers that will improve their understanding of the topic (Davis, 2009; Nelken, 2009).

Questioning is most appealing to activists and pragmatists and offers some appeal to the auditory learner; however, it offers very little to other types. We must turn to other methods in order to extend our appeal to the remaining types of learners. See Table 4.4 for an overview of the advantages and drawbacks of the questioning method.

DISCUSSION

Discussions can occur at any point during instruction, serve a variety of functions, and be initiated in a number of ways. Well-constructed and thoughtful questions can often serve as a jumping-off point for the more in-depth conversations typical

Table 4.4. The Questioning Method	
Advantages	**Drawbacks**
Creates a more interactive experience for the learner.	Only the more outgoing learners may actively participate.
Encourages higher levels of thinking—analysis, synthesis, and evaluation.	Questions need to be carefully structured so that they are inviting critical analysis, leading to higher levels of thinking.
Helps learners organize their thoughts.	The instructor may impose his or her organization on learners through the way questions are structured and/or ordered.
Helps guide learners through the material being addressed.	It may move learners through the material faster than they can process it.
Offers instructors opportunity to correct misconceptions.	Only some misconceptions will surface during the activity, because not everyone will have the opportunity to respond.
Offers instructors opportunity to monitor comprehension.	The instructor will be monitoring only a portion of the learners' comprehension, i.e., those who respond.
Some appeal to auditory learners, who like hearing other people's answers.	It has limited appeal to kinesthetic learners, although it does offer a more active change of pace. It has little or no appeal to visual learners.
Appeals to activists, who like the quick pace usually associated with questioning; some appeal to pragmatists, who like the problem-solving aspect of the approach.	It does not appeal to reflectors, who are overwhelmed by the quick pace usually associated with questioning. It has limited appeal to theorists unless questions are directed at theoretical issues.

of the discussion format. As mentioned earlier, the concept mapping technique is also a good lead-in for a more detailed discussion of the topic. Discussions can be triggered by an intriguing and/or provocative quote or a topical video or audio clip or by presenting the learners with a real-life problem to be solved. Discussions move instruction further into the indirect format as the instructor acts as moderator and facilitator, encouraging and supporting the learners in their explorations of the material (Brookfield, 1995; Cruickshank, Jenkins, and Metcalf, 2009; Davis, 2009; McKeachie and Svinicki, 2006). Effective discussions are multidirectional, with dialogue flowing between instructor and learners and among the learners themselves.

Discussions can be completely instructor-led and moderated, or they can be done in small groups. If using the small groups idea, try to leave time for some sort of feedback and closure experience. Have as many of the groups as possible report back so that everyone can benefit from these more private discussions. These feedback sessions often trigger additional discussion as groups compare their comments and perhaps even are asked to defend them against conflicting opinions from other groups. The feedback element also allows us to monitor the learning that occurred during the discussions, help clarify any remaining confusion, and correct any misconceptions that learners might still have. Whether we are moderating a full class discussion or facilitating feedback after a small group discussion period, remember that our role is to encourage an open and equitable exchange of ideas among our learners. It is often a good idea for instructors to refrain from contributing their own ideas until the discussion has wrapped up completely. Voicing our opinion too soon may shut down further discussion, as learners may view us as the expert and our opinions as irrefutable (Cruickshank, Jenkins, and Metcalf, 2009; Davis, 2009; Grassian and Kaplowitz, 2009).

Learners may be reluctant to participate actively, especially if they are nervous about expressing their point of view in such an open forum. It's important to set the stage ahead of time in order to counteract their fears. Any kind of icebreaker in which learners get the chance to find out something about each other can ease the tension and stimulate more active discussions. Once learners have expressed themselves during the icebreaker, they may be more willing to do so when asked to discuss more course-related topics (McKeachie and Svinicki, 2006; Marlow and Page, 2005; Nelken, 2009). Allowing learners a few minutes to think about and write down their thoughts before the more active exchange of ideas occurs can also help the shyer, more reflective people to be more willing to express their ideas to others—whether to the full class or in a small group setting. Finally, make sure that ground rules for the discussion (and perhaps for all interactions during the session) are in place that reinforce the idea of a learning community in which all comments are welcome, everyone is respectful to his or her fellow learners' contributions, and where no one is allowed to dominate the discussion, thereby giving everyone an equal chance to participate (Brookfield, 1990; Cruickshank, Jenkins, and Metcalf, 2009; Davis, 2009; McCombs and Miller, 2007). To reinforce the idea that all ideas are welcome, go around the room and solicit one comment from each person before the discussion begins. If someone starts dominating the discussion, step in and say, "Thank you for your comments, but let's hear from someone else as well." Just making sure everyone raises his or her hand and waits to be recognized before speaking can help ensure everyone is getting the chance to participate.

Discussions help learners develop their communication skills as well as providing a more active way to acquire information. As learners exchange ideas, they can learn how to articulate their own ideas, think through problems, organize supportive evidence for their point of view, and listen to and be respectful of a diversity of ideas, opinions, and perspectives (Brookfield, 1990; Davis, 2009;

McKeachie and Svinicki, 2006). As such they add to the inclusiveness and learner-centered nature of instruction.

Discussions provide opportunities for a bit more active involvement than the lecture approach and as such can help engage the more kinesthetic and activist learners. However, it is still a step removed from actually working with the material. Theorists and pragmatists may each be attracted to this approach, depending on the type of material under discussion (theoretical concepts versus real-life problem solving). Auditory learners may be engaged as they listen to others express themselves but are generally less comfortable when it comes to sharing their own ideas. Reflectors often find the pace of the discussion leaves little time to actually think about the topics at hand. See Table 4.5 for an overview of the advantages and drawbacks of the discussion method.

Table 4.5. The Discussion Method	
Advantages	**Drawbacks**
Offers opportunity to review and extend comprehension of the material.	It can fail if learners are unwilling to participate or have not sufficiently grasped the material.
Helps highlight key concepts and ideas.	Learners may ignore important concepts and ideas not addressed by discussion.
Can address complex issues.	Learners must be ready to deal with the complexity of the issues being discussed.
Can stimulate critical examination of material covered.	Learners may be reluctant to question the authority of the instructor and/or the written text.
Encourages learners to express their own opinions and perspectives.	Some learners find it uncomfortable to express their ideas in a group setting.
Encourages multiway interactions between learners and teacher and among learners.	The discussion is frequently dominated by the most outgoing and opinionated learners.
Can be used to address real-life issues and authentic problems.	Learners may lack the experiences needed for these types of discussions.
Increases appeal for the kinesthetic learner. Although not actual "doing," there is a bit more active learning going on. Some appeal for the auditory learner as he or she listens to other people's comments.	It has very little appeal for the visual learner.
Appeals to pragmatists, especially when the discussion focuses on problem solving in the real world. Some appeal for the theorist; particularly if the discussion focuses on theoretical issues.	It has limited appeal for reflectors, who may not have time to formulate ideas in the time allotted. While activists may enjoy expressing their own ideas, they will grow impatient when others are offering theirs.

PRACTICE

Allowing learners to try out their newly developing skills and knowledge is yet another way to break up instruction and widens its appeal to the more kinesthetic, activity-oriented learners in the group. It also provides an opportunity for learners to mentally process the information and material just addressed in the other methods and to then move it into their long-term memory storage. Furthermore, instructors can monitor learning progress as they watch their learners trying to apply their newly acquired skills and knowledge (Grassian and Kaplowitz, 2009; Smart and Csapo, 2007; Veldof, 2006).

Practice can be guided or more freeform (Freilberg and Driscoll, 2005). Guided practice is usually associated with the demonstration/modeling method. In guided practice, learners are invited to follow along with the demonstration on their own computers or other equipment/resources. While this does add an element of active involvement, learners are still not at liberty to proceed at their own pace. Because people vary in their abilities, some learners are unable to keep up, while others try to forge ahead of the group. This can cause a problem for instructors, as they are forced to go back and repeat steps in order to clarify the information for those who have fallen behind while trying to retain the attention of those who have stayed in sync with the demonstration. Furthermore, some learners find it difficult to "watch," "listen," and "do" all at the same time. Many instructors make the guided practice optional. That way, those who enjoy this type of activity can follow along, while those who need to watch and listen first before doing can opt out of the practice.

An alternative is to insert a more freeform practice period after one of the other already discussed techniques (Cruickshank, Jenkins, and Metcalf, 2009; Saskatoon Public Schools, 2010). Handouts or other types of support material are often supplied to help the learners remember the steps in the process being practiced. Learners generally appreciate these handouts, taking the documents with them as reminders and reviewing for later reference.

Freeform practice segments can be done individually, in pairs, or in small groups. Individual practice is appealing to learners who wish some privacy during their initial interactions with the material. On the other hand, working in pairs or in small groups increases the likelihood that more of the material from the lecture and/or demonstration will be remembered, at least by someone in the group. It also creates a more social and collaborative learning environment in which people are encouraged to support each other's learning. It offers yet another learning opportunity for those who did not quite get it the first time. Plus, peers can often frame things in ways that their fellow learners are better able to comprehend. Those who are doing this peer coaching also gain from the experience, as they are forced to think about the material and then articulate it in a way that can be understood by someone else (Slavin, 2011).

Instructors have the option of assigning actual topics or tasks for learners to accomplish during practice or to allow learners to select what they want to work on themselves. There are advantages and drawbacks to both ideas. Allowing the learners to pick their own topics/activities increases the relevance of the task and therefore learners' motivation to complete it. However, learner-selected topics/tasks don't always work. So, learners can become discouraged and frustrated, feeling that they will never be able to learn the material in question. Furthermore, learners may spend most of their practice time trying to come up with a topic/task, leaving little time for the actual practice. Providing learners with a topic/task that has been checked out in advance in terms of its potential for success eliminates these problems but lowers the relevance of and motivation for the task. A compromise could be to provide a list of possible topics/tasks from which the learners may choose but also telling them they can use their own ideas if they like.

Practice, especially the freeform version, appeals to many different types of learners. With its "doing" aspect it appeals to both kinesthetic and activist learners. Pragmatists like the real-world problem-solving aspects, and even reflectors find practice a nice break from trying to absorb the information being addressed via other techniques, especially if sufficient time is allocated for the practice period. If the setup for the practice segment is done carefully, even theorists can see the benefit as they try to apply the more theoretical material to the actual activity. Practice offers a nice break from the more verbal types of instruction and can also serve as a comprehension check for the instructor who can watch learning (or the possible lack of it) in action. Rather than asking learners if they "got it," instructors can monitor progress as they observe learners try out their newly acquired information and abilities. See Table 4.6 for an overview of the advantages and drawbacks of the practice method.

COLLABORATIVE GROUP WORK

Collaborative group work is one of the mainstays of LCT. Putting the learning experience more into the learner's own hands, it represents a further movement toward the indirect end of the teaching spectrum. Collaborative group work can be as simple as having learners get together to discuss an issue or as complex as having them working to solve an authentic, real-world problem (Barkley, Cross, and Major, 2004; Johnson and Johnson, 1999; Slavin, 1990). Regardless of the task set for the group, the distinguishing feature of this method is that the learners are exploring the material for themselves rather than having it presented to them (Saskatoon Public Schools, 2010). The idea of letting the learners loose on the material often makes some instructors very uncomfortable. They view it as giving up control over the class. But the truth is that using collaborative group work requires the instructor to keep an even tighter rein on things. Because group

| Table 4.6. The Practice Method ||
Advantages	**Drawbacks**
Allows learners to actively engage with the material.	Because not everyone progresses at the same pace, some learners may finish before others and become bored, while others feel pressured because it is taking them longer to complete the task.
Reinforces information addressed in other formats—lecture, questioning, modeling/ demonstration, discussions, etc.	Learners can become frustrated if their practice sessions are unsuccessful.
Can provide instructor with assessment data as he or she watches learners practice newly acquired skills and knowledge.	It is hard for instructors to monitor multiple learners during the practice session.
Allows learners time to process newly acquired material and then to store in their long-term memory.	Learners may not be using the best approaches to the problem and therefore may be storing incorrect or less effective techniques and strategies.
Very appealing to kinesthetic learners; can also have a certain amount of appeal to visual learners.	It is not very appealing to auditory learners.
Very appealing to activists, who like the action-oriented nature of practice, and pragmatists, especially if learners are allowed to practice solving real-world problems. Also some appeal for reflectors, who can use the practice time to think about material and then see how it can be used on real problems.	It is not appealing to theorists, who are more interested in the big-picture ideas associated with the material.

work can take more time than other methods, the instructor must be vigilant in keeping groups on track and on schedule (Grassian and Kaplowitz, 2009). Instructors need to determine, in advance, how long the exercise should take and make that time frame clear to the learners during the initial setup for the work. Learners also seem to appreciate ongoing time checks to further keep them on track. Instructors who use this method generally walk around in order to monitor the groups' progress and sometimes join the individual group conversations to clarify issues and/or to answer questions.

Collaborative group work really exemplifies the CPR principles of LCT. Learning is done in a collaborative setting in which learners are encouraged to exchange ideas and work together to produce a final product that represents the best of all points of view. Learners are expected to participate in the exercise, contribute to the discussions and problem solving going on in the group, and engage in the shared, social construction of knowledge (Bain, 2004; Cruickshank, Jenkins, and

Metcalf, 2009; Lowyck and Poysa, 2001; Weimer, 2002). Groups are purposefully made small enough and time frames for the exercise are set long enough so that everyone should have the chance (and are expected) to express his or her views (Davis, 2009; Slavin, 2011). Furthermore, because most collaborative group work includes some kind of reporting back from each small group to the class at large, learners are held responsible not only for the learning going on in their particular small group but also for that of everyone in the larger group. Collaborative group work can be seen as CPR in action (Grassian and Kaplowitz, 2009).

Using collaborative group work activities really stresses the learning community aspect of LCT. Furthermore, it clearly demonstrates the "guide on the side" philosophy of teaching by putting learners in the driver's seat as they interact with the material to be learned. It increases learners' engagement with the material, allows them to work together to jointly construct knowledge, and helps them organize the material in a way that makes sense both to the group as a whole and to its individual members. The instructor's role moves from presenter of information to one of facilitator for the exchange of ideas (Barkley, Cross, and Major, 2004; Cooper et al., 2000; Eggen and Kauchak, 2010; Johnson, Johnson, and Smith, 2007). Instructors' responsibilities include:

- Creating a task that is neither too easy to be challenging nor too hard to be frustrating.
- Describing the task and clearly explaining what is expected of the group.
- Making sure that the learners have the necessary preparation to successfully complete the assigned task.
- Monitoring the group's progress as they work on the task.
- Moderating the post-task feedback from groups and any discussion that arises as a result of this feedback.
- Wrapping up the exercise by providing a summary of the feedback and/or discussion, putting the material into context of what has preceded it, and using the results of the exercise as a jumping-off point for the next instructional segment as needed.

While collaborative group work has many advantages and is extremely appealing to those committed to the LCT approach, it is not without its challenges. Many of the tasks that fall under this heading take up a bigger chunk of class time than would some of the more direct, teacher-centered methods. Therefore, consider very carefully what part of the material should be devoted to this type of activity. Think about how long learners will need to complete the activity. Then consider what portion of the expected learning outcomes (ELOs) might be accomplished by this group work. It is helpful to refer to Bloom's taxonomy for educational objectives when planning activities (Anderson and Krathwohl, 2001; Bloom, 1956).

An activity that is directed at some of the higher levels of complexity (analysis, synthesis, or evaluation) might warrant a longer, more complex activity than those directed at the lower levels (knowledge, comprehension, or application). In other words, make sure that the time spent on the activity has the appropriate amount of educational payoff and is in keeping with the ELOs set for the instruction.

Some of the methods already discussed could be easily turned into collaborative group work. For example, learners could be asked to engage in some sort of idea sharing in small groups as a preparation for a larger group discussion. Concept maps can also be developed in small groups instead of or in addition to a full group concept mapping exercise (Boxtel et al., 2002). Questions also could be considered in small groups prior to a full group discussion. And groups could be formed for any hands-on practice experiences. The advantage of these group interactions (whether they are prior to or instead of a full group experience) is that they give learners the chance to exchange ideas and discuss possible solutions in the smaller, somewhat safer-feeling environment. This often encourages the quieter learners to volunteer in the larger setting, because they have already tried out their ideas with their colleagues in the small group. See Table 4.7 for

Table 4.7. The Collaborative Group Work Method	
Advantages	**Drawbacks**
Actively involves learners in the material.	It takes more time than more didactic, teacher-directed approaches.
Gives learners a chance to practice newly acquired skills and apply newly constructed knowledge.	Developing effective group work experiences requires a great deal of instructor preparation time.
Offers a break from sensory input, allowing material to move from short- to long-term memory storage.	The more open and freeform nature of group work can lead to learners developing misconceptions or errors in the way they are viewing (and thus storing) the information.
Helps to create a social learning environment in which learners can share their various perspectives and learn from each other.	The more quiet, shy learners might feel uncomfortable sharing ideas in the small group setting. However, they may also be more likely to do so in the smaller group than in the full group at large.
Very appealing to kinesthetic learners; auditory learners also like the discussion elements associated with most group work.	It appeals to visual learners only if the group is working on something that can be seen.
Very appealing to activists, who like the hands-on elements; also appealing to pragmatists, but only if exercise has some kind of practical application element.	It is less appealing to reflectors unless some "quiet" thoughtful time is built into the process. It is also less appealing to theorists unless the exercise is asking learners to apply theory to practice.

an overview of the advantages and drawbacks of the collaborative group work method.

Many types of collaborative, group work activities have already been developed. Take a look at books and articles on collaborative learning, active learning, creating constructivist classrooms, and developing learning communities for inspiration and suggestions. Here are a couple of examples from that literature.

Think/Pair/Share

This is one of the most popular and adaptable of the collaborative group work ideas. It can be used with any size group and with a variety of tasks. The basic format for this activity is to present learners with a question, issue, problem to be solved, or activity to complete and then give them all a minute or two to work on their own. Next they are told to exchange ideas with a partner for another few minutes. In the final stage (Share), pairs of learners are asked to report the results of their discussions and/or present their solutions to the task at hand. A variation of this technique adds a fourth component—"Square." In the Think/Pair/Square/Share version, each pair is asked to share its results with one other pair and then the Squares are asked to report back during the "Share" portion. Although this variation adds extra time to the activity, it allows for an exchange of ideas among more learners and is especially useful in larger settings in which time constraints may limit the number of pairs/squares that can report back to the full group (Grassian and Kaplowitz, 2009; Saskatoon Public Schools, 2010).

Either version works well in groups of 25 or less, especially if the room is set up in pods with four to six learners clustered around a small table. However, with a little thought and planning, it can be equally effective in the larger auditorium/lecture hall setting. Learners can turn to someone next to them or in the row behind them to form the pairs (and later the squares if appropriate). This technique is appealing to a variety of learners. It allows the reflectors to think about the material before having to exchange ideas with another learner. Activists, pragmatists, and kinesthetic learners like the more "doing" aspects. Auditory learners (and to some extent theorists) enjoy the discussions that generally accompany both the small group segment and the larger group feedback portion. So, all in all, this is a real opportunity to engage just about all types of learners in a relatively short period of time. Think/Pair/Share activities are generally allocated about 10 to 15 minutes of class time—one or two minutes for thinking, two to five minutes for pairing, and five to eight minutes for sharing. Adding the Square segment would increase the time commitment by about five to eight minutes.

Jigsaw

This is a great technique for exposing learners to a larger body of information than is possible in the Think/Pair/Share approach. However, because of the logistics of the technique it is not easily adapted to the large auditorium/lecture hall setting. In this technique, the class is divided into a specific number of small groups—usually four or five depending on the number of learners involved. Each group is presented with a segment of a problem to be solved (Aronson, 1978; Cruickshank, Jenkins, and Metcalf, 2009; Saskatoon Public Schools, 2010). For example, in an ILI setting each group could be told it needs to find authoritative material on a topic selected for the class. Each group is assigned a specific resource to explore (i.e., encyclopedias, books, newspaper or popular magazines, scholarly journals, web search engines such as Google, or possibly a variety of different databases). Groups then spend a set amount of time searching their assigned resource for information on the topic. During that time, groups also must complete a form that lists the advantages and disadvantages of using their resource for the topic under discussion with the idea that members of individual groups will be teaching others about the assigned resource.

So far this seems like any small group activity. The next step, however, is what earns it the "jigsaw" label. Once the small groups have completed their assignment, the learners are asked to count off—say, 1, 2, 3, 4, 5 if the original groups had five people each. Once everyone has his or her designated number, learners are asked to regroup according to their numbers. The result is that the new groups should now have representatives from each of the original groups. The newly formed groups are asked to share what they learned about each of the resources from the first portion of the exercise with each other (Brown and Campione, 1996; McKeachie and Svinicki, 2006; Smith, 2000). These reconstructed groups could also be given a second task in which learners are not only sharing knowledge but are asked to apply it as well. In the ILI example described earlier, the jigsaw groups would be asked to make recommendations about what type of topics should be researched using each of the various types of resources.

Jigsaw is a great technique to use as a means to address a lot of theoretical material in a more engaging and interactive fashion. Each group could be assigned a portion of the material to be covered. In full-term, credit courses, they could be asked to work on material from the assigned readings. In the one-shot situation, each group could be given some material to review, discuss, and summarize for the second (jigsaw) segment.

Not only is the jigsaw method a great way to address lots of information at once, it also creates a situation in which learners are asked to interact with others in a new, more creative way. Learners come to understand the information better because they are asked to teach it to others. Asking learners to move to new groupings also presents the opportunity for them to work with people they may not ordinarily interact with. Learners tend to sit with people they know and with whom they are familiar. The jigsaw method forces learners to leave these safe groupings and engage with a wider variety of people. Plus the physical act of moving to a new group often recharges attention levels and creates a break for those who find sitting in one place for too long tiresome.

But despite all its advantages, the jigsaw method must be considered carefully before being incorporated into an instructional session. Clearly it is a time-consuming type of activity. It also requires a great deal of logistical planning. Finally, the physical setting can make or break this approach. Classrooms need to be in a configuration that promotes easy movement from place to place within the space. Learners may also be reluctant to leave their personal items, especially laptops, in their original space because others will be working there. So learners may not be happy with the choice of having to leave their stuff behind or carrying it to the new grouping. Be prepared for some grumbling and discontent, because this technique will probably be very unfamiliar to most learners. However, the educational payoff is great, and once learners settle into the new groupings and start to exchange ideas with the new group's members, they may get a better idea of why they were asked to do this outlandish thing and begin to see the instructional benefits of the method.

Pass the Problem

As in the jigsaw method, the class is divided into a specific number of small groups, with each group assigned a part of a larger problem or issue upon which to work. However, in Pass the Problem, groups remain intact during the entire exercise. It is the problem that moves (Aronson, 1978; Cruickshank, Jenkins, and Metcalf, 2009; Saskatoon Public Schools, 2010).

Groups spend the first round of the exercise working on their piece of the larger problem. Each group's recommendations are recorded in some way. At the end of round one, each group passes its problem and solution/recommendations to the group to its left. The new group then reviews what the previous group(s) has written and adds its own comments. The "problems" are passed in subsequent rounds until each problem returns to the group in which it started. The original group then summarizes all the written comments for that particular problem or issue. The advantage of this technique is that everyone gets a chance to view, think about, and comment on all the parts of the problem. It also reinforces the idea of social construction of knowledge as each group adds its own perspective on the pieces of the problem—with the net result being a solution built by the entire class. The first round tends to be the longest one, as each group mulls over its segment. Because the number of new ideas tends to diminish as more groups review the material, subsequent rounds are usually shorter than the initial one.

Pass the Problem is another way to have learners interact with a lot of material in a relatively short period of time. For example, if the topic is evaluating the quality of material found by using a variety of online resources, each group could be assigned a particular resource, supplied with the list of evaluation attributes to consult (i.e., authority, timeliness, organization, biases, etc.), and asked to evaluate the assigned resource. The groups then "pass" their assigned resource and comments to the next group for further investigation. While the first group will be doing the most extensive review, by the end of the full exercise, each group will have been exposed to all the resources under review. Pass the Problem creates an interactive way for learners to work with multiple resources in a much more engaging fashion than either the lecture or demonstration method of presenting the material.

Problem-Based/Case-Based Learning

Although generally associated with medical, law, or business schools, this approach is starting to be used in other educational venues because of the "authentic" or real-life nature of the material that serves as the basis for the exercise and the social (small group) aspect of the experience. In problem-based/case-based learning, a large group of learners is divided into smaller groups (between four and ten people in each group). Groups are then presented with an open-ended authentic problem to solve or a case study to review and address. Each group is generally expected to work on its own with some minimal direction or facilitation provided by either the class instructor (in smaller settings) or tutors selected by the instructor and assigned to each group (in larger settings) (Clouston, 2005; Davis, 2009; Jonassen, 1997, 2000; Macklin, 2008). The exercise begins with a discussion of the following questions to stimulate thinking about ways to address the problem/case:

- What do we know?
- What do we need to know?
- How will we find out?

This is followed by some kind of information-gathering period during which the group members try to collect information that will help them solve the problem/case. When used in full-term courses, groups often split up the "searching for information" aspect, with people sharing what they found at a future meeting. Groups then use the combined information to come up with a solution to the problem or a way to approach the case under review. Finally, the group prepares some kind of report that is shared with the instructor and perhaps with the other small groups as well (Clouston, 2005; Johnson, Johnson, and Smith, 2007; McKeachie and Svinicki, 2006; Smith, 2000).

Although most often associated with full-term settings, the problem-based/case-based approach can be easily adapted to the "one-shot" situation as well. The procedure remains the same. The larger group is divided into several small groups, all of whom are working on the same problem or case. Groups discuss the issues involved and decide how to proceed. The ensuing "solution" discussions can be done in just the "what we think we would do" hypothetical mode, or learners could try to gather some of the necessary information using resources made available to them in the classroom—via either computers or the actual physical items. Encyclopedias, reference-type books, scholarly books and articles, as well as authoritative websites sponsored by government or nonprofit agencies, associations, and organizations are all possible sources of online information. Obviously access to these resources depends on the license agreements set up within the institution. The available online resources can be augmented by bringing in appropriate samples of material not accessible electronically. As in the full-term version, the exercise is closed by some sort of feedback period. In the one-shot scenario, the number of groups that can provide "feedback" may be limited because of time constraints. The more time that can be provided for sharing the better, because each group may have approached the issues from different perspectives. Providing some way for groups to share their findings in an online setting—maybe via a wiki or a discussion board—can expand the effectiveness of the exercise.

A modified jigsaw element can also be added to this approach. Rather than having each group use every resource available, individual groups could be asked to concentrate on a different resource and report back to the full group not only on what they found but also on how well the resource seemed suited to the problem/case under review. Or each group could be asked to work on a different element of the full problem/case.

Adding an element of creativity to the feedback portion can also increase learners' engagement with the exercise. One classroom instructor asked his learners to prepare a short PowerPoint presentation on the information they had gathered. All the groups were working on the same case but in the jigsaw-type format. So each group had a different piece of the full case to address, although everyone was allowed to use any resource available to them via the classroom computers. Learners were also given lists of appropriate (instructor and librarian vetted) resources from which to choose. This was a one-shot situation that lasted about two hours. And yes, learners were able to perform the required research and create an informative and graphically appealing PowerPoint presentation to share with the rest of the class during this fairly short time frame.

In a "no-tech" version, all groups are supplied with flip-chart paper or poster board and some craft material, such as felt markers, crayons, stickers, colored paper, glue sticks, press-on letters, numbers, and/or shapes, and asked to create a poster summarizing what they found. Adding this more "right-brain" or visual element to the exercise can really energize the group and widens the appeal of the experience to more types of learners, especially those who like the "doing" elements it brings in. It introduces an unexpected element to the instruction and seems to appeal to people of all ages and at all grade levels. The PowerPoint example was done in a medical school environment and the poster session exercise was used with graduate students, and it might even be more appealing to undergraduates. It certainly would add an element of fun to K–12 instructional efforts and to public library ILI sessions as well.

Designing realistic, comprehensible, engaging, yet feasible problems and cases is key to the success of this technique. Good problems/cases take time, effort, and expertise to develop and need regular reviews to make sure the content is up-to-date and remains relevant. However, this technique challenges learners to take responsibility for their own and their fellow group members' learning and moves them toward becoming more self-directed and metacognitively aware learners, skills necessary for becoming lifelong learners (Bransford et al., 2005; Johnson, Johnson, and Smith, 2007; McKeachie and Svinicki, 2006; Smith, 2000).

REFLECTION

Reflection is probably the method most neglected by instructors. Given the time constraints of many of our instructional endeavors, we find it hard to allow time for quiet contemplation. But because promoting lifelong learning is an important aspect of information literacy, we need to give our learners an opportunity to reflect on what they are learning and how they are learning and to develop a better understanding of their own approaches to that learning. In other words, we need to offer learners the chance to develop metacognitive skills (Costa and Kallick, 2000; Grassian and Kaplowitz, 2009; McCombs and Miller, 2007; Thompson, Licklider, and Jungst, 2003). Obviously, reflection is the most indirect of all the methods discussed so far. The learner is doing all the work without any input from the instructor or from fellow learners (Cruickshank, Jenkins, and Metcalf, 2009; Davis, 2009; Eggen and Kauchak, 2010). This is both the power of, and the problem with, reflection.

Reflection offers learners the chance to process material and make it their own. It allows for transfer from short- to long-term memory storage. And it gives learners time to think about the information to be transferred and organize it in a way that makes sense to them. However, if the instructor does not monitor reflections somehow, the information being stored may include misinformation and misconceptions. This is where the instructor must engage in an interesting balancing act. On the one hand, reflections should be confidential and private in order to promote honesty and the development of real insight. On the other hand, the instructor has a responsibility to make sure the reflections reflect reality. Here again, the relationship we developed with learners is key. They should trust us enough to be willing and happy to have us read their reflections and offer feedback. Learners should be graded only on the fact that they completed the reflections. The content is not up for evaluation. Providing a nongraded environment for our learners' reflections goes a long way to building trust and fostering their willingness to take these reflection exercises seriously.

Learners can be offered the opportunity to reflect at any point in instruction. If we are going to have a long-term relationship with our learners, we can ask for an opening reflection on what they expect to get from the class and a closing one that discusses if they got what they expected. Or we can ask them to set some ELOs for themselves in their opening reflections and comment on whether or not they have attained these ELOs in the closing one. Many instructors ask learners to keep a journal throughout the course that monitors ongoing progress (McAdoo and Manwaring, 2009; McGinness and Brien, 2007; Meyers and Jones, 1993; Saskatoon Public Schools, 2010). Journals are collected at set periods during the course or are turned in at the end. Because these reflective journals contain learners' thoughts on the material, it is important to try and return them at some point so that learners have them for future reference.

Any of the closure exercises discussed later, such as the One-Minute Paper and the 3-2-1 cards (Angelo and Cross, 1993) can serve as reflections in both long-term classes and the one-shot setting. They can be used at the end of an individual class meeting in the long-term class or at the end of the one-shot session. For more on these types of exercises, see the Ending It All section.

It is usually best to allow for anonymity when using a reflection exercise in the one-shot instructional setting in order to encourage more honest and open comments. Learners can be given the option of including their e-mail addresses if they want a personal response. Instructors should also try to review the reflections to identify common themes and questions and then provide feedback to the group in some manner. If this is a "guest shot" in a classroom teacher's course, send the feedback to the teacher for distribution. If there is a course website, try to get permission to post comments there. In the single workshop setting, such as those used in the public library, designate a portion of the library's website as the place to respond to the types of questions and issues highlighted by the reflections.

Reflecting on the material and the learning experience is important to all types of learners, but it is especially useful to the reflectors whose needs are so often overlooked. In our rush to "get through" the material, we don't offer nearly enough time for learners to "stop and smell the roses," so to speak. The more contemplative learners are often the quiet ones—those who do not actively participate in the sessions and so whose opinions, perspectives, and ideas are not voiced. To be truly learner-centered in our instructional endeavors, we need to create a place for all our learners to contribute and share in the experience. Providing some reflection space creates a more inclusive atmosphere and invites this frequently forgotten group a chance to shine. See Table 4.8 for an overview of the advantages and drawbacks of the reflection method.

Table 4.8. The Reflection Method	
Advantages	**Drawbacks**
Can provide learners the time to process material and move it to long-term storage.	Learners may develop misconceptions or errors as they reflect on the material and thus could be storing incorrect information.
Helps learners develop metacognitive skills by asking them to think about their learning experiences.	Most learners are unfamiliar with the concept of metacognition and may need instruction in how to reflect appropriately and fruitfully on the material.
Promotes lifelong learning as learners acquire more insight into how they learn and the learning process itself.	Learners may not see the value at first. Instructors can help by reviewing reflections and offering nonjudgmental, constructive feedback. However, providing this feedback can be time-consuming for the instructor.
Highly appealing to reflectors, who are often neglected in our instructional endeavors; theorists may find it appealing if they are allowed to concentrate on the theoretical aspects of the material in their reflections.	It has only limited appeal to the activists and the pragmatists, who prefer more active problem-solving learning experience.
Because most reflections take the form of written material, visual learners may be somewhat engaged; the writing element may have some minimal appeal to the kinesthetic and/or activist learners as well.	It has little appeal for auditory learners because of the quiet, introspective nature of the activity.

A WORD ABOUT DISCOVERY

Although not a method in its own right, the idea that learners do best when allowed to "discover" information on their own is fundamental to the constructivist philosophy of learning. So it stands to reason that the more indirect the method, the greater the element of discovery. Because LCT relies heavily on constructivist ideas and these more indirect methods, it is no surprise that the Discovery approach is closely associated with the learning-centered approach. In some ways this association has served as an impediment to the approach's acceptance. Instructors are concerned that if they adopt LCT practices, they will lose control of their class, the learners, and the instructional situation in general. As already discussed in terms of the individual indirect methods, the truth is that LCT practices require that the instructor take an even more active role in the process. Learner-centered instructors do not just step back and let the learners loose on the material. They create carefully constructed situations that allow learners to actively work with the material to be learned and moderate, facilitate, and guide their learners through the experience (Cruickshank, Jenkins, and Metcalf,

2009; Freilberg and Driscoll, 2005; Grassian and Kaplowitz, 2009; Prince and Felder, 2006).

Discovery, as an approach, is often seriously misunderstood. Jerome Bruner, who first promoted it as a learning approach, based his ideas on cognitive/constructivist learning theories (Bruner, 1961). His writing on the subject, especially his work on scaffolding (Bruner, 1966; Wood, Bruner, and Ross, 1976) make it clear that Discovery is not just meant as the type of random trial and error associated with behaviorist learning theory. Learners are given ample support and direction both prior to and during the Discovery experience (Davis, 2009; Prince and Felder, 2006; Rosenshine and Guenther, 1992; Simons and Klein, 2006). This is not a "sink or swim" or "find it out on your own" approach. It is a carefully organized and monitored learning activity created by the instructor with a clear and valid intent for what the learners will gain from the exercise (Eggen and Kauchak, 2010; Innes, 2004).

The literature criticizing the approach (Kitshner, Sweller, and Clark, 2006; Mayer, 2004) discusses what the authors call "Pure Discovery" in which learners are told to explore the material with little or no instructor guidance or support. However, a closer look at the literature (both that of the critics as well as the supporters) shows that the more constructivist or Guided Discovery approach in which instructors carefully prepare the learners for the experience, provide scaffolding for it, and monitor their learners progress throughout the activity has been proven to be a successful approach to learning (Brown and Campione, 1994; Dean and Kuhn, 2007; Gagnon and Collay, 2001; Marlow and Page, 2005).

ENDING IT ALL

Breaking up instruction as you go along is just one way to enhance your instructional effectiveness. Leaving time for some sort of closure experience is another. How you end an instructional session is very important. If you are still trying to present material as your learners are packing up their bags and rushing out the door, you are really just wasting everyone's time. They are no longer "with you," and nothing further is being absorbed. But if you leave a bit of time at the end for some fun, engaging, and interactive type of closing exercise, everyone will benefit. Your learners will remain excited about the material and will leave your sessions energized and hopefully inspired to find out more about the topic. These types of exercises can also serve as informal assessment techniques, helping you gain some insight into what your learners have gotten out of the instructional experience and highlight ways you might improve your future instructional efforts (Barr and Tagg, 1995). For more on assessment, see Chapter 5.

The One-Minute Paper (Angelo and Cross, 1993) has already been alluded to as a way for learners to reflect on material. This technique can be used at any point in the lecture but is most typically saved for the end, because it is a good way to get learners to summarize the entire session for themselves (Harwood, 1996; Maier and Panitz, 1996; Stead, 2005).

Typically the One-Minute Paper consists of asking the learners two questions:

1. What are one or two things that you learned from today's instruction?

2. What are some questions you still have about today's instruction?

A variation on this approach asks the learners:

- What was surprising to you about today's session?

3-2-1 Cards takes a slightly different approach. This method also takes the form of questions, but in this case the questions are:

- What are three things you learned in this instruction?

- What are two things you would still like to learn more about?

- What is one thing you would change about this instruction?

3-2-1 Cards not only provides information about the contents of the instruction, it also provides great needs assessment data that helps suggest ways to improve the session itself.

In both versions learners are asked to write down their answers. Instructors then collect the forms and offer feedback either via e-mail, or in person if they are lucky enough to be seeing the learners again. In typical ILI situations, especially one-shots, this exercise can be done orally by asking learners to just call out their answers to the questions. Answers are recorded on the board or on flip-chart papers (Grassian and Kaplowitz, 2009).

A variation on this exercise is the What Stuck? game. In this adaptation the class is divided into small groups. The groups are given five minutes to come up with as many items as they can about the material that was addressed during the session. If feasible, the groups are asked to list their answers on flip-chart paper and post them on the walls. Once the five minutes are up, the lists are read, the number of entries is totaled, and a winner is declared. The winning team can be awarded small prizes, and, in the spirit of "everyone is a winner," small tokens can be presented to the rest of the group as a reward for participating.

Prizes can range from elaborate to simple—depending on how many learners are in the class and on available funds. Vendors for the resources being addressed are often willing to supply pens, bookmarks, Post-it pads, or other items that can be used as prizes. Candy bars, magnets, and other small, fairly inexpensive items can also be used, as well as promotional material available from local, state, and national library associations. The advantage of these closing exercises is that learners are reviewing the material from the preceding session for themselves rather than having it reviewed for them.

Another way to structure instruction in order to include a closure experience is to use the KWL method (Maier and Panitz, 1996; Ogle, 1986). KWL stands for the following three questions:

1. What do I know?
2. What do I want to learn?
3. What did I learn?

Learners are directed to write down their answers to the first two of these questions at the beginning of the session and then are given time to compose their answers to the third at the end. The advantage of this technique is that it focuses learners' attention on what they want to get out of the session, thus increasing their motivation and attention. The KWL approach puts people in a "learning" frame of mind in which they expect to gain something from the instructional experience. Many instructors who use the One-Minute Paper share the closure questions at the beginning of the session for the same reason—to set an expectation of learning and to alert learners to the fact that they are going to be called on to be accountable (if only to themselves) about what they have gained from the instructional experience.

Finally, many online games are now available for instructional use. Templates using PowerPoint software for *Jeopardy!*, *Who Wants to Be a Millionaire?*, and other familiar game shows are available for educational use (Internet4Classrooms, 2011; Tech Teachers, 2006). Furthermore, games are beginning to be created specifically for ILI purposes. One example, *Bibliobouts*, pits teams of learners against each other as they gather resources and create bibliographies (Bibliobouts, 2011; Danforth, 2011). These are all great ways to help learners review the material, apply what they learned, and end instruction on an "up" note.

MIXING IT UP

Clearly all these teaching methods have their advantages and their drawbacks. None of them is perfect for every situation or for every type of learner. So, with all these options available, what can be done to make instruction as effective as possible? The answer—Variety! Variety! Variety! Not only is variety the spice of life, it is absolutely crucial to creating effective instruction (Grassian and Kaplowitz, 2009). Using an assortment of methods increases the chances of reaching the widest possible range of learners—especially if the methods that seem most appealing to different types of learners is kept in mind (Brookfield, 1990; Cruickshank, Jenkins, and Metcalf, 2009; Davis, 2009). Try to include something for visual, auditory, and kinesthetic learners. Make an effort to incorporate activities that appeal to activists, pragmatists, theorists, and reflectors. Look for activities such as Think/Pair/Share that seem to be enjoyed by a number of different types of learners. And remember that the change of pace offered by varying activities also reenergizes learners and can recapture flagging attention (Jensen, 1998).

Here's one approach to planning that can help to increase the instruction's "mixing it up" potential. Start by creating the ELOs for the instruction as usual. Then look at each one to see what type of method/activity might help learners attain that outcome. Create at least one activity for each of the outcomes. Try to select a variety of different methods—ranging from direct to indirect—in order to appeal to different types of learners. Then arrange those activities into a cohesive and logical order. Once you do that, you might find that you are well on your way to having developed your instruction. Create introductions for each activity and segues between them that help the learners see how each piece relates to the one that preceded it, and voila, you have created your outline for the session. Furthermore, you may be able to use some, if not all, of these activities to monitor and assess learners' progress toward those ELOs. See Chapter 5 for more on using activities as assessment.

FINAL REMARKS

As discussed in previous chapters, our role as learner-centered teachers is to Listen, Engage, and Inspire. We do this by using methods that allow us to listen to our learners (prior to, during, and after instruction), engage them by providing opportunities to actively interact with the material, and inspire them to keep on learning after they leave us. The various methods described in this chapter offer us the ability to do all of this and provide our learners with instructional experiences that move them closer to becoming lifelong learners. While most of the methods reviewed were created for use in the face-to-face setting, many of them can be adapted for the online setting as well. See Chapter 7 for more on how to use these modified methods to create a LCT online environment.

We listen to our learners by gathering information about them and their information needs either prior to or at the start of each instructional encounter. We listen to them during our interactions with them by paying careful attention to their questions, monitoring their attention levels, and respectfully responding to their comments. By using a variety of methods we endeavor to capture and sustain our learners' attention and to appeal to a broad spectrum of learners. And we try to incorporate relevant and appropriate examples into our instruction so that learners can see how what they are learning in our ILI also relates to their real lives. Finally, we model our enthusiasm both for the material being addressed and for learning in general with the hope that our learners "catch the bug" and are inspired to continue to be effective, efficient, thoughtful, creative, and reflective learners throughout their lives.

REFLECTIONS

1. Consider the various methods reviewed in this chapter.
   a. Which of these methods appeal to you the most as a learner? Why?
   b. Which ones appeal to you most as a teacher? Why?
   c. Did you pick the same ones when you were the learner and when you were the teacher? If so, what do you think might be the advantages and disadvantages of using only your preferred learning methods when you teach?
2. Now review the methods again, but this time select one or two of the methods that do not appeal to you either as the learner or the teacher.
   a. Why are these methods less appealing to you?
   b. Is there anything you could do to modify these methods so that you might feel more comfortable with them?
3. Finally, select a method that you have never used before but are interested in trying. The next time you are planning your instruction, think about where you might use this method. You may wish to start small—maybe using it in only a five- to ten-minute segment.

As you become more comfortable with the new method, you might wish to expand its use. Or you could try adding another new method. If you keep doing this, your instructional bag of tricks will keep expanding, and your instructional offerings will become more varied, interesting, and engaging.

EXPLORATIONS

Barkley, Elizabeth F., K. Patricia Cross, and Claire Howell Major. 2004. *Collaborative Learning Techniques: A Handbook for College Faculty.* San Francisco: Jossey-Bass.

This book has lots of great suggestions for creating a collaborative learning environment.

Cooper, James L., and Pamela Robinson. 2000. "Getting Started: Informal Small-Group Strategies in Large Classes." *New Directions for Teaching and Learning* 81: 17–24.

The authors provide examples of how to create small group learning experiences in a large lecture hall–type setting.

Cruickshank, Donald R., Deborah B. Jenkins, and Kim K. Metcalf. 2009. *The Act of Teaching.* 5th ed. New York: McGraw-Hill.

This book contains excellent chapters on a variety of instructional approaches, including presentation, discussion, cooperative learning, discovery learning, and constructivist approaches.

Eggen, Paul, and Don Kauchak. 2010. *Educational Psychology: Windows on Classrooms.* Upper Saddle River, NJ: Merrill.

Eggen and Kauchak offer practical suggestions about how to apply psychological and educational theory in the classroom.

Freilberg, H.J., and A. Driscoll. 2005. *Universal Teaching Strategies.* Boston: Allyn and Bacon.

The authors cover many different techniques for teaching.

Johnson, David W., and Roger T. Johnson. 1999. *Learning Together and Alone: Cooperative and Individualistic Learning.* Boston: Allyn and Bacon.

This is a good place to begin learning about the many ways that you can incorporate cooperative learning opportunities into your teaching.

Maier, Mark H., and Ted Panitz. 1996. "End on a High Note: Better Endings for Classes and Courses." *College Teaching* 44, no. 4: 145–148.

Here are lots of great suggestions about how to close your sessions in an interesting and dynamic fashion.

Marlow, Bruce A., and Marilyn L. Page. 2005. *Creating the Constructivist Classroom.* Thousand Oaks, CA: Corwin Press.

This book takes the ideas behind the constructivist approach and shows how to apply them to actual teaching practices.

Marzano, Robert J., Debra J. Pickering, and Jane E. Pollock. 2001. *Classroom Instruction That Works: Research-Based Strategies for Increasing Student Achievement.* Alexandria, VA: Association for Supervision and Curriculum Development.

This as another good book for learning how to take theoretical and research-based ideas and apply them to your practice.

Ruhl, Kathy L., Charles A. Hughes, and Patrick J. Schloss. 1987. "Using the Pause Procedure to Enhance Lecture Recall." *Teacher Education and Special Education* 10, no. 1: 14–18.

Here is an interesting exploration of how simply pausing in your presentation can enhance learning. Although quite old, it is a valuable article to read because it offers suggestions about how the lecture method can be improved.

Smith, Karl A. 2000. "Going Deeper: Formal Small-Group Learning in Large Classes." *New Directions for Teaching and Learning* 2000, no. 81: 25–46.

This is a great article for those who teach in large lecture hall–type settings. Smith offers wonderful suggestions on how to incorporate active and collaborative learning techniques into these types of classes.

REFERENCES

Anderson, Lorin W., and David R. Krathwohl. 2001. *A Taxonomy of Learning, Teaching and Assessing: A Revision of Bloom's Educational Objectives.* Boston: Allyn and Bacon.

Angelo, Thomas A., and K. Patricia Cross. 1993. *Classroom Assessment Techniques: A Handbook for College Teachers.* 2nd ed. *The Jossey-Bass Higher & Adult Education Series.* San Francisco: Jossey-Bass.

Aronson, Elliot. 1978. *The Jigsaw Classroom.* Beverly Hills, CA: Sage.

Ausubel, David P. 1960. "The Use of Advance Organizers in the Learning and Retention of Meaningful Verbal Material." *Journal of Educational Psychology* 51, no. 2: 267–272.

Bain, Ken. 2004. *What the Best College Teachers Do.* Cambridge, MA: Harvard University Press.

Barkley, Elizabeth F., K. Patricia Cross, and Claire Howell Major. 2004. *Collaborative Learning Techniques: A Handbook for College Faculty.* San Francisco: Jossey-Bass.

Barr, Robert B., and John Tagg. 1995. "From Teaching to Learning—A New Paradigm for Undergraduate Education." *Change* 27, no. 6: 13–25.

Bibliobouts. 2011. Bibliobouts. http://bibliobouts.org/.

Bligh, Donald A. 2000. *What's the Use of Lectures?* San Francisco: Jossey-Bass.

Bloom, Benjamin Samuel. 1956. *Taxonomy of Educational Objectives: The Classification of Educational Goals. Handbook 1: Cognitive Domain. Handbook 2: Affective Domain.* 2 vols. New York: McKay.

Boxtel, Carla Von, Jos Van Der Linden, Erik Roelofs, and Gijbert Erkens. 2002. "Collaborative Concept Mapping: Provoking and Supporting Meaningful Discourse." *Theory into Practice* 41, no. 1: 40–46.

Bransford, John D., et al. 2005. "Theories of Learning and Their Role in Teaching." In *Preparing Teachers for a Changing World: What Teachers Should Learn and Be Able to Do,* edited by Linda Darling-Hammond and John D. Bransford, 40–87. San Francisco: Jossey-Bass.

Brookfield, Stephen D. 1990. *The Skillful Teacher: On Technique, Trust and Responsiveness in the Classroom.* San Francisco: Jossey-Bass.

Brookfield, Stephen. 1995. *Becoming a Critically Reflective Teacher.* 1st ed. *The Jossey-Bass Higher & Adult Education Series.* San Francisco: Jossey-Bass.

Brown, Ann L., and Joseph C. Campione. 1994. "Guided Discovery in a Community of Learners." In *Classroom Lessons: Integrating Cognitive Theory and Classroom Practice,* edited by Kate McGilly, 229–270. Cambridge, MA: MIT Press.

———. 1996. "Psychological Learning Theory and the Design of Innovative Environments: Procedures, Principles and Systems." In *Contributions of Instructional Innovations to Understanding Learning,* edited by Leona Schauble and Robert Glaser, 289–325. Mahwah, NJ: Lawrence Erlbaum.

Bruner, Jerome. 1961. "The Act of Discovery." *Harvard Educational Review* 31, no. 1: 21–32.

———. 1966. *Toward a Theory of Instruction.* Cambridge, MA: Belknap Press of Harvard University.

Clark, Ruth C., and David Taylor. 1994. "The Cause and Cure of Worker Overload." *Training* 31, no. 7: 40–43.

Clouston, Teena J. 2005. "Facilitating Tutorials in Problem-Based Learning: Students' Perspectives." In *Enhancing Teaching in Higher Education,* edited by Peter Hartley, Amanda Woods, and Martin Pill, 48–58. London: Routledge.

Cooper, James L., Jean MacGregor, Karl A. Smith, and Pamela Robinson. 2000. "Implementing Small-Group Instruction: Insights from Successful Practitioners." *New Directions for Teaching and Learning* , no. 81: 63–76.

Cooper, James L., and Pamela Robinson. 2000. "Getting Started: Informal Small-Group Strategies in Large Classes." *New Directions for Teaching and Learning* 2000, no. 81: 17–24.

Costa, Arthur L., and Bena Kallick. 2000. "Learning through Reflection." In *Assessing and Reporting Habits of Mind,* edited by Arthur L. Costa and Bena Kallick, 15–28. Alexandria, VA: Association for Supervision and Curriculum Development.

Cruickshank, Donald R., Deborah Bainer Jenkins, and Kim K. Metcalf. 2009. *The Act of Teaching.* 5th ed. Boston: McGraw-Hill.

Danforth, Liz. 2011. "Gamification and Libraries." *Library Journal* 136, no. 3: 84.

Davis, Barbara Gross. 2009. *Tools for Teaching.* 2nd ed. San Francisco: Jossey-Bass.

Dean, David Jr., and Deana Kuhn. 2007. "Direct Instruction VS Discovery: The Long View." *Science Education* 91, no. 3: 384–397.

Denman, Mariate. 2005. "How to Create Memorable Lectures." *Speaking of Teaching* 14, no. 1: 1–5.

Di Vesta, Francis J., and Deborah A. Smith. 1978. "The Pausing Principle: Increasing the Efficiency of Memory for Ongoing Events." *Contemporary Educational Psychology* 43, no. 3: 288–296.

Duffy, Donna K. 1995. *Teaching within the Rhythms of the Semester.* San Francisco: Jossey-Bass.

Eggen, Paul, and Don Kauchak. 2010. *Educational Psychology: Windows on Classrooms.* Upper Saddle River, NJ: Merrill.

Fox, Jane, and Dot Morrison. 2005. "Using Concept Maps in Learning and Teaching." In *Enhancing Teaching in Higher Education,* edited by Peter Hartley, Amanda Woods, and Martin Pill, 39–47. London: Routledge.

Freilberg, H. Jerome, and Amy Driscoll. 2005. *Universal Teaching Strategies.* Boston: Allyn and Bacon.

Gagnon, G.W., and M. Collay. 2001. *Designing for Learning: Six Elements in Constructivist Classrooms.* Thousand Oaks, CA: Corwin Press.

Grassian, Esther, and Joan Kaplowitz. 2009. *Information Literacy Instruction: Theory and Practice.* 2nd ed. New York: Neal-Schuman.

Harwood, William S. 1996. "The One-Minute Paper: A Communication Tool for Large Lecture Classes." *Journal of Chemical Education* 73, no. 3: 229–230.

Honey, Peter, and Alan Mumford. 1995. *Capitalizing on Your Learning Style.* HRDQ http://www.hrdq.com.

Innes, Robert B. 2004. *Reconstructing Undergraduate Education.* Mahwah, NJ: Lawrence Erlbaum.

Internet4Classrooms. 2011. *PowerPoint Game Templates Links.* Internet4Classrooms. http://www.internet4classrooms.com/technology_tutorials/powerpoint_game_templates_technology_tutorials.htm.

Jensen, Eric. 1998. *Teaching with the Brain in Mind.* Alexandria, VA: Association for Supervision and Curriculum Development.

Johnson, David W., and Roger T. Johnson. 1999. *Learning Together and Alone: Cooperative and Individualistic Learning.* Boston: Allyn and Bacon.

Johnson, David W., Roger T. Johnson, and Karl A. Smith. 2007. "The State of Cooperative Learning in Postsecondary and Professional Settings." *Educational Psychology Review* 19, no. 1: 15–29.

Jonassen, David H. 1997. "Instructional Design Models for Well-Structured and Ill-Structured Problem-Solving Learning Outcomes." *Educational Technology Research and Development* 45, no. 1: 65–94.

———. 2000. "Revisiting Activity Theory as a Framework for Designing Student-Centered Learning Environments." In *Theoretical Foundations of Learning Environments,* edited by David H. Jonassen and Susan M. Land, 89–121. Mahwah, NJ: Lawrence Erlbaum.

Kaplowitz, Joan. 2008. "The Psychology of Learning: Connecting Theory to Practice." In *Information Literacy Instruction Handbook,* edited by Christopher N. Cox and Elizabeth B. Lindsay, 26–49. Chicago: ALA.

King, Alison. 1993. "From Sage on the Stage to Guide on the Side." *College Teaching* 41, no. 1: 30–35.

Kitshner, Paul A., John Sweller, and Richard E. Clark. 2006. "Why Minimal Guidance During Instruction Does Not Work: An Analysis of the Failure of Constructivist, Discovery, Problem-Based, Experiential, and Inquiry-Based Teaching." *Educational Psychologist* 41, no. 2: 75–86.

Kolb, David A. 1984. *Experiential Learning: Experience as the Source of Learning and Development.* Englewood Cliffs, NJ: Prentice Hall.

Lowyck, Joost, and Johanna Poysa. 2001. "Design of Collaborative Learning Environments." *Computers in Human Behavior* 17, no. 4: 507–516.

Macklin, Alexis Smith. 2008. *Problem-Based Learning. In Information Literacy Instruction Handbook,* edited by Christopher N. Cox and Elizabeth B. Lindsay, 56–65. Chicago: ALA. ACRL.

Maier, Mark H., and Ted Panitz. 1996. "End on a High Note: Better Endings for Classes and Courses." *College Teaching* 44, no. 4: 145–148.

Marlow, Bruce A., and Marilyn L. Page. 2005. *Creating the Constructivist Classroom.* Thousand Oaks, CA: Corwin Press.

Marzano, Robert J., Debra J. Pickering, and Jane E. Pollock. 2001. *Classroom Instruction That Works: Research-Based Strategies for Increasing Student Achievement.* Alexandria, VA: Association for Supervision and Curriculum Development.

Mayer, Richard E. 2004. "Should There Be a Three-Strike Rule Against Pure Discovery Learning? The Case for Guided Methods of Instruction." *American Psychologist* 59, no. 1: 14–19.

Mayer, Richard E., and Roxanne Moreno. 2003. "Nine Ways to Reduce Cognitive Load in Multimedia Learning." *Educational Psychologist* 38, no. 1: 43–52.

McAdoo, Bobbi, and Melissa Manwaring. 2009. "Teaching for Implementation: Designing Negotiation Curricula to Maximize Long-Term Learning." *Negotiation Journal* 25, no. 2: 195–215.

McCombs, Barbara L., and Lynda Miller. 2007. *Learner-Centered Classroom Practices and Assessments: Maximizing Student Motivation, Learning, and Achievement.* Thousand Oaks, CA: Corwin Press.

McGinness, Claire, and Michelle Brien. 2007. "Using Reflective Journals to Assess the Research Process." *Reference Services Review* 35, no. 1: 21–40.

McKeachie, Wilbert J., and Marilla Svinicki. 2006. *McKeachie's Teaching Tips*. 12th ed. Boston: Houghton-Mifflin.

Meyers, Chet, and Thomas B. Jones. 1993. *Promoting Active Learning: Strategies for the College Classroom*. 1st ed. The Jossey-Bass Higher & Adult Education Series. San Francisco: Jossey-Bass.

Mezeske, Richard J. 2007. "Concept Mapping: Assessing Pre-service Teachers' Understanding and Knowledge." In *Beyond Tests and Quizzes: Creative Assessment in the College Classroom*, edited by Richard J. Mezeske and Barbara A. Mezeske, 8–25. San Francisco: Jossey-Bass.

Miller, George A. 1956. "The Magic Number Seven, Plus or Minus Two: Some Limits on Our Capacity for Processing Information." *Psychological Review* 63, no. 2: 81–97.

Minstrell, Jim, and Virginia Stimpson. 1996. "A Classroom Environment for Learning: Guiding Students' Reconstruction of Understanding and Reasoning." In *Contributions of Instructional Innovations to Understanding Learning*, edited by Leona Schauble and Richard Glaser, 175–202. Mahwah, NJ: Lawrence Erlbaum.

Nelken, Melissa I. 2009. "Negotiating Classroom Practices: Lessons from Adult Learning." *Negotiation Journal* 25, no. 2: 181–194.

Ogle, Donna M. 1986. "K-W-L: A Teaching Model That Develops Active Reading of Expository Text." *The Reading Teacher* 39, no. 6: 566–570.

Prince, Michael J., and Richard M. Felder. 2006. "Inductive Teaching and Learning Methods: Definitions, Comparisons, and Research Bases." *Journal of Engineering Education* 95, no. 2: 123–138.

Ramsden, Paul. 1988. "Studying Learning: Improving Teaching." In *Improving Learning: New Perspectives*, edited by Paul Ramsden, 13–31. London: Kogan Page.

Romance, Nancy R., and Michael R. Vitale. 1999. "Concept Mapping as a Tool for Learning: Broadening the Framework for Student-Centered Learning." *College Teaching* 47, no. 2: 74–79.

Rosenshine, Barak, and Joseph Guenther. 1992. "Using Scaffolds for Teaching Higher Level Cognitive Strategies." In *Teaching for Thinking*, edited by James W. Keefe and Herbert J. Walberg, 35–47. Reston VA: National Association of Secondary School Principals.

Rowe, Mary Budd. 1976. "The Pausing Principle: Two Invitations to Inquiry." *Research in College Science Teaching* 5, no. 4: 258–259.

———. 1980. "Pausing Principles and Their Effects on Reasoning in Science." *New Directions for Community Colleges*, no. 31: 27–34.

Ruhl, Kathy L., Charles A. Hughes, and Patrick J. Schloss. 1987. "Using the Pause Procedure to Enhance Lecture Recall." *Teacher Education and Special Education* 10, no. 1: 14–18.

Saskatoon Public Schools. 2010. *Instructional Strategies Online 2004–2009*. Saskatoon Public Schools. http://olc.spsd.sk.ca/de/pd/instr/index.html.

Simons, Krista D., and James D. Klein. 2006. "The Impact of Scaffolding and Student Achievement Levels in a Problem-Based Learning Environment." *Instructional Science* 35, no. 1: 41–72.

Slavin, Robert E. 1990. *Cooperative Learning: Theory, Research and Practice.* Englewood Cliffs, NJ: Prentice Hall.

———. 2011. *Educational Psychology: Theory into Practice.* 10th ed. Upper Saddle River, NJ: Prentice Hall.

Smart, Karl L., and Nancy Csapo. 2007. "Learning by Doing: Engaging Students through Learner-Centered Activities." *Business Communication Quarterly* 70, no. 4: 451–457.

Smith, Karl A. 2000. "Going Deeper: Formal Small-Group Learning in Large Classes." *New Directions for Teaching and Learning,* no. 81: 25–46.

Stead, David R. 2005. "A Review of the One-Minute Paper." *Active Learning in Higher Education* 6, no. 2: 118–131.

Tech Teachers. 2006. *Jeopardy Templates and Other Games.* Tech Teachers, Inc. http://www.techteachers.com/jeopardytemplates.htm.

Thompson, Janette, Barbara Licklider, and Steven Edward Jungst. 2003. "Learner-Centered Teaching: Postsecondary Strategies That Promote Thinking Like a Professional." *Theory into Practice* 42, no. 2: 133–141.

Veldof, Jerilyn. 2006. *Creating the One-Shot Library Workshop: A Step by Step Guide.* Chicago: American Library Association.

Weimer, Mary Ellen. 2002. *Learner-Centered Teaching: Five Key Changes to Practice.* San Francisco: Jossey-Bass.

———. 2003. "Focus on Learning. Transform Teaching." *Change* 35, no. 5: 49–54.

Wood, David, Jerome Bruner, and Gail Ross. 1976. "The Role of Tutoring in Problem Solving." *Journal of Child Psychology and Psychiatry* 17, no. 2: 89–100.

Chapter 5

How Will Learning Be Measured?—Learner-Centered Assessment

I have been impressed with the urgency of doing. Knowing is not enough; we must apply. Being willing is not enough; we must do.

—Leonardo da Vinci

TAKING THE GUESSWORK OUT OF LEARNER-CENTERED TEACHING, OR HOW DO I KNOW IT WORKED?

When it comes right down to it, the ultimate goal of learner-centered teaching (LCT) is that learners attain the expected learning outcomes (ELOs) set for the instruction. Unless we have some way of measuring that attainment, we have no way of knowing if our teaching has been effective. So, assessing our learners' accomplishments is a crucial element in LCT. Assessment can take many forms, and, as in teaching, some techniques are more learner-centered than others. Instructors who work from the learner-centered perspective are more interested in using assessment to support their learners than in judging them. Whether or not actual grades are involved, learner-centered assessment is all about guidance. In assessment jargon, we are more interested in formative than in summative assessment. As such, assessment becomes much more integral to the instructional process itself (Marlow and Page, 2005; Saulnier et al., 2008; Weimer, 2002). So, let's examine how we can use assessment to support our learners' educational journey.

USING LEARNER-CENTERED ASSESSMENT TO LISTEN, ENGAGE, AND INSPIRE

As has been previously discussed, learner-centered instructors listen to, engage, and inspire their learners. The choices they make when selecting assessments helps them accomplish these three tasks. Here are some of the ways in which assessment can support the principles of LCT.

Listening via Assessment

Learners can convey a great deal about what they know, what they need to know, and what they have learned if we just give them a chance to tell us. Listening starts with finding out as much as we can about our learners through various types of needs assessments. Although this may not be what is commonly thought of when considering the topic of assessment, gathering this data is the first step in the assessment process. The information we obtain from our needs assessments tells us how to select the most appropriate and relevant ELOs for our instruction. Once we have determined these ELOs, we need to find ways for our learners to show us they have attained these outcomes. This is where instructional assessment comes in.

Learner-centered assessment provides opportunities for learners to exhibit their grasp of whatever has been included in the instructional endeavor. It can take many forms and can take place at different times—during the instruction itself, at the end of an instructional session and/or course, and at some later point after the instruction is over (Huba and Freed, 2000). Regardless of the format and the timing, the goal of learner-centered assessment is twofold—as a way for learners to exhibit what they have accomplished and as a means to provide feedback to them. Feedback, in the learner-centered assessment paradigm, not only provides information on whether learners "got it right or wrong" but also offers constructive comments about how learning can be improved (Eggen and Kauchak, 2010; Shepard, 2006; Shute, 2008). So, in a way, learner-centered assessment becomes part of the instructor–learner conversation that is the cornerstone of LCT (McKeachie and Svinicki, 2006; Weimer, 2002).

Engaging via Assessment

The types of assessments we select can either support our LCT efforts or seem to be separate from them. Research has shown that learners are more attentive and motivated if the material being taught has some connection to their real life. The more our assessments seem to mimic real-world situations, the more integral they become to learning itself. These more authentic types of assessment both engage the learners at a higher level and create a better instructional experience. Because the assessment has some real-world application, learners become better equipped to transfer the instructional experience to later life experiences (Davis, 2009; Paris, 1998). Furthermore, the more authentic assessments can tap into higher cognitive processes such as synthesis, analysis, and evaluation (Montgomery, 2002; Saulnier et al., 2008; Wiggins, 1996). As such they provide a better picture of learning than assessments that just measure right and wrong answers (i.e., objective, aka forced-choice, tests). Authentic assessments offer us the chance to provide better, more supportive feedback to our learners—letting the learners know not only if their responses are "correct" or "incorrect" but also what steps they might need to take to improve.

Inspiring via Assessment

Learner-centered assessments, especially those that are more "authentic" in nature, are what the educational literature refers to as "unstructured." This means that they are open ended enough to offer the possibilities of multiple solutions. There is no one right answer—merely many possible ways to solve the problem. As such, learner-centered assessment allows for more diversity of thought and honors the ways in which learners can differ in their approaches. So, once again, we are modeling our dedication to allowing all voices to be heard and encouraging our learners to be flexible and open minded to the ideas and perspectives of their fellow learners. Furthermore, this recognition that there are many equally acceptable roads to a possible solution helps our learners feel more confident about their own abilities, which in turn should encourage them to apply what they learned in the future. People who experience success during instruction leave feeling good about themselves and about the instructional endeavor as well. Their self-efficacy (the belief in one's own abilities) improves, and their self-confidence for future learning is enhanced. Thus learner-centered assessment helps inspire people to become lifelong learning learners.

LEARNER-CENTERED ASSESSMENT: CREATING OPPORTUNITIES TO COLLABORATE, PARTICIPATE, AND TAKE RESPONSIBILITY

If assessment is to be learner-centered, it must rest on the same collaboration, participation, and shared responsibility (CPR) principles that underlie LCT itself. If we view assessment as part of the learning process itself, it becomes easier to transform our assessment methodologies so that they reflect a more learner-centered focus. We can design our assessments so that they offer opportunities for learners to collaborate both with us and with their fellow learners. Assessment tasks in the learner-centered scenario require active participation on the part of the learners and also allows them to take more responsibility not only for the learning itself but also for assessing that learning. There are many ways we can apply CPR to our assessment efforts. Here are just a few suggestions. Other ideas will be highlighted during the rest of this chapter as we delve more deeply into the "how-to-do-it" aspects of learner-centered assessment.

Collaboration and Assessment

The emphasis on feedback and formative rather than summative assessment that characterizes learner-centered assessment illustrates collaboration in action.

Instructors use assessments as ways to communicate with their learners, offering advice for improvement along with evaluative comments on the quality of the work. Furthermore, as will be seen in later sections of this chapter, many learner-centered assessments are done in collaborative group or team settings. Whether working with the learners one on one or in groups or teams of learners, the instructors' aim is to offer constructive feedback that supports, encourages, and furthers learning. Assessment used in this way becomes yet another example of the collaborative aspect of LCT.

Participation and Assessment

While any kind of assessment (including the paper-and-pencil, forced-choice test) has some element of participation, the more learner-centered assessments up the ante on learner participation. Rather than forcing learners to choose the one and only "right" answer from several options, learner-centered assessments ask the learner to demonstrate what they have learned and to apply it to a question, issue, or problem. Learners don't just say what they think they might do in a given situation; they actually show it. Offering learners opportunities to demonstrate what they have learned via discussions, in-class exercises, problem-based or case study activities, and the like encourage learners to do more than scratch the surface of the topic. The level of thinking and participation in these types of assessment tasks requires learners to delve deeply into the material and use higher cognitive skills, such as analysis, synthesis, and evaluation. This active participation element also offers learners the opportunity to think about the material in their own way and to offer solutions from their own individual perspectives.

Learners can be invited to be active participants in assessment in other ways as well. They could be allowed to choose from several different types of assessments (writing a paper, giving a speech, doing a demonstration, creating a webpage, etc.) each of which would exhibit their learning. At the very least, giving learners the option to work on their own topic increases their participation quotient. Learners can also be asked to assess each other's work—perhaps by commenting on draft versions of an assignment, discussing various possible ways to approach and solve a problem in a small group setting, or by assessing their fellow team-mates' efforts on a group project. This not only adds an element of participation to the assessment process, it also encourages learners to take more responsibility for everyone's learning, which leads to the "R" in CPR.

Responsibility and Assessment

One of the goals for both LCT and information literacy instruction (ILI) is to encourage a lifelong learning mind-set in our learners. To accomplish this goal, we must encourage our learners to be introspective about and able to reflect upon their own learning experiences. Furthermore, we want them to take responsibility not only for their own learning but also for the learning of everyone who is sharing the instructional experience with them. As seen in the previous two sections, the collaboration and participation elements of LCT lead to an environment of shared responsibility. Learners are encouraged to self-assess and to review their fellow learners' projects, products, and discussion comments and to provide constructive feedback and suggestions for improvement (Shepard, 2006).

Whenever possible, learners are allowed to work on topics of their own choice. They are offered options about how they wish to learn and how that learning will be assessed. In full-term, for-credit courses, learners may be allowed to decide the point value for a selection of their assignments or to pick which assignments they will undertake for a given number of points (Mezeske, 2007; Mundhenk, 2004; Smith, 2007). In the first example, learners are told that they have 50 percent of their grade to work with and may allocate portions of that percentage to four of the course assignments. Each assignment must be given a minimal amount (say 5 or 10 percent), and the total for all four assignments has to add up to 50 percent. This gives learners the opportunity to emphasize their strengths and minimize the amount of time spent working in ways that are less appealing. Those who like writing can give more points to papers, while those who prefer verbal exchanges may allocate more points to discussions (in-person or online), speeches, debates, and other types of oral projects.

In the second option, the instructor offers learners a choice between several different assignments, due at various points during the course, but all of equal point value. There could be a paper, a book or website review, an assignment in which learners create a website or run a blog on a topic, or they could go out and interview relevant experts in the field and report their findings to their fellow learners. This approach not only gives learners the chance to pick the type of assignment/assessment format that most appeals to them, because the tasks are due at different points during the term, they can also decide when during the course they want to do the work for the allotted number of points.

Even the one-shot sessions typical of ILI can be injected with some of these elements of responsibility. We often allow learners to work on topics of their own choice during exercises and activities. Creating collaborative, small group learning experiences in our one-shot sessions also encourages the idea of shared responsibility. And as we incorporate more learner-centered activities (discussions, debates, interactive question-and-answer segments) we are in fact telling our learners that they must be involved in their own learning. We no longer are willing to view our learners as passive recipients, who just sit there with glazed expressions as we pontificate on the material. Instead, we are asking them to think, to analyze, to synthesize, and to construct information for themselves. When learners are allowed to take a bigger role in their own learning, what they have learned has greater meaning. Furthermore, learners become more confident in their own abilities and more willing to apply what they have learned beyond the instructional setting—and have taken yet another step toward becoming lifelong learners.

PLANNING FOR LEARNER-CENTERED ASSESSMENT: THE TEACHING TRIPOD

Now that we have established the role of assessment in LCT, you are probably asking yourself, "How do I create a learner-centered assessment experience?" To answer this question, we are going to have to take a little side trip into the topics of instructional design and planning as well as examine some basic concepts related to assessment in general. Let's start with the planning process— more specifically, the relationship between ELOs, instructional activities, and assessment. Keep in mind that we want to find out how successful our learners have been in attaining the information and knowledge we set out to share with them. So, effective instructors—especially those dedicated to learner-centered teaching—always begin with the development of ELOs. These ELOs will then guide us as we develop both how we will share the material with our learners and how we will assess their experience.

When presented with the idea of having to create outcomes and then assess those outcomes, many information literacy instructors initially may feel overwhelmed. But when we are developing outcomes and designing assessments what we are trying to do is answer the following two questions:

1. What do we want our learners to be able to do following instruction?

2. How will we know they can do it?

The first question informs the development of our instructional ELOs. The second encourages us to create opportunities for us to assess our learners' success in attaining those ELOs. Because assessments are being viewed as opportunities to observe learners exhibit what they have learned, this outcomes-driven approach places a greater emphasis on learning by doing or active/participatory learning. To see how this plays out in LCT, we need to take a brief look at two categories of assessment—Assessment with an uppercase "A" and assessment with a lowercase "a."

Instruction librarians often lament that they do not have the time, resources, or expertise to undertake systematic assessment. With our often quite limited contact time, especially in our one-shot endeavors, there does not seem to be any time available to assess our learners. We barely have time to address all the content we feel they need. But that is only if you think in terms of the uppercase version (Assessment) or the more formal techniques that include data collection, analysis, evaluating and making judgments about the date, and writing up the results and recommendations. There are certainly times that call for this type of assessment, say, when you are researching the comparative effectiveness of two different instructional methodologies such as online versus face-to-face (F2F) formats, are trying to determine the long-term effect of your instructional interventions, or need to justify your programs to your administrators.

LCT deals more with the lowercase version of assessment—the assessment that we can and generally do engage in as we teach. The goal of this type of assessment is to check if our learners are attaining the outcomes we have set for them. And we do this type of assessment by incorporating opportunities into the instruction itself to observe learners exhibiting the behavior set out in our ELOs. Active, learner-centered techniques and methodologies can help us create these opportunities. And they provide us with the answers to our two questions: "What will they be able to do?" and "How will we know they can do it?" Learner-centered activities and exercises enable us to know what they can do because we are watching them do it (Tollefson and Osborn, 2008).

TEACHING TRIPOD—STEP ONE: CREATING EXPECTED LEARNING OUTCOMES

Aligning ELOs with instructional activities and assessment is sometimes referred to as "backwards design" (Shepard, 2006; Tollefson and Osborn, 2008; Wiggins, 1998). We start with where we want our learners to go and then design our instruction with that end goal in mind. In other words, we decide what our overall goal is for the instruction and then ask ourselves what behaviors would our learners exhibit that would show us they have reached that goal. So, we ask ourselves that first question, "What do we want our learners to be able to do following instruction?"

The answers to this question help us create our ELOs. Keep in mind that an instructional goal represents the overall intent for the instruction. So it can be written in general terms such as "understand," "know," or "become familiar with." To assess whether learners have reached the instructional goal, something more is needed—a way to "see" this understanding, knowing, or familiarity. Remember, in LCT we are concerned about what people are learning. It is not enough to present, cover, or address the material. We want to find a way of determining that our learners have developed new skills, abilities, and knowledge as a result of our instruction. And that is where ELOs come in. They help us articulate how learners will exhibit their new skills, abilities, and knowledge and set the stage for assessing their success.

Those who have never worked with ELOs before may feel overwhelmed by the task. Although much has been written about the topic and various models exist about how to structure outcomes, most people agree that ELOs should meet the following criteria:

- ELOs are written from the learner's rather than the teacher's perspective. That is, they are about what the learner will do, not what the teacher will be teaching.

- ELOs must be observable and measurable. Instructors need to be able to see that learners can "perform" the expected behavior.

- ELOs are written in the active rather than the passive voice. This ensures that the outcome can be observed and measured.

The more we work with ELOs, the better we get at creating them. We also start to build up a sort of library of outcomes that can be modified and repurposed for different instructional situations. After all, wanting our learners to be able to effectively search social science databases is not all that different from wanting our learners to be able to effectively search databases in the sciences or the arts and humanities.

A dip into the literature on this topic will show that some authors use the term "objectives" instead of or interchangeably with "outcomes." Others differentiate between the two concepts. Both objectives and outcomes describe learner behavior, and both describe what learners should be able to do following instruction. In the strictest protocol, objectives describe the behaviors learners exhibit following instruction, and outcomes describe how learners will show they have attained that objective. For example, if the goal was that learners would know how to critically evaluate websites, the following objective and outcome might be created:

- Objective: After instruction, learners will be able to determine the quality of a specific website.

- Outcome: Learners will demonstrate their ability to determine website quality by applying a list of criteria to specific websites in order to rate these sites as useful for their own research needs.

Many instructors feel this distinction between objectives and outcomes is too subtle to be useful and combine both into one statement. The more current literature seems to be leaning toward the combination approach and calling the whole statement an outcome. Each of us must make that decision for ourselves. Whether we distinguish between them or combine them into one statement, it's important to make sure that the statement or statements include a description of the behavior the learner will exhibit (behavioral objective) and how he or she will demonstrate that behavior (the observable and measurable outcome). Here's a formula that might be useful when constructing objective/outcome statements:

- After instruction, learners will be able to (insert behavior to be exhibited) by (insert way that behavior will be observed).

Of course, the critical issue in all this is deciding what learners should be able to do and then coming up with a way to describe that behavior. Many instructors turn to Bloom's *Taxonomy of Educational Objectives* (Anderson and Krathwohl, 2001; Bloom, 1956, 1984) for assistance. The original taxonomy, and its 2001 update, organizes learning into competency levels from basic knowledge at the simplest end to the more complex synthesis, analysis, evaluation, and, in the 2001 update, creation. Each goal level has specific objectives/outcomes associated with it. The taxonomy even includes suggestions for active voice verbs (list, define, describe, apply, compare, explain, design, evaluate, conclude, etc.) that are appropriate for each level.

TEACHING TRIPOD—STEP TWO: SELECTING INSTRUCTIONAL ACTIVITIES

Once outcomes have been developed it is time to decide what to include in the instruction that will enable learners to attain those observable and measurable outcomes. The "measurable" characteristic is often of great concern to instructors. In their minds, being measurable equates with quantifiable and therefore places some kind of restrictions on what outcomes they can select. But in reality all that is needed is to be able to "see" learners "do" what was described in the outcomes. We are not necessarily interested in grades or counting correct responses on a test. We just want to observe our learners in action. In other words, we are now moving on to the "How will we know they can do it?" question. So, the next step is to create opportunities in which learners can be observed performing the outcomes. This is the second leg of the teaching tripod—selecting instructional activities. Review the outcomes, and ask, "What activities can I include in the instruction that will give learners the opportunity to exhibit that they have successfully attained the ELOs?" Remember to include an observational opportunity of some kind for each of the ELOs created. Otherwise there is no way of knowing if learners have attained that outcome. Although each activity selected does not have to be tied to a specific outcome, if an activity is not outcome related, consider why it is being included. What purpose does it serve? This is a good way to trim the fat in your instruction—emphasizing activities that support outcomes and only including other activities as time permits. That is the wonderful thing about having observable, learner-centered outcomes. They help to guide the selection of instructional activities and, as will be seen in the discussion of the teaching tripod's final step, suggest ways for assessing learning as well (Grassian and Kaplowitz, 2009, 2010).

Observation opportunities can be created *during*, at the *end* of, or *after* the instructional endeavor. Small group exercises, hands-on practice, worksheets, discussions, and questioning are all examples of "observational opportunities" that occur *during* instruction itself. Feedback forms such as the One-Minute Paper or 3-2-1 cards are "observational opportunities" that are placed at the *end* of a session. Any kind of follow-up contact with learners or course instructors would count as *after* types of observational opportunities, as could examinations of learners' products (papers, projects). Citation analysis of the bibliographies used for these products would also be an example of an *after* observation. See Chapter 4 for more on these instructional methods.

But before moving on to the third leg of our teaching tripod, let's take a moment to discuss overt versus covert behaviors. Advocates of outcome-driven instruction and LCT assert that you must be able to observe your learners performing the ELOs. Critics of the approach feel its emphasis on visible behavior creates a focus on only the most observable skills. How then can outcomes be created that help determine changes in learners' affect? How will you know if they have become more comfortable in using resources or if they have gained self-confidence, reached a higher level of self-efficacy as a result of the instructional experience, and are ready to take more responsibility for their own learning? These are all valid ELOs, especially in the LCT perspective (Grassian and Kaplowitz, 2009).

While it is true that we cannot see these affective changes, we can create observational opportunities that help us to infer that these changes in feeling states have occurred (Grassian and Kaplowitz, 2009). For example, if we want to "see" changes in how learners feel about doing research following instruction, we can do a concept mapping exercise at the start of instruction and another one at its conclusion and compare the results. See Chapter 4 for more on concept mapping. Or we can "observe" these changes by including questions in our *end* activity directed at determining any changes in affective states at this point. Instructors often used the five- or six-point Likert scales (strongly agree to strongly disagree continuum surveys) to measure change in affective states. We could distribute these surveys at the *end* of instruction itself or send them out to learners at some point *after* instruction has occurred. An advantage to the *after* scenario is that we could be gathering information about how learners feel at a point when they have actually tried to apply what they have learned from the ILI to some kind of paper or project.

Selecting instructional activities that allow us to see how well our learners have attained the ELOs set for them helps us to structure our instructional endeavors. What we do with the information gathered from these observations will contribute to our assessment efforts described in the next section.

TEACHING TRIPOD—STEP THREE: ASSESSING EXPECTED LEARNING OUTCOMES

It turns out that if we adopt a learner-centered approach to instruction, and incorporate ways for learners to exhibit the attainment of ELOs, we are already doing a lot of assessment with little or no extra effort on our part. We may not think of these activities as assessment, but we do use them as such. We check for comprehension and offer constructive feedback to our learners as they interact with the material during exercises and small group activities, as well as when we moderate discussions and facilitate interactive questioning segments. In other words, we are informally assessing our learners' grasp of the material we are sharing with them during these instructional activities. We also use the information gathered from these assessments to make midstream corrections during instruction—clarifying, repeating, or paraphrasing material that learners do not seem to be correctly comprehending. And we consider ways in which we can improve and revise our instruction in order to improve its effectiveness in the future. So instructional activities can serve a dual role—supporting learning and also assessing that learning. But that is only if we view them as such. So, as we design our instruction and select activities from the various methods available to us, we must also think about the assessment potential each might provide us. And we must determine if the activities we have selected are sufficient to assess each of our instruction's ELOs, or if we need to incorporate additional "observation opportunities," aka assessments. To make that determination, we need to know a bit more about assessment methodology and the issues that are associated with that methodology. So let's take a closer look at these methodological concerns.

ASSESSMENT 101: AN OVERVIEW OF SOME BASIC PRINCIPLES

If we look at the literature associated with educational assessment, we will see that a vast array of assessment techniques, instruments, and methodologies are available to us. So, how do we pick the right assessment for the task at hand? There are lots of things to consider as we make our assessment decisions. We must ask ourselves:

1. What is the reason for the assessment?
2. What is the question we are trying to answer with the assessment?
3. What are the pros and cons of various types of assessment methods?
4. What, if any, logistical constraints exist that might affect our assessment decisions?

Let's take a closer look at each of these issues.

What Is the Reason for the Assessment?

In general, we assess for two main reasons. Let's call them "learning" and "accountability." We assess to find out if our instruction has been effective. So we try to find ways to determine if our learners have attained the ELOs we have set for the instruction. We use the results of these assessments as a way to help learners improve their accomplishments as well as a means to highlight places in our instructional methodology that might need some revision and improvement. So this first type of assessment is directed at assessing the learning itself. Using formal assessment vocabulary, this type would be called *formative* assessment. But we also assess to document the value of our ILI endeavors. We assess to gather data that we can present to our administrators, institutions, accreditation agencies, and other stakeholders in our communities that demonstrate the value of our endeavors and the contributions that ILI makes to our learners' lives. This second type of assessment is directed at accountability issues and is often referred to as *summative* assessment (Cruickshank, Jenkins, and Metcalf, 2009; Eggen and Kauchak, 2010; Grassian and Kaplowitz, 2009; Shepard, 2006).

In some ways this learning versus accountability goes back to the discussion of assessment with a lowercase "a" versus that with an uppercase "A." We are including lowercase a learning type formative assessments in instructional encounters whenever we include those "observational opportunities" that allow us to watch our learners in action. But we may only do uppercase A summative assessments when we are engaged in more formal data collection, research, and report generating types of experiences—for example, those that might be required during accreditation processes or when we need to justify our current ILI budget or request additional funding. Although some of the same assessment techniques can be used for both types, how we collect the data and what we do with it once it is collected differ. For example, techniques like the One-Minute Paper or 3-2-1 cards are generally thought of in terms of "learning" assessments, but if we collected the information provided by them and summarized it in some way they could be turned into accountability assessments that can be included in reports to our stakeholders.

What Is the Question We Are Trying to Answer with the Assessment?

Next we need to consider what we are trying to find out about our learners. In general, the intent of all types of assessment is to help us determine if our learners have attained the ELOs set for the instruction. But remember Bloom's hierarchy of competency levels. ELOs for any given instructional endeavor vary depending on which of these levels were selected as the goal or goals for that endeavor. In most cases instruction goals will represent multiple levels, and thus various types of ELOs will be needed to address these different levels of complexity.

According to Donald Kirkpatrick (1998), assessments can be divided into four levels, each of which answers a different question about the learners' competencies. Each of the four levels (Reaction, Learning, Behavioral, Results) provides a different answer to the general question, "What did my learners get from the instruction?" (Grassian and Kaplowitz, 2009, 2010; Veldof, 2006). Table 5.1

Table 5.1. An Interpretation of Kirkpatrick's Levels of Assessment		
Level	Question Addressed	Description
Reaction	Did they like it?	• The assessment measures what learners thought of the session—not what they learned. • It frequently takes the form of Likert scales (strongly agree to strongly disagree). • It is often referred to as a "happiness scale," because it measures only opinions about instruction, not what was learned from it. • It provides some valid data. If learners dislike the learning environment and/or the presenter, they will be less engaged in the process. • Factors that contribute to "unhappiness" need to be examined and revised.
Learning	Did they get it?	• The assessment requires learners to perform in some fashion either during the instruction itself or after the fact. • How learners demonstrate their grasp of the concepts is usually under the control of the instructor. • The instructor presents the learner with a situation and asks the learner to apply what has been learned, or the learner is presented with some kind of instrument that tests comprehension. • Although a step above the "happiness scales," it still does not measure how the learner will react when presented with a situation in her or his own life.
Behavioral	Can they do it?	• The assessment examines the process used to perform, the product that results from the performance, or both. • It is sometimes referred to as an "authentic assessment," because learners are asked to apply what they have learned in a real-life situation. • It examines whether the learners' method of solving the problem has changed as a result of the instruction. • Examples include analyzing papers, projects, or other assignments produced by learners after instruction or comparing those produced before to those done after instruction.
Results	Does it matter?	• This is the most difficult assessment to undertake, because it measures the effect of the instruction on the learners' lives. • Did the instruction lead to better retention rates or higher overall grade point average in college? Did K–12 students get into better schools and/or do better when they got there? Did the instruction contribute to learners getting a higher-paying job? Did the company's productivity, sales figures, or market share improve? • These types of assessments require instructors to collaborate with people and groups to discover the instructional impact on their learners. • Because these are more complicated to accomplish, results assessments are often done infrequently or not at all.

presents an overview of Kirkpatrick's work that illustrates what kind of information each assessment level can provide.

Reaction Assessments

Each level of assessment looks at a different aspect of what learners gained from an instructional encounter. One of the most common mistakes instructors make is to use an assessment at one level to answer the question addressed by another. For example, many instructors distribute some kind of *reaction* assessment (surveys, questionnaires, One-Minute Papers, 3-2-1 cards) either at the end of instruction or at some later date. In addition to the general "Did they like it?" type questions, instructors also include questions that ask if people who participated in the instruction felt they had learned anything and/or if they intended to use those new insights in their future pursuits. While on the surface these questions seem to be gathering data about learning itself, in reality reaction assessments indicate only what people think they learned or might do. There is no real demonstration of the attainment of the instructional ELOs and so no real measure of learning. However, many researchers and practitioners erroneously use the results of reaction assessments as measures of learning. To truly assess learning, we must incorporate assessments that exemplify some of the other levels.

Learning Assessments

Many of the exercises and activities that are often incorporated into instruction can also be viewed as *learning* assessments. Even though they may not originally have been thought of as such, these activities allow instructors to watch learners as they try to apply some new skill or knowledge acquired from the instruction. So they can provide instructors with assessment information while offering practice opportunities for the learners. Although providing a clearer picture of what learners are now able to do, assessments at this level suffer from a degree of artificiality. The situation is completely under the instructor's control. He or she sets up the situation, provides the materials, and tells learners what they have to accomplish. Although success at these tasks offers some insight into learners' attainment of ELOs, it is still unclear if learners will take these newly acquired skills, knowledge, and abilities into their real lives. When faced with a similar problem out in the real world, will these learners continue to apply what they learned from our instruction, or will they revert back to their old, less effective, pre-instructional habits?

Behavioral Assessments

Behavioral assessments help to counter the artificiality associated with learning assessments. Whether they take place during instruction itself or are associated with papers, projects, or other learner-created products after the fact, these assessments ask learners to demonstrate learning in a more real-life situation. Learners are being asked to apply what they learned beyond the restrictive, artificial constraints associated with learning assessments. They must answer real questions, solve real problems, and come up with real solutions, which is why they are often referred to as "authentic" learning and assessment experiences. These authentic types of "observational opportunities" require higher levels of thinking, such as analysis, synthesis, and evaluation, and ultimately the creation of new information/knowledge. Although most people associate behavioral assessments with the post-instructional types of assignments, they can also be incorporated into instruction itself. Real-world, authentic case studies or problems can serve as the basis for instructional activities and can add an element of reality to the instructional situation. Although learners are not actually performing in the real world, the fact that they are working on real issues/problems/cases provides a better idea of how they might operate once they are on their own.

Results Assessments

Results assessments are the hardest and most complicated to create, coordinate, implement, and interpret and so remain the ones that instructors tend to overlook or avoid. Unfortunately, that means there is little evidence about the long-term effectiveness of our instructional efforts. In terms of ILI there is very little in the way of results-based assessment data to support our belief that an information-literate person will be more likely to succeed in life. More research needs to be done on this in order to provide librarians with even more evidence of the necessity of ILI sessions, courses, and programs.

Making the Right Decision

To ensure that we select the most appropriate assessment methods and tools for our purposes, we need to know a bit more about the various types of assessments available. Each method/tool has its advantages and its drawbacks (Cruickshank, Jenkins, and Metcalf, 2009; Oakleaf, 2008). Making the right assessment decision depends on knowing the type of information/data provided by the various tools and the limitations of each (Eggen and Kauchak, 2010; Grassian and Kaplowitz, 2009; Gratch-Lindauer, 2007; Linn and Gronlund, 2005). And because of our LCT approach, we need to examine our assessment options to see which ones allow our learners to have a more collaborative, participatory, and responsible role in the assessment process (Saulnier et al., 2008).

A Brief Overview of Assessment Instrument Characteristics

An in-depth discussion of the many and varied assessment tools available is beyond the scope of this book. See the Reflections section at the end of this chapter for ways to further explore this topic. In general, it is helpful to think of assessment tools as falling into six categories (Cruickshank, Jenkins, and Metcalf, 2009; Grassian and Kaplowitz, 2009). See Table 5.2 for information on these categories.

Table 5.2. Categorizing Assessment Tools		
Category	Description	Examples
Forced choice	• Assessments in which there is only one correct answer • Answers determined in advance by test designer/instructor • Learners' responses either right or wrong	• Multiple choice • Matching • True/false • Fill in the blanks
Surveys and questionnaires	• Offer a range of options for respondents to choose from • Tend to be used for demographic, opinion, and attitude information	• Likert scales • Multiple-choice or fill-in-the-blanks questions that gather general information about learners and their thoughts on issues and subjects
Open ended	• Allow for more options in responding • Specific right answers determined in advance by instructor	• Short answer or essay
Interviews and focus groups	• Allow for discussion of process as well as skills • No right or wrong response, though questions are structured in advance • Skilled facilitator needed in order to encourage interviewees to express themselves freely on the topic under discussion	• Any kind of question-and-answer exchange between person doing the assessment and the respondents • Interviews usually done one on one • In focus groups, multiple respondents queried at the same time
Classroom assessment techniques (CATs) (Angelo, 1998; Angelo and Cross, 1993)	• Generally take the form of exercises, worksheets, and other classroom activities interspersed within instruction itself • Provide practice opportunities as well as feedback to both learners and instructor on how well learners are performing	• One-Minute Paper • 3-2-1 cards • Empty outline • Additional examples given in Angelo's and Angelo and Cross's publications
Authentic assessments	• Assessments that are based in reality • Learners presented with real-life, important questions or reality-based problems to solve • Explore both process and product • Correct solutions not determined in advance • Instructor provides some direction and constraints, but learners encouraged to solve problems in their own way • Allow for diversity in approach and solutions	• Problem-based learning • Case studies

Another way to think about these different types of assessments is how well or how little they reflect reality and how much the test administrator or instructor can regulate or control the testing and/or scoring situation. In general, assessment techniques that are high in control are low in relevance and vice versa. The six tool types described in Table 5.2 vary in regard to these two parameters, with forced choice representing the highest in control and lowest in relevance and authentic assessment representing the other extreme (very high in relevance but low in control). Generally speaking, the more latitude learners have over their performance and ability to customize their solutions, the higher the relevance and the lower the control (Grassian and Kaplowitz, 2009). We can call this the "control/relevance continuum," as depicted in Table 5.3.

Clearly, adhering to LCT principles would suggest the use of assessments that give learners more control over the situation and that are highly relevant to them. As learners are offered more control over the ways in which their learning is assessed, they are also being given the opportunity to take more responsibility for their own learning. Rather than acting as judge and jury, learner-centered instructors use assessment to collaborate with their learners, offer feedback that supports learning, and give their learners the chance to actively participate in the assessment process (Baron, 1998; Bransford, Darling-Hammond, and LePage, 2005; Ercikan, 2006). Furthermore, the more relevant the assessment is to real-world applications, the more motivated the learners will be, and the higher the likelihood that what is learned will transfer to new situations later in life (Huba and Freed, 2000).

LCT principles also emphasize criterion-referenced over norm-referenced approaches to assessment. In norm-referenced assessments learners' scores are compared to each other, and the relevant position of each learner is given a score as a result of this comparison. This is the so-called "grading on the curve" approach. Norm-referenced assessment is the antithesis of LCT, because it is more concerned with relative position than it is with individual learning and as such is not always a good measure of learning success. Learners' scores tell us the relative ranking of our learners but not necessarily what they have learned or are able to do

Table 5.3. The Control/Relevance Continuum						
	Forced Choice	Surveys/ Questionnaires	Open Ended	Interviews/ Focus Groups	Classroom Assessment Techniques	Authentic Assessment
Control	High	High	High	Moderate	Moderate	Low
Relevance	Low	Low	Low	Moderate	Moderate	High

Source: Grassian, Esther, and Joan Kaplowitz. 2009. *Information Literacy Instruction: Theory and Practice*. 2nd ed. Table 11.2, p. 212. New York: Neal-Schuman.

following instruction. Criterion-referenced assessments, on the other hand, compare learners' work to an objective standard (Cruickshank, Jenkins, and Metcalf, 2009; Eggen and Kauchak, 2010). In the case of ILI, we might use the ACRL's *Information Literacy Competency Standards for Higher Education* (ACRL, 2000), AASL's *Standards for the 21st-Century Learner* (AASL, 2007), standards set within a discipline such as Chemistry or Psychology (APA Board of Educational Affairs [BEA] Task Force on Psychology Major Competencies, 2007; American Chemical Society, 2002), or by individual institutions, organizations, states, and so forth as the standards to which we will compare our learners' work (Grassian and Kaplowitz, 2009).

Rubrics

Another way to transform assessment procedures so that they are more in line with LCT principles is to develop scoring rubrics and share those rubrics with learners (Grassian and Kaplowitz, 2009). Rubrics are based on standards such as those described earlier. They are not judgmental but rather are intended to measure the learners' performance against those standards (Eggen and Kauchak, 2010). Rubrics consist of performance criteria, descriptions of how learners will demonstrate that performance, and generally include levels of proficiency (e.g., basic, proficient, advanced) with the highest level indicating performance at or very close to professional standards (Cruickshank, Jenkins, and Metcalf, 2009; Teaching, Learning, and Technology Group, 2008; Wiggins, 1998). Websites such as Rubistar (4Teachers, 2008) can provide invaluable assistance as you get started in your development of ILI rubrics. Although intended for classroom teachers, Rubistar's interactive tool can be customized to your ILI situation. Sharing rubrics with learners gives them a better idea of the level of performance expected of them. This in turn helps them to take a bit more control over and responsibility for their own learning (Marzano, 1998; Shepard, 2006; Tollefson and Osborn, 2008).

Armed with your knowledge of assessment tools and techniques, you are just about ready to make your final selections among your various options. But there is still one more issue to address. As with so many things in life, there is the absolutely perfect and ideal selection and the compromises that must be made due to practical considerations. So let's now turn to the very last of our concerns—logistical issues.

Logistical Concerns

What, if any, logistical constraints exist that might affect the assessment decisions? This is the moment we need to take a breath and consider the reality of our situation. Some of the things to consider follow:

- Amount of time available for assessment tasks during instruction
- Amount of time needed to develop customized assessment material

- Any costs that might be involved and how those costs will be covered (e.g., printing surveys or other paper-based material)

- Special expertise needed to develop assessment and/or analyze the data (e.g., facilitator for focus group interviews)

- For formal, summative assessment projects—the stakeholders who will want copies of the final report and how you will present that information (e.g., format of the report—written narrative, verbal presentation, tables and charts, etc.) (Grassian and Kaplowitz, 2009)

We may truly wish to do some kind of behavioral or results level assessment but do not have the time, the budget, or access to the learners that is needed. Or maybe we want to do a lot of CATs during instruction, but our contact time is limited. So we can include only a select few. Be realistic. Some assessment is better than no assessment. Don't despair because everything can't be done. The crucial component is that we assess the attainment of all the ELOs in some way and use the information gathered from those assessments to enhance the learning experience and identify ways in which to improve instruction for the future.

DOUBLE DUTY: USING INSTRUCTIONAL ACTIVITIES FOR ILI ASSESSMENT

Many of the assessment techniques described earlier might seem more appropriate for full-term, for-credit types of ILI. Generally speaking, information literacy instructors who teach one-shot sessions tend to rely most heavily on surveys/questionnaires and CATs. They do so because they are not usually involved in grading their learners' efforts. This nongrading element has its good side and its bad. While some learners may feel less motivated without the grading element, the absence of the grading element allows us to take a more learner-centered, nonjudgmental, supportive approach to our assessments. And many of the instructional activities discussed in the previous chapter can serve as less formal ways to assess our learners. As we discussed in step two of the teaching tripod, "Selecting Instructional Activities," we choose activities not only to offer our learners a chance to interact with the material in some way but also as a way for us to monitor our learners' attainment of ELOs—in other words, to assess how well they are grasping the material being addressed. Table 5.4 shows how each of the methods described previously can also serve as "observation opportunities," aka assessments.

FINAL REMARKS

Assessment is a crucial element in LCT. If we neglect to include any kind of assessment, we cannot be sure that our learners are getting anything out of the

Table 5.4. Using Instructional Activities for Assessment

Instructional Activity	Assessment Potential
Lecture	• Effective lecturers continually monitor their learners' attention levels. • Glazed or confused expressions, yawns, and long-distance stares are all indications you are losing your audience and need to stop, regroup, and maybe insert some other more learner-centered type of activity.
Modeling/demonstration	• As with the lecture, this more instructor-centered technique may not hold learners' attention for long periods of time. • Watch for any restlessness or other signs of disinterest, such as those described in the previous section on the lecture method, and try to do something that will reinvigorate learners. • Try asking your learners to do some of the modeling or demonstrating. You will be able to watch them perform (assess) as well as increase interest in the material.
Questioning	• Interactive Q&As can serve as comprehension checks and as ways to identify errors in understanding, misconceptions, and confusion. • Questioning offers you the opportunity to provide constructive feedback as well as gives you a chance to review, revise, and otherwise clarify previously addressed material.
Discussion	• Similar to Q&As, monitoring discussions allows you to assess how well the material is being grasped and offer suggestions, feedback, corrections, etc. • Discussions also offer the opportunity for learners to start assessing each other as they reply to (or even refute) other learners' comments.
Practice	• Watching your learners as they attempt to apply their newly acquired skills, knowledge, and abilities is a great way to assess how well they are attaining ELOs. • As you observe their attempts, you can offer suggestions for ways in which they can improve their efforts. • If done in pairs or in small groups, practice offers peer assessment opportunities as well. • You can also provide worksheets for learners to complete as they practice and collect some or all of them to add to your assessment data collection.
Collaborative group work	• Techniques such as Think/Pair/Share, Jigsaw, Pass the Problem, and other small group exercises offer all the same assessment opportunities as those described in relation to discussion. • Additionally, incorporating elements of authentic problem-based or case-based scenarios into small group activities/exercises increases the relevance of the situation. • As groups report back on the results of their collaborations, you (and members of other groups) can offer constructive feedback and suggestions for improvement. • Furthermore, you might ask for some written product from the groups that you can collect and analyze for additional assessment data.

(Continued)

Table 5.4. Using Instructional Activities for Assessment *(Continued)*	
Instructional Activity	**Assessment Potential**
Reflection	• While most reflections are meant to be private and confidential, they can still be used as a source of assessment data. • Research journals can be collected from time to time and reviewed for assessment purposes. • Online reflections can also be monitored in this fashion. • However, you need to reassure your learners that these reflections will not be graded in any way. You are reviewing them as a way to offer support, not to be judgmental or critical. • In addition to acting as ways for learners to reflect upon the instructional experience, One-Minute Papers, 3-2-1 cards, and other learner feedback forms that are completed at the end of an instructional experience can also offer you insight into what your learners are taking away with them.

instructional experience we are sharing with them. However, expanding the notion of assessment to include a variety of "observational opportunities" allows us to look beyond the formal types of assessment and transforms assessment into something that is not only integral to learning, but that goes on throughout the learning situation.

While much of the material in this chapter was discussed in terms of the F2F instructional setting, many of the assessment techniques can be easily adapted to the online instructional setting. See Chapter 6 for more on assessment issues in online instruction. Regardless of whether we are engaged in F2F or online instruction, assessment should not be overlooked. If we use the three steps of the teaching tripod as the model for our instructional design efforts, assessment not only becomes second nature, it also becomes part and parcel of the planning process. Once we determined the ELOs for our instruction, we immediately begin to think about how our learners will exhibit attainment of those ELOs via the activities during, at the end of, or at a later date following instruction. In doing so, we have not only created opportunities for our learners to interact with the material and participate in their own learning, but we have also incorporated ways to assess that learning.

REFLECTIONS

1. Think about a topic you are planning to teach. Develop the ELOs for this instruction. Remember to write these from the learners' perspective, to use the active voice, and to make sure these outcomes are observable and measurable (either formally or informally). Try using the formula, "After instruction, learners will be able to (insert behavior to be exhibited) by (insert way that behavior will be observed)."

2. Now create an instructional activity for each of the ELOs that will allow your learners to interact with the material being addressed. Can any of these instructional activities serve double duty as instruction and assessment opportunities? Which ones? Which specific ELO does each of these activities address?

3. Once you have decided which of your instructional activities can also serve as assessment opportunities consider whether or not you need to add additional assessment opportunities. In other words, have you included something that can serve as an assessment of each of the ELOs you have specified for this instruction? If not, what additional assessment opportunities do you need to include?

4. Next think about the type of assessment data you are interested in collecting (formative or summative), the purpose for your assessment (learning, accountability, or both), and what questions you are trying to answer with your assessment (i.e., Kirkpatrick's levels: Reaction, Learning, Behavioral, Results). Review the activities/assessments you have selected against Kirkpatrick's four levels to make sure your choices are supplying the data required to answer your question(s), and revise your work as needed.

5. Once you have completed these four steps, you will have a rough outline for your instruction. Put the activities/assessment opportunities into a logical order. Then develop talking points or descriptive background material that learners will need to know in order to complete the various learning and assessment tasks. Make sure you have also included segues that link the various instructional segments. These segues should serve as a review of previous material and an introduction to the next content segment.

6. Congratulations! You have now successfully created your instructional endeavor. Don't forget to monitor its effectiveness in order to highlight any places that might need improvement in the future. And keep a lookout for how elements of this instruction might be recycled into other instructional endeavors.

EXPLORATIONS

Anderon, Lorin W., and David Krathwohl, eds. 2001. *A Taxonomy for Learning, Teaching, and Assessing: A Revision of Bloom's Taxonomy of Educational Objectives.* New York: Longman.

This is the latest update of the classic Bloom's *Taxonomy*—foundational work for outcomes-based teaching and assessment.

Angelo, Thomas A., and K. Patricia Cross. 1993. *Classroom Assessment Techniques: A Handbook for College Teachers.* 2nd ed. *The Jossey-Bass Higher Education & Adult Education Series.* San Francisco: Jossey-Bass.

This book started it all when it comes to classroom assessment techniques.

Battersby, Mark, and Learning Outcomes Network. 1999. *So What's a Learning Outcome Anyway?* ERIC Centre for Curriculum, Transfer and Technology. ED430611.

This is a great introduction to outcomes, why they are so important, and how to write them.

Burkhardt, Joanna, Mary C. Macdonald, and Andrea J. Rathemacher. 2003. *Teaching Information Literacy: 35 Practical Standards-Based Exercises for College Students.* Chicago: ALA.

The authors provide excellent suggestions on how to make your instruction more learner-centered and engaging.

Cruickshank, Donald R., Deborah B. Jenkins, and Kim K. Metcalf. 2009. *The Act of Teaching.* 5th ed. New York: McGraw-Hill.

This book covers all aspects of teaching, including how to write outcomes and how to develop appropriate assessments.

CyberCampus. 2010. *RadioJames Objective Builder.* Golden Gate University. http://www.radiojames.com/ObjectivesBuilder/.

This is an online, interactive guide to creating learning objectives/outcomes.

Driscoll, Amy, and Swarup Wood. 2007. *Developing Outcomes-Based Assessment for Learner-Centered Education.* Sterling, VA: Stylus.

This is a good discussion of the relationship between outcomes and assessment.

Grassian Esther, and Joan Kaplowitz (2009). *Information Literacy Instruction: Theory and Practice.* 2nd ed. New York: Neal-Schuman.

This book includes discussions of outcomes, teaching techniques, assessment, and active learning as well as many other ILI topics.

Huba, Mary E., and Jann E. Freed. 2000. *Learner-Centered Assessment on College Campuses.* Boston: Allyn and Bacon.

The authors provide great suggestions for learner-centered teaching and assessment and highlight the relationship between outcomes and assessment.

Kirkpatrick, Donald. 1998. *Evaluating Training Programs: The Four Levels.* San Francisco: Berret-Koehler.

Kirkpatrick introduces the concept of the four levels of assessment.

Lorenzen, Michael. 2001. "Active Learning and Library Instruction." *Illinois Libraries* 83, no. 2: 19–24.

This is an excellent overview and great discussion of how we can apply active learning in the library setting.

Neeley, Teresa Y., ed. 2006. *Information Literacy Assessment: Standards-Based Tools and Assignments.* Chicago: American Library Association.

Neeley ties assessment to the ACRL information literacy standards.

Oakleaf, Megan. 2008. "Dangers and Opportunities: A Conceptual Map of Information Literacy Assessment Approaches." *portal: Libraries and the Academy*, 8, no. 3: 233–253.

This provides a brief overview of the pros and cons of using various types of assessment techniques.

Radcliff, Carolyn J., Mary Lee Jensen, Joseph A. Salem, Jr., Kenneth J. Burhanna, and Julie A. Gedeon. 2007. *A Practical Guide to Information Literacy Assessment for Academic Librarians.* Westport, CT: Libraries Unlimited.

This is a comprehensive examination of various types of assessment techniques geared to a teaching librarian audience.

Veldof, Jerilyn. 2006. *Creating the One-Shot Library Workshop: A Step-by-Step Guide.* Chicago: American Library Association.

This well-organized discussion of the development process provides good material on outcomes and assessment.

Weimer, Mary Ellen E. 2002. *Learner-Centered Teaching: Five Key Changes to Practice.* San Francisco: Jossey-Bass.

This is an in-depth discussion of Weimer's philosophy of teaching and learning and includes a thorough examination of learner-centered assessment.

Wiggins, Grant. 1998. *Educational Assessment: Designing Assessments to Inform and Improve Student Performance.* San Francisco: Jossey-Bass.

Wiggins presents an excellent discussion of why we assess, the use of authentic assessment techniques, and the importance of feedback to the learning process.

REFERENCES

ACRL. 2000. *Information Literacy Competency Standards for Higher Education.* American Library Association. http://www.ala.org/ala/mgrps/divs/acrl/standards/information literacycompetency.cfm.

AASL. 2007. *Standards for the 21st-Century Learner.* American Library Association. http://www.ala.org/ala/aasl/aaslproftools/learningstandards/standards.cfm.

American Chemical Society. 2002. *Chemical Information Retrieval.* American Chemical Society. http://portal.acs.org/portal/fileFetch/C/CTP_005584/pdf/CTP_005584.pdf.

Anderson, Lorin W., and David R. Krathwohl. 2001. *A Taxonomy of Learning, Teaching and Assessing: A Revision of Bloom's Educational Objectives.* Boston: Allyn and Bacon.

Angelo, Thomas A., 1998. *Classroom Assessment and Research: An Update on Uses, Approaches and Research Findings.* San Francisco: Jossey-Bass.

Angelo, Thomas A., and K. Patricia Cross. 1993. *Classroom Assessment Technique: A Handbook for College Teachers.* 2nd ed. San Francisco: Jossey-Bass.

APA Board of Educational Affairs (BEA) Task Force on Psychology Major Competencies. 2007. *APA Guidelines for the Undergraduate Psychology Major.* Washington, DC: American Psychological Association.

Baron, Joan Boykoff. 1998. "Using Learner-Centered Assessment on a Large Scale." In *How Students Learn: Reforming Schools through Learner-Centered Education,* edited by Nadine M. Lambert and Barbara L. McCombs, 211–240. Washington, DC: American Psychological Association.

Bloom, Benjamin Samuel. 1956. *Taxonomy of Educational Objectives: The Classification of Educational Goals. Handbook 1: Cognitive Domain.* Handbook 2: Affective Domain. 2 vols. New York: McKay.

———. 1984. *Taxonomy of Educational Objectives.* Boston, MA: Allyn and Bacon.

Bransford, John D., Linda Darling-Hammond, and Pamela LePage. 2005. "Introduction." In *Preparing Teachers for a Changing World: What Teachers Should Learn and Be Able to Do,* edited by Linda Darling-Hammond and John D. Bransford, 1–39. San Francisco: Jossey-Bass.

Cruickshank, Donald R., Deborah Bainer Jenkins, and Kim K. Metcalf. 2009. *The Act of Teaching.* 5th ed. Boston: McGraw-Hill.

Davis, Barbara Gross. 2009. *Tools for Teaching.* 2nd ed. San Francisco: Jossey-Bass.

Eggen, Paul, and Don Kauchak. 2010. *Educational Psychology: Windows on Classrooms.* Upper Saddle River, NJ: Merrill.

Ercikan, Kadriye. 2006. "Developments in Assessment of Student Learning." In *Handbook of Educational Psychology,* edited by Patricia A. Alexander and Philip H. Winne, 929–952. Mahwah, NJ: Lawrence Erlbaum.

4Teachers. 2008. RubiStar. 4Teachers.org. http://rubistar.4teachers.org/index.php.

Grassian, Esther, and Joan Kaplowitz. 2009. *Information Literacy Instruction: Theory and Practice.* 2nd ed. New York: Neal-Schuman.

———. 2010. "Information Literacy Instruction." In *Encyclopedia of Library and Information Science,* edited by Marcia J. Bates and Mary Maack. http://www.informaworld.com/smpp/section?content=a917629725&fulltext=713240928.

Gratch-Lindauer, Bonnie. 2007. "The Role of Assessment." In *Proven Strategies for Building an Information Literacy Program,* edited by Susan Curzon and Lynn Lampert, 257–277. New York: Neal-Schuman.

Huba, Mary E., and Jann E. Freed. 2000. *Learner-Centered Assessment on College Campuses.* Boston: Allyn and Bacon.

Kirkpatrick, Donald. 1998. *Evaluating Training Programs: The Four Levels.* San Francisco: Berret-Koehler.

Linn, Robert L., and Norma Gronlund. 2005. *Measurement and Assessment in Teaching.* 9th ed. Upper Saddle River, NJ: Prentice Hall.

Marlow, Bruce A., and Marilyn L. Page. 2005. *Creating the Constructivist Classroom*. Thousand Oaks, CA: Corwin Press.

Marzano, Robert J. 1998. "Cognitive, Metacognitive, and Conative Considerations in Classroom Assessment." In *How Students Learn: Reforming Schools through Learner-Centered Education*, edited by Nadine M. Lambert and Barbara L. McCombs, 241–266. Washington, DC: American Psychological Association.

McKeachie, Wilbert J., and Marilla Svinicki. 2006. *McKeachie's Teaching Tips*. 12th ed. Boston: Houghton-Mifflin.

Mezeske, Barbara A. 2007. "Getting Creative in a Required Course." In *Beyond Tests and Quizzes: Creative Assessment in the College Classroom*, edited by Richard J. Mezeske and Barbara A. Mezeske, 26–38. San Francisco: Jossey-Bass.

Montgomery, Kathleen. 2002. "Authentic Tasks and Rubrics: Going Beyond Traditional Assessments in College Teaching." *College Teaching* 50, no. 1: 34–39.

Mundhenk, Leigh. 2004. "Toward an Understanding of What It Means to Be Student-Centered: A New Teacher's Journey." *Journal of Management Education* 28, no. 4: 447–462.

Oakleaf, Megan. 2008. "Dangers and Opportunities: A Conceptual Map of Information Literacy Assessment Approaches." *portal: Libraries and the Academy* 8, no. 3: 233–253.

Paris, Scott G. 1998. "Why Learner-Centered Assessment Is Better Than High Stakes Testing." In *How Students Learn: Reforming Schools through Learner-Centered Education*, edited by Nadine M. Lambert and Barbara L. McCombs, 189–209. Washington, DC: American Psychological Association.

Saulnier, Bruce M., et al. 2008. "From Teaching to Learning: Learner-Centered Teaching and Assessment in Information Systems Education." *Journal of Information Studies Education* 19, no. 2: 169–173.

Shepard, Lorrie. 2006. "Classroom Assessment." In *Educational Measurement*, edited by Robert L. Brennan, 623–646. Westport, CT: Praeger.

Shute, Valerie J. 2008. "Focus on Formative Feedback." *Review of Educational Research* 78, no. 1: 153–189.

Smith, Thomas. 2007. "Exams as Learning Experiences: One Nutty Idea after Another." In *Beyond Tests and Quizzes: Creative Assessment in the College Classroom*, edited by Richard J. Mezeske and Barbara A. Mezeske, 71–83. San Francisco: Jossey-Bass.

Teaching, Learning, and Technology Group. 2008. *Rubrics*. The TLT Group. http://www.tltgroup.org/resources/Flashlight/Rubrics.htm.

Tollefson, Kaia, and Monica K. Osborn. 2008. *Cultivating the Learner-Centered Classroom: From Theory to Practice*. Thousand Oaks, CA: Corwin Press.

Veldof, Jerilyn. 2006. *Creating the One-Shot Library Workshop: A Step by Step Guide*. Chicago: American Library Association.

Weimer, Mary Ellen. 2002. *Learner-Centered Teaching: Five Key Changes to Practice*. San Francisco: Jossey-Bass.

Wiggins, Grant. 1996. "Practicing What We Preach in Designing Authentic Assessment." *Educational Leadership* 54, no. 1: 18–25.

———. 1998. *Educational Assessment: Designing Assessments to Inform and Improve Student Performance*. San Francisco: Jossey-Bass.

Part III

Applying Learner-Centered Teaching in Practice

Chapter 6

Creating the Face-to-Face Learner-Centered Experience

> I know that I cannot teach anyone anything. I can only provide an environment in which he can learn.
>
> —Carl Rogers

Now that we have reviewed the theoretical basis for learner-centered teaching (LCT) as well as the practical aspects of teaching and assessment, we need to turn our attention to applying all this to our teaching practice. This chapter, and the two following it, will discuss how to apply LCT practices in three different settings. In this chapter we will deal with the face-to-face (F2F) learning environment. Chapter 7 will discuss the online learning environment, and Chapter 8 will deal with how to get the best of both worlds by using a blended learning format. Although LCT can be applied in any of the three formats, each chapter will concentrate on how best to use LCT approaches in the specific format under discussion.

Regardless of format, using LCT principles means we need to decide how we will listen, engage, and inspire our learners. And we need to consider how best to do that in each of these learning environments. Furthermore, we need to think about how to work within that setting to create an atmosphere of collaboration, participation, and responsibility. We must be focused on our learners as we guide and facilitate their learning. We must promote active engagement, ownership, and responsibility in all our interactions (F2F or online) with our learners and create a safe, nonjudgmental climate for their learning experience (Eggen and Kauchak, 2010; McCombs and Miller, 2007; Vella, 2000). The principles remain the same, but the ways in which we apply them depend on whether we are sharing the same physical space with our learners or reaching out to them using more virtual, online technologies. Both F2F and online approaches have their advantages and drawbacks. Interestingly enough, research seems to indicate that there are no significant differences between F2F and online learning. Both can be equally effective. But that effectiveness is greatly dependent on the skills of the instructors to actively engage their learners (Alonso Diaz and Blazquez Entonada, 2009). In other words, it is not the delivery mode that is key to effectiveness. It is our ability to maintain a learner-centered focus as we use that delivery mode that determines the effectiveness of the instructional offering. So, as we review F2F, online, and blended instruction in this and subsequent chapters, let's focus on how following LCT principles can contribute to effectiveness by enhancing the advantages and compensating for the drawbacks for each of the three delivery modes.

ADVANTAGES AND DRAWBACKS OF THE F2F FORMAT

This chapter will concentrate on the F2F format, which is still the one most widely used for information literacy instruction (ILI). Whether we are meeting with our learners in a one-shot situation or are working with them in a long-term, for-credit course, the F2F environment tends to be the most familiar both to our learners and to us as instructors. However, our interactions with our learners during these F2F meetings need to be designed in such a way that we maximize the LCT aspects of the experience. Before we talk about how to do that, let's look at the advantages and drawbacks of this mode of instructional delivery as depicted in Table 6.1.

The biggest advantage of the F2F environment is that it allows for personal and immediate interactions between instructors and learners and among learners themselves. We can offer our learners a variety of ways to interact with the material, and we can observe them as they do so. Because we share the same physical space with our learners, we can monitor their learning on the spot and offer immediate feedback that will further support and encourage them in their grasp of the material. Our adherence to LCT principles can create an even more effective F2F experience for our learners. The ways in which we interact with our learners, the types of methods we select for our instructional endeavors, and the opportunities we give our learners to collaborate with us and each other, to be active participants in the learning process, and to take responsibility for their own and others' learning can go a long way to enhance the advantages of the F2F format.

The major advantage of F2F instruction (everyone in the same place at the same time) is also its biggest drawback. Because everyone must be physically present, the format lacks flexibility. It also suffers from time constraints. Whether we are teaching a one-shot class or have the luxury of working with our learners in a full-length course, there are still limits to our actual F2F contact time. So we must make hard decisions about how much we can address in the time frame allotted. There always seems to be more to include than time permits. Although LCT does not offer any specific fixes for these time constraints and

Table 6.1. Advantages and Drawbacks of the F2F Format	
Advantages	**Drawbacks**
It encourages personal and immediate exchanges between teacher and learners.	There is limited contact time, which places constraints on what can be addressed in the time frame.
Both learners and instructors are familiar with the format and therefore are comfortable with it.	It lacks flexibility. Instructor and learners must be physically in the same place at the same time.
High levels of interactive learning are possible.	Instructors may vary in their ability to capture and sustain learners' attention and to work in an interactive setting.
Instructors have more opportunities to interact with, monitor, and facilitate learners' progress through the material.	Outgoing, spontaneous learners can dominate discussions. Shyer, more introverted learners may not feel comfortable participating in activities.
It has the potential of appealing to different types of learners if a mix of methods is used.	Success depends on the skill of the instructor in using a variety of methods. Instructors who concentrate on only one or two methods may be appealing to only a portion of their learners.
Feedback can be immediate and therefore more likely to reinforce correct responses.	Time limits on activities means learners are not always able to work at their own pace. Faster learners finish early and may get bored. Slower learners may not be able to finish in the time frame allotted and get frustrated and/or lost.

lack of flexibility, if we focus on our learners and their instructional needs, we may be able to compensate a bit for these drawbacks. We can use LCT principles to make the most of the time we have. First, we must be very selective about how much we include in our F2F experience. Trying to do too much is not a good thing. Remember the "less is more" rule. It is better to teach a few things well than many things poorly or not at all (Grassian and Kaplowitz, 2009; Marlow and Page, 2005; Veldof, 2006). Don't forget the issue of cognitive overload referred to earlier in this book. Trying to cram too much into the time frame is counter-productive to learning. Take advantage of the many benefits of collaborative, participatory activities. Truly be the "guide on the side," who facilitates learning, and learners will not only have acquired new skills, knowledge, and abilities, they will also have taken more responsibility for their own learning and will have moved closer to being lifelong learners.

Although we cannot extend the F2F contact time or diminish the lack of flexibility associated with this format, we can think about supplementing the experience with handouts, webpages, and other material that learners can use prior to or following the F2F meeting. This not only increases the flexibility of the format, it also helps to appeal to learners who may not find the fast pace of a learner-centered F2F experience quite their style. Furthermore, offering some of the information in these "other than verbal" ways can free up time during the F2F meeting for even more learner-centered activities.

ATMOSPHERE—CREATING AN LCT ENVIRONMENT

Adhering to LCT principles can create an F2F learning experience that is effective, engaging, and motivating for our learners. Much of the success of this format relies on us. How we present ourselves to our learners and interact with them is crucial to the creation of a learner-centered climate for our F2F instructional endeavors. So, let's take a look at what we can do to make this happen.

Before They Arrive

Creating a learner-centered climate begins even before our learners walk in the door. If possible, try to contact them prior to the F2F meeting. Send them a welcoming e-mail. Or ask them to complete some kind of survey that will help gather a bit of needs assessment data about who they are and what their needs might be. Refer them to a webpage designed to provide them with background information for the instruction. To whatever extent possible, try to reach out to learners and make them feel welcome. In a full-length course, make sure that the language in the syllabus (online or in print) is friendly and supportive. Whenever possible, phrase the documents in a friendly and collaborative fashion (Marlow and Page, 2005). Emphasize the "we are all in it together" idea. Instead of saying, "learners or students will," talk directly to them by saying "you will" (Mundhenk, 2004). Making some kind of personal contact with our learners is even more crucial in the one-shot situation. We have a very short window for establishing a learner-centered climate during that single meeting. Making contact with learners ahead of time will help them arrive at the F2F meeting feeling like they know us already.

Arranging the Room

How the classroom is arranged also sends a message. If possible, avoid having learners sit in the formal, auditorium arrangement in which everyone is facing forward. This creates the impression that they are an audience, there to listen to us, rather than a part of a learning community with whom we wish to work collaboratively (Brogan, 2009; LePage, Darling-Hammond, and Akar, 2005). The best setup for LCT is one in which learners can be arranged in groups of four to six, preferably around small tables (Cruickshank, Jenkins, and Metcalf, 2009; Keefe and Jenkins, 2002). An alternative is the inverted "U" shape in which learners are seated in a semicircle or around a large seminar table so that they can see each other. To further promote the "we are all in it together" idea, we should try to sit at the side rather than at the head of the group (Davis, 2009). Clearly this is not always possible. We are often working in either auditorium settings or in computer classrooms and have little or no control over the room arrangement. But if given the choice, try to arrange to work in a space that is physically amenable to LCT. And keep LCT principles in mind if given the chance to design an instructional space. Make it as flexible as possible so that it can accommodate a variety of activities.

When we do have to work in a fixed seating environment with all the learners facing front, try to diminish the "them versus us" aspect by standing as close as possible to your "audience." Moving around a bit during more lecture-type segments also helps to make everyone in the room feel involved and included, as does making eye contact with all parts of the room—not just with those seated in the T-zone (front row and middle section of the room) (Biggs, 1999a; Bransford, Darling-Hammond, and LePage, 2005). And don't forget to walk around the room during small group activities. As we check in on how our learners are doing, we can correct any misconceptions and make suggestions that will help them successfully complete the assigned task.

When They Arrive

Continue creating this inclusive atmosphere by getting to the instructional space a few minutes before learners are scheduled to arrive (Cruickshank, Jenkins, and Metcalf, 2009; Oswald and Turnage, 2000; Smith, 1991). We can use this time to make sure everything is set up the way we want it. Plus we will be there to greet learners as they enter the room. Chatting casually with learners as they arrive helps to create a friendly and welcoming environment. It also makes learners feel more comfortable with us and may even encourage them to participate at a higher level during the instruction itself. We have shown ourselves to be nice, friendly people who want only to help them, thus reducing any anxiety they may have about the instructional situation.

In the one-shot situation we can use this "getting to know you" time to find out more about what brings the learners to the instruction (Brookfield, 1990). In the school or academic setting, this is a good time to check about any assignment learners may have. We could be in for a big surprise if it turns out that there has been some kind of confusion about what we thought the assignment was and the actual assignment. It is better to find this out at the start than to spend our precious contact time addressing inappropriate material. Using this technique in other library settings (e.g., public or special) can also help us clarify what our learners hope to gain from the instructional experience and will help us focus our session on their specific learning needs.

If we are working in the full-length course setting, we can devote a portion of the first class meeting to having learners get to know each other, thus beginning the process of creating a learning community atmosphere for the course. This first class meeting is also the time to introduce the concept of LCT and explain that the class will be run according to learner-centered principles. Arriving early for each meeting is still a good idea, even in this longer format. Learners may wish to chat informally about issues related to the course or use the opportunity to strengthen their connections to us.

How We Present Ourselves

We have already established our interest in our learners by arriving early and engaging them in informal conversation. We need to continue to make them feel welcome, comfortable, and supported throughout the instructional session. One way we do this is through our body language, gestures, and vocal qualities (McKeachie and Svinicki, 2006). Eye contact has already been mentioned as a way to maintain a connection with our learners. Where we stand, how we move, and the way in which we hold ourselves all send a message, as does the tone and intonations we use as we speak. Whenever possible, we should talk in a conversational tone. If we are to maintain the idea of a collaborative learning community, then we should be talking with our learners, not at them (Cruickshank, Jenkins, and Metcalf, 2009; Grassian and Kaplowitz, 2009).

Remember that we are trying to engage and inspire our learners. So our tone should be upbeat and enthusiastic. Effective instructors are passionate about the material (Combs, 2004; Cruickshank, Jenkins, and Metcalf, 2009; Eggen and Kauchak, 2010). After all, if we don't care, why should our learners? Our excitement could be catching, and even the most blasé of learners will start to wonder what is so intriguing about the material for it to cause all this enthusiasm.

LCT also encourages us to have high expectations for our learners and their ability to succeed at the tasks at hand (Cruickshank, Jenkins, and Metcalf, 2009; McCombs and Miller, 2007; Weimer, 2002). We demonstrate that belief in every interaction we have with our learners. If we truly adopt this attitude, it will show in every aspect of our instruction—how we talk with our learners, how we respond to their questions, and by the methods we choose to use during the instructional experience (Eggen and Kauchak, 2010; McCombs and Miller, 2007; Vella, 2000). And this belief will become contagious. Our learners will gain more self-confidence in their own skills and abilities. If we believe that our learners can succeed, then so will they (Grassian and Kaplowitz, 2009).

How We Interact with Them

Talking directly to our learners rather than reading from our notes or repeating what is on our PowerPoint slides is another way to ensure that we are being learner-centered in our approach. It is hard to maintain an upbeat demeanor and to exhibit our connection to our learners if we are just reciting some prewritten material. While it is fine to have notes or to refer to slides in order to make sure that the material is organized and complete, we should consider them prompts rather than predetermined scripts. If we rely too heavily on our notes, we might find it difficult to be flexible and react appropriately to our learners' questions and/or comments (Brookfield, 1990; Grassian and Kaplowitz, 2009). Including anecdotes and examples from our own life adds a nice personal touch and can also help learners relate to the material. Learners strongly connect to these glimpses into our lives, which provide familiar and accessible ways for them to deal with the information we are sharing with them. Revealing the problems we had in mastering the material demonstrates that even we experts had to overcome some obstacles and that a certain number of missteps are inevitable and to be expected (Brookfield, 1990).

Remember that we are trying to encourage a sense of community in our learners. This means everyone is expected to participate and to take responsibility for the accomplishments of the whole group—whether in full group discussions or in small group activities. Make sure that everyone feels part of the larger group by encouraging even the shyer learners to participate. Merely standing near these more reticent learners may help them feel more comfortable about joining in. Another approach is to ask if anyone who has not already contributed to the conversation would like to make a comment. While our more outspoken learners will be ready and willing to speak up, our quieter learners may be waiting for a nonthreatening opportunity to join in (Davis, 2009). It is up to us to provide that opportunity and to invite them to add their voices to the discussion. As mentioned earlier in this book, allowing learners to work in small groups or to engage in some quiet reflection before an interactive conversation or activity can also encourage more learners to participate actively in larger group discussions. See Chapter 4 for more on how to be inclusive and encourage participation while using a variety of instructional methods.

Don't forget the importance of constructive feedback as well. Offer encouraging and supportive feedback as soon as possible after a learner's response. Make sure the feedback has a positive emotional tone, is specific to the work at hand, and helps support learning (Eggen and Kauchak, 2010). See Chapter 5 for more on the effective use of feedback as part of both formative and summative assessments.

HOW TO BUILD A LEARNER-CENTERED F2F EXPERIENCE

While setting the right tone and creating a warm, welcoming, inclusive, and supportive atmosphere are crucial to creating a learner-centered instructional experience, we still need to think about what is actually going to happen during our F2F interactions with our learners. In other words, what information do we wish to share with our learners, and how will we go about giving them opportunities to interact with and learn about that material? This takes us back to the teaching tripod referred to in Chapter 5. We start by creating the expected learning outcomes (ELOs) for the class and/or course. Then we develop instructional activities that will allow learners to actively participate in their own learning in order to attain these ELOs. Finally, we look for ways to observe our learners as they interact with the material (during, at the end of, or after instruction) so that we can assess their attainment of the ELOs and offer constructive feedback as appropriate (Eggen and Kauchak, 2010; Grassian and Kaplowitz, 2009).

But how do we actually structure the session? What do we include and in what order? Although many of us follow a linear approach as we develop our instruction, we could adopt a somewhat more nonlinear way of thinking that really helps us emphasize the LCT nature of our instruction. In this approach to creating instruction, we start with developing a hook or sponge activity to draw learners into the topic as they enter the room. We then move on to work on our "big finish," an upbeat and stimulating closing experience that helps learners reflect upon and review what has happened in the session. Once we have created our attention-getting opening and snazzy big finish, we can move on to designing instructional activities that allows learners to work with the material to be learned and move them toward the attainment of the ELOs we have set for them. Let's look at each of these segments in turn.

Get Their Attention

Whether we are meeting with our learners multiple times in a full-length course or will have the opportunity to work them only once or twice, what we do in the first five minutes of any class can make or break a session. Having gotten to the instructional space early and greeted learners as they arrive, we now need to get them involved in the material to be addressed. We want to build rapport, set the learner-centered tone, and grab learners' attention right off the bat. We do this by creating what is often referred to as a "hook," "sponge," or "gotcha" activity— one that "soaks" up our learners as they arrive and immediately gets them involved (Freilberg and Driscoll, 2005; Grassian and Kaplowitz, 2009). These activities serve many purposes. They act as a preview of what is to come, start learners thinking about the material to be addressed, and hopefully engage and intrigue them (Eggen and Kauchak, 2010; Hunter, 1985). Furthermore, because we are beginning with a learner-centered activity, we are putting our learners on notice that this is not going to be a typical "we talk and you listen" type of experience.

A hook, sponge, or gotcha can take many forms. A tried and true approach is to give out 3 × 5 cards and ask learners to write down one question they might have about the library, doing information-gathering research, the assignment they have been given, or whatever else might be relevant to the instructional session.

Give learners a couple of minutes for this activity. Collect the cards, skim them quickly, and use their own questions as a way into the material. Learners rarely ask something so completely off topic that we do not know the answer or that would take us away from the material we wish to share. But if that happens, we can just tell the questioners that we need to look into their question and will get back to them later. More often than not the questions will be directed at just what we were going to say. But instead of addressing this material in a kind of canned, lecture-like format, we use the learners' own questions to enter into a dialogue with them, showing them that we really care about their needs and concerns (Grassian and Kaplowitz, 2009).

Another approach is to have a list of possible topics on the board and ask learners to put check marks next to the ones they would like the session to address and then structure the session around the most requested topics. This approach asks us to be flexible, as we will be organizing our session on the spot in response to what our learners have selected. However, because the learners have picked topics of interest to them, they are generally more attentive to us. And because we have designated the possible topics, we should be more than ready to address them. Furthermore, giving learners a voice in what will be addressed certainly reinforces the learner-centered philosophy we are trying to promote (Grassian and Kaplowitz, 2009).

Another use of the cards is to get at the more "feeling" aspect of doing research. Ask learners to describe previous information-gathering experiences (good or bad) and how they felt when doing them (Cunningham and Carr, 2008). Or use the concept mapping idea described in Chapter 4 to get at learners' feelings about having to do research. One more approach is to put a thought-provoking quote or statement on the board and get learners to react to it (Bain, 2004). One ILI example might be, "The Internet is like a great, big garbage dump. Most of what you find there is worthless trash. It takes time and effort to dig through the junk to find anything of value." Learners will probably offer a wide range of reactions to this statement, all of which can be used as a jumping-off point for the rest of the session.

Because many of our learners feel they already know how to find information, why not have them prove it? Give them a very brief quiz or set them an information-seeking task before any instruction has taken place. Learners may quickly discover that they do not know as much as they thought they did and so will be more inclined to participate in the instruction. These activities can also act as a kind of on-the-spot needs assessment, helping us gather a bit more information about what our learners know or don't know about the topics we plan to address (Grassian and Kaplowitz, 2009).

To make the quizzes even more interactive, try using clickers or other types of audience response software. Project the questions, and then have learners respond via these devices (Davis, 2009). A no-tech alternative is to just ask them to raise their hands. We can gather both needs assessment data (how many research papers have you done?) and topical information (if you needed background information on a topic, which of the following resources—books, encyclopedias, websites, newspaper/magazine articles—would be your best choice?) using this audience participation approach.

No matter what attention-getting activity is used, make sure that it is relevant and appropriate to the instructional material. Otherwise, it becomes a silly game that eats up valuable contact time. Furthermore, rather than winning our learners over, we risk losing their respect if our activities don't seem to make sense or support learning (Grassian and Kaplowitz, 2009).

Have a Big Finish

The last few minutes of an F2F instructional encounter are just as important as the first few. What we do during those last few crucial minutes can round off the instruction in a positive and useful way or can undermine everything we have just done (Cruickshank, Jenkins, and Metcalf, 2009; Biggs, 1999a, 1999b). So we must plan this final segment carefully and make sure we leave time for it. We want to ensure that the end of the session is as valuable as what went before. And we certainly don't want to be in a position where we are yelling at our learners, trying to squeeze in just one more thing as they are packing up and attempting to escape out the door (Grassian and Kaplowitz, 2009). We want them to leave inspired, energized, and confident that they have learned what they need to be successful beyond their time with us.

So we need to create some kind of closure experience that helps wrap things up in a positive way and that allows learners to reflect on and summarize for themselves what they got out of the instructional encounter (Davis, 2009). Several closure activities were already described in Chapters 4 and 5. The One-Minute Paper and the What Stuck? game are just two examples. See Angelo and Cross's (1993) work on Classroom Assessment Techniques for more ideas.

Collaborative activities can also serve in this closure capacity. Do a modified Think/Pair/Share. Ask learners to pair up and tell their partners what they thought was the thrust of the session and how they might apply what they learned in the future. Give them two or three minutes to do this and then ask for some of the pairs to share their ideas (Grassian and Kaplowitz, 2009).

The "big finish" helps end the session exactly how it started—in a fun, energized, and learner-centered fashion. Rather than running out the door, thrilled that they have escaped our clutches, our learners leave excited about their newfound abilities and may even be anxious to try them out. Many learners even stick around and continue to chatter with each other or approach us to ask us for more information. By creating a big finish, we have managed to sustain high levels of energy and attention levels from the first moments of contact to the very last.

What Goes Between

Having created a catchy opening and an upbeat and invigorating ending, we still need to fill in the space that makes up the bulk of our instruction. Here is where we return to our ELOs to create activities that allow our learners to interact with the material to be learned. Try to come up with an activity that will help learners attain each of those outcomes. As we select an activity to address each of the ELOs and put them into some rational order, we are actually creating an outline for our instruction.

Don't forget to create logical segues between each of the segments of the instruction. Many instructors like to start off with a brief introduction that lets the learners know what to expect from the session. The nature of this introduction will vary depending on what was done during the hook/sponge/gotcha segment. However, whatever was done in that attention-getting piece should serve as a jumping-off point for the introduction. If we can't tie the introduction to what happened during that opening segment, we may not have selected the right kind of hook.

Introductions are used to set the stage for the instruction and put it in context for the learners. This is the time to appeal to the "What's in it for me?" factor. Let the learners know exactly what they will gain by participating in the instruction. Make it as personal and relevant as possible. We can present the conceptual framework for the session and/or share the ELOs during the introduction as long as we tie these ideas to the learners' specific information literacy needs. One way to make the introduction a bit more interactive is to ask learners the following questions about the specific information needs that have brought them to the instructional session:

- What do you know?

- What do you need to know?

- How will you find out?

We can use the answers to these questions to introduce the concepts and resources that will be addressed during instruction and to show how this material will help them find out what they need to know. Regardless of what is included in the introductory segment, we need to make sure we are sustaining the attention level created in the hook/sponge/gotcha activity. Try to make this introductory segment as succinct and brief as possible. Just present hints of what is to come. Remember that we want to avoid spending too much time with our voice being the dominant one in the room. We want to move quickly into a more collaborative, participatory format where the learners' voices prevail (Grassian and Kaplowitz, 2009).

Once we have captured their attention and have set the stage for the session, we now move into the heart of the instruction—the time during which the learners are allowed to work with the material to be learned. Returning to the "less is more" rule, make sure there is enough time during the session for learners to successfully accomplish all the activities selected. Divide up the time appropriately. Get as much out of each activity as possible. When selecting an activity, weigh the length of time it will take against the value of the experience as a way for learners to attain one or more ELOs. Can some of the ELOs be accomplished through handouts, webpages, or other resources that learners can access before or after instruction? Use precious contact time for learners to work on material that is best learned collaboratively, in an active, participatory fashion, and that benefits from our input, feedback, and support.

It is often difficult, especially when we are first starting out as information literacy instructors, to decide what to include in our sessions. Think like a novice. What are the most important things you needed to know when you first learned this information? Make sure this material is given sufficient attention during the F2F encounter. However, no matter how good our intentions might be, we might still be tempted to try and fit in more material than might rationally fit into the time frame. One way to handle this is to take a tiered approach to our instruction. As we develop our notes, we can divide the material into three levels or tiers. The first tier addresses the "absolutely must know" material—that stuff that a novice needs to be able to successfully attain the ELOs. The second level contains the "nice to know" material—the slightly more advanced material that is not absolutely necessary but might be useful under certain circumstances. Finally, there is the "kind of interesting but not crucial" information. This third level would address the special "bells and whistles" of the material—those resource features or nifty tricks that are not needed on a regular basis but do come in handy in special situations. For example, if the topic was how to effectively and efficiently search a particular database, the tiers might look like this:

- Tier one—need to know
  - Keyword versus controlled vocabulary searching
  - Truncation
  - Boolean operators

- Tier two—nice to know
  - Author searching
  - Using subject heading links to launch new searches
  - Using limits to narrow search results

- Tier three—kind of interesting but not crucial to know
  - Citation tracing
  - Using search history to combine searches
  - Exploding search terms to broaden results

Once we have designated levels to the material, it is helpful to indicate them in some way and to make timing notations to indicate when it is time to move on to the next segment. We can highlight our notes in three different colors to help us easily identify the three levels. As we move through our session, we can keep an eye on the clock and then add levels two and three material depending on how quickly learners have grasped level one material or skip it if time is running short. Even if we miscalculate and move too quickly through the level one material, we can always return to some of the skipped items at the end of the session—as time permits (Grassian and Kaplowitz, 2009; McKeachie and Svinicki, 2006; Veldof, 2006). However, remember to make sure that these "extras" don't take away from the time allocated to the big finish activity.

Finally, we need to make sure that we are not moving too quickly from one segment to another by including some kind of check for comprehension before moving on to new material. Lucky for us learner-centered instructors, these checks can be seamlessly included in the activities we choose for our learners. As we observe our learners interacting with material—during discussions, question-and-answer exchanges, collaborative learning activities, or other types of exercises—we also gain insight into their levels of comprehension. LCT approaches, if implemented correctly, create ample opportunities for us to monitor progress, to offer constructive and supportive feedback, and therefore to keep a sharp eye on how well our learners comprehend the material at hand.

SPECIAL CONSIDERATIONS FOR THE LEARNER-CENTERED F2F EXPERIENCE

Much of what has just been discussed is as applicable to the online and blended format as it is to the F2F one. But the very nature of F2F instruction creates some special challenges and opportunities for the learner-centered teacher. Here are some of the things we need to consider when working in the F2F delivery mode.

Think outside the F2F Box

Although the F2F setting offers a very welcoming setting for LCT with its potential for personal and immediate interactions between instructor and learners, it also offers many challenges. We have already touched on the problem of having limited contact time with our learners, one of the main drawbacks for the F2F experience. We must be very cautious to avoid the "tyranny of coverage" fallacy. We cannot cover everything in the limited amount of time we have with our learners—tempted as we might be to try. So we must pick and choose carefully and concentrate on the "added value" experiences that we can offer to our learners in the F2F mode. What opportunities can we provide in the F2F setting that will improve their skills, knowledge, and abilities as critical and knowledgeable information seekers, information creators, and information sharers? And how can we use our time with our learners to help them become more confident, self-directed, lifelong learners?

Once we have selected the learning experiences best suited to the F2F setting, we need to expand our ideas beyond the actual in-person contact time. In other words, we need to "think outside the F2F box" by looking for ways our learners can access necessary information through other modes such as print or online. Examples of these ideas have been interspersed throughout this chapter. The bottom line is that we need to match the material with the delivery mode. If we want learners to know about the scope and coverage of a variety of different databases, is it more efficient to talk about it in the F2F session or to create a handout and/or a web guide that might provide that material? Could we create an activity for the F2F session that introduces the idea that different databases cover different things but leaves the details for a supplementary print or web presentation? Handout and/or web guides offer the added advantage of being available beyond the F2F session—for learners to refer to and refresh their memories long after they have left our presence.

We can also extend our contact time by creating some pre-F2F meeting experiences for our learners. Sending learners some preliminary questions or having them do some exercise prior to the F2F meeting can act as a presession attention-getting device, which can be expanded on during those first few minutes of the actual F2F meeting (Prince and Felder, 2006).

Push-Back from Learners

Whether we are meeting with our learners only once or twice or have the luxury of multiple sessions over the entire term, we may find that our learner-centered ideas are met with suspicion and maybe even some hostility. Our learners probably have spent most of their educational lives in the more traditional teacher-centered environment. So they may be quite unprepared for the more active role we give them in an LCT situation. They may even resent us for asking them to do so much of the work. So, in addition to drawing them into the material itself, we need to provide them with some insight into why we are asking them to be collaborative, participatory, and responsible learners. As stated earlier, we can and should devote a portion of the first session in a full-length ILI course to introducing the concepts of and reasons for LCT. We have a much harder task in the one-shot situation. We don't really have time to devote to an extensive discussion of

LCT. So we just need to model the principles instead. Here again, we can use any presession communication with our learners as a way to introduce them to LCT. But, for the most part, we just need to jump in and start interacting with them in a learner-centered way from the moment they enter the instructional space. Our being there early to chat with them and provide whatever type of hook/sponge/gotcha activity we create should clue them in fairly rapidly that our approach is going to be a bit different from what they have experienced in other instructional settings. Although we may still encounter some less than completely cooperative learners, our more engaging, interesting, and lively approaches should draw in most of our learners. The resultant high energy level might even get those reluctant learners to join in the fun.

Our Guest Role in Someone Else's Class

Related to the previous point is the fact that our learner-centered style may not match up with that of the primary course instructor when we are working as a guest in someone else's class or team teaching with a classroom instructor. Learners who are accustomed to spending F2F time listening to the course instructor and taking notes on what he or she is presenting may need a little shaking up to get them to participate in our more activities-based instruction. We need to use those first few minutes to alert them to the fact that we expect them to be active participants and not passive recipients. And we must continue to reinforce this idea throughout our time with them. The fact that we are not their course instructors (or graders) can sometimes act in our favor. Because we are just visitors, learners may allow us a bit more latitude for what might appear to them as wild and crazy ideas.

Levels of Learners

No group of learners is entirely homogenous in background, experience, and expertise. Regardless of the environment in which we work, our learners will vary in how much information-gathering research they have done before meeting with us and in the types of resources they have used for this research. This is especially true in a public library where the range of learners can be extremely large. Although the range may be narrower in school and academic settings, we should still expect to see variations among our learners. No matter what the environment, we should also expect learners to vary in the ways in which they prefer to learn and in the pace at which that learning takes place. LCT approaches actually address these issues. With its emphasis on collaborative learning, more knowledgeable learners can offer assistance and support to those who have less experience. This not only helps the less experienced learners, but it keeps the more knowledgeable ones from losing interest in the session. Instead of finishing before everyone else and then having to sit around and wait for the rest to catch up, these more experienced learners are offered an active role in the instruction. Furthermore, teaching someone else how to do something is a great way to solidify that material for the "teacher." Having to restate the material in a way that is understandable to someone else makes those more knowledgeable learners really examine their own understanding of the material. This creates a win–win for all involved.

The LCT emphasis on "mixing it up" also helps to address the variations in our learners' makeup, especially regarding differences in learning styles. Including a lot of different types of experiences (lecture, modeling, question-and-answer exchanges, discussion, and/or collaborative group work) ensures that we have incorporated something for everyone into our session.

FINAL REMARKS

LCT is an ideal format for F2F instruction. We can use the techniques and principles associated with LCT to strengthen the advantages of this delivery mode while compensating for some of its drawbacks. The trick is to be learner-centered in our thinking as we create the F2F experience. The ways in which we communicate with our learners (before, during, and after) instruction, set up the learning space, and create opportunities for our learners to participate and take responsibility for their own learning through collaborative/small group activities, all must support LCT ideals. Our focus is always on the learner, and our goal is to create the very best learning situation possible for all concerned. LCT environments may appear noisier and more chaotic than the more formal teacher-centered situation as learners are actively (and sometimes loudly) interacting with the material and each other. But we learner-centered instructors love the apparent madness because we are confident that our thoughtful and thorough planning has created a situation in which learning happens.

REFLECTIONS

1. Learner-centered instructors are described as those who:
    a. Are enthusiastic and passionate about the material.
    b. Are focused on the learner.
    c. Are supportive.
    d. Create a warm and welcoming instructional atmosphere.
    e. Build rapport with their learners.
    f. Give immediate and constructive feedback.
    g. Encourage everyone to participate.
    h. See teaching as a partnership between learners and instructor.

    i. Offer learners choices and the opportunity to take responsibility for their own learning.

    j. Believe that all learners can succeed.

Take an honest look at yourself. How do you think you rate on these characteristics? Try rating each one on a scale from one to five, with one being "Not at All" and five being "Extremely." If you score four or five on any characteristic, congratulations and keep up the good work. If you score three or less, try to think about what you can do to improve your score. Return to the list of LCT characteristics after about six months and reflect on any changes you may have made in your instructional practice. Keep doing this at regular intervals to take your LCT practice temperature and to look for places that might need improvement.

2. Think about one of your typical F2F sessions. Does it have a snappy opening that captures learners' attention? Have you included an upbeat and energizing closing? Do the types of activities that make up the bulk of the instruction actively involve your learners? Have you included something that addresses each of the ELOs for the session? Are your learners' voices more prominent than yours in the session?

    a. If you answer no to any of these questions, can you revise your instruction to make it more learner-centered?

    b. Try your hand at creating an attention-getting hook/sponge/gotcha for the beginning of the session.

    c. Think about ways to end the session on a positive and inspiring note.

    d. Look for opportunities where you can turn responsibility for the learning over to the learners themselves.

You may wish to start small and concentrate on just one of these aspects. As you become more comfortable with each one, try adding another learner-centered element. Once you have done this for one instructional experience, you may find it more natural to do so for some of your other ones.

EXPLORATIONS

Angelo, Thomas A., and K. Patricia Cross. 1993. *Classroom Assessment Techniques: A Handbook for College Teachers.* 2nd ed. San Francisco: Jossey-Bass.

    The authors include lots of suggestions for classroom activities that both engage the learners and act as ways to assess their learning.

Bain, Kenneth. 2004. *What the Best College Teachers Do.* Cambridge, MA: Harvard University Press.

Bain offers good advice about how to connect with learners in a learner-centered fashion. The book contains inspirational conversations with exemplary college teachers who discuss techniques and methods they actually use in the classroom.

Burkhardt, Joanna, Mary C. Macdonald, and Andree J. Rathemacher. 2003. *Teaching Information Literacy: 35 Practical Standards-Based Exercises for College Students.* Chicago: ALA.

This work includes lots of examples of activities that can be used in the information literacy instruction setting.

Davis, Barbara Gross. 2009. *Tools for Teaching.* 2nd ed. San Francisco: Jossey-Bass.

Davis covers all aspects of teaching. She places special emphasis on the actual "how to do it" aspects of working with learners in an interactive, learner-centered fashion.

Johnson, David W., Roger T. Johnson, and Karl A. Smith. 1991. *Active Learning: Cooperation in the College Classroom.* Edina, MN: Interaction Book Company.

The authors provide a thorough and informative discussion of how to incorporate collaborative/cooperative learning experiences into instruction.

Maier, Mark H., and Ted Panitz. 1996. "End on a High Note: Better Endings for Classes and Courses." *College Teaching* 44, no. 4: 145–148.

This is an excellent discussion of how to close instruction in a positive and upbeat fashion.

Marlow, Bruce A., and Marilyn L. Page. 2005. *Creating the Constructivist Classroom.* Thousand Oaks, CA: Corwin Press.

This work contains lots of practical advice about how to apply constructivist (and learner-centered) principles in the classroom.

McCombs, Barbara L., and Linda Miller. 2007. *Learner-Centered Classroom Practices and Assessments: Maximizing Student Motivation, Learning, and Achievement.* Thousand Oaks, CA: Corwin Press.

McCombs and Miller offer lots of suggestions about how to make instruction more learner-centered. They include self-assessment instruments to help teachers reflect on their own practices.

Palmer, Parker J. 1998. *The Courage to Teach: Exploring the Inner Landscape of a Teacher's Life.* San Francisco: Jossey-Bass.

This is a classic in the field and a must read for all who wish to be effective and compassionate teachers.

Veldof, Jerilyn. 2006. *Creating the One-Shot Library Workshop: A Step-by-Step Guide.* Chicago: American Library Association.

> Veldof addresses the special case of the one-shot workshop and includes ideas about how to make instruction more engaging and participatory. The guide also contains tips on how to develop and structure instructional sessions.

Vella, Jane. 2000. *Learning to Listen. Learning to Teach.* 2nd ed. San Francisco: Jossey-Bass.

> Vella discusses creating a learner-centered environment by listening to and communicating with the learners—before, during, and after an instructional session.

Weimer, Mary Ellen. 2002. *Learner-Centered Teaching: Five Key Changes to Practice.* San Francisco: Jossey-Bass.

> Weimer talks about what makes instruction learner-centered and offers advice about how to adopt a learner-centered focus for one's own instructional endeavors.

REFERENCES

Alonso Diaz, Laura, and Florentino Blazquez Entonada. 2009. "Are the Functions of Teachers in E-learning and Face-to-Face Environments Really Different?" *Educational Technology and Society* 12, no. 4: 331–343.

Angelo, Thomas A., and K. Patricia Cross. 1993. *Classroom Assessment Techniques: A Handbook for College Teachers.* 2nd ed. *The Jossey-Bass Higher & Adult Education Series.* San Francisco: Jossey-Bass.

Bain, Ken. 2004. *What the Best College Teachers Do.* Cambridge, MA: Harvard University Press.

Biggs, John B. 1999a. *Teaching for Quality Learning at the University.* Buckingham, Great Britain: Open University Press.

———. 1999b. "What the Student Does: Teaching for Enhanced Learning." *Higher Education Research and Development* 18, no. 1: 57–75.

Bransford, John D., Linda Darling-Hammond, and Pamela LePage. 2005. "Introduction." In *Preparing Teachers for a Changing World: What Teachers Should Learn and Be Able to Do,* edited by Linda Darling-Hammond and John D. Bransford, 1–39. San Francisco: Jossey-Bass.

Brogan, Chris. 2009. *Audience or Community.* ChrisBrogan.com. June 3. http://www.chrisbrogan.com/audience-or-community/.

Brookfield, Stephen D. 1990. *The Skillful Teacher: On Technique, Trust and Responsiveness in the Classroom.* San Francisco: Jossey-Bass.

Combs, Barbara L. 2004. "Learner-Centered Teachers' Approaches to Literacy Instruction: Are They Best Practice?" In *Celebrating the Power of Literacy,* edited by Jo Ann R. Dagan, Patricia E. Linder, Mary Beth Sampson, and Barrie A. Brancato, 122–138. Logan, UT: College Reading Association.

Cruickshank, Donald R., Deborah Bainer Jenkins, and Kim K. Metcalf. 2009. *The Act of Teaching.* 5th ed. Boston: McGraw-Hill.

Cunningham, April, and Alison Carr. 2008. "Research as a Cognitive Process." Paper presented at *SCIL Works 2008: Putting Theory into Practice—The Why Behind Instructional Strategies.* Claremont, California, April 25.

Davis, Barbara Gross. 2009. *Tools for Teaching.* 2nd ed. San Francisco: Jossey-Bass.

Eggen, Paul, and Don Kauchak. 2010. *Educational Psychology: Windows on Classrooms.* Upper Saddle River, NJ: Merrill.

Freilberg, H. Jerome, and Amy Driscoll. 2005. *Universal Teaching Strategies.* Boston: Allyn and Bacon.

Grassian, Esther, and Joan Kaplowitz. 2009. *Information Literacy Instruction: Theory and Practice.* 2nd ed. New York: Neal-Schuman.

Hunter, Madeline. 1985. *Mastery Teaching: Increasing Instructional Effectiveness in Elementary and Secondary Schools, Colleges, and Universities.* El Segundo, CA: TIP Publications.

Keefe, James W., and John M. Jenkins. 2002. "A Special Section on Personalized Instruction." *Phi Delta Kappan* 83, no. 6: 440–448.

LePage, Pamela, Linda Darling-Hammond, and Hanife Akar. 2005. "Classroom Management." In *Preparing Teachers for a Changing World: What Teachers Should Learn and Be Able to Do,* edited by Linda Darling-Hammond and John D. Bransford, 327–357. San Francisco: Jossey-Bass.

Marlow, Bruce A., and Marilyn L. Page. 2005. *Creating the Constructivist Classroom.* Thousand Oaks, CA: Corwin Press.

McCombs, Barbara L., and Lynda Miller. 2007. *Learner-Centered Classroom Practices and Assessments: Maximizing Student Motivation, Learning, and Achievement.* Thousand Oaks, CA: Corwin Press.

McKeachie, Wilbert J., and Marilla Svinicki. 2006. *McKeachie's Teaching Tips.* 12th ed. Boston: Houghton-Mifflin.

Mundhenk, Leigh. 2004. "Toward an Understanding of What It Means to Be Student-Centered: A New Teacher's Journey." *Journal of Management Education* 28, no. 4: 447–462.

Oswald, Tina A., and Martha Turnage. 2000. "First Five Minutes." *Research Strategies* 17, no. 3: 347–351.

Prince, Michael J., and Richard M. Felder. 2006. "Inductive Teaching and Learning Methods: Definitions, Comparisons, and Research Bases." *Journal of Engineering Education* 95, no. 2: 123–138.

Smith, Terry C. 1991. *Making Successful Presentations: A Self-Teaching Guide.* 2nd ed. New York: Wiley.

Veldof, Jerilyn. 2006. *Creating the One-Shot Library Workshop: A Step by Step Guide.* Chicago: American Library Association.

Vella, Jane. 2000. *Learning to Listen. Learning to Teach.* 2nd ed. San Francisco: Jossey-Bass.

Weimer, Mary Ellen. 2002. *Learner-Centered Teaching: Five Key Changes to Practice.* San Francisco: Jossey-Bass.

Chapter 7

Creating the Online Learner-Centered Experience

With Hillary Kaplowitz

> Nothing makes the earth seem so spacious as to have friends at a distance.
>
> —Henry David Thoreau

WHY TEACH ONLINE?

Our learners live and work in an online-enhanced world. They communicate, network, shop, entertain themselves, and do all or part of their jobs while using a variety of electronic devices—cell phones, iPods, PDAs, laptops, desktop computers, and so forth. So, it is no wonder that they want to do their learning online as well (Fox, 2007; Palloff and Pratt, 2007). In keeping with learner-centered principles, we need to accommodate those desires and move our instructional efforts to extend beyond the face-to-face (F2F) delivery mode.

Online educational offerings have been steadily increasing over the past few years—especially in higher education where students can earn their undergraduate and graduate degrees without ever setting foot in a physical classroom (Park and Choi, 2009). Online instruction is reaching out to the K–12 world as well, with many high schools requiring students to take at least one online course in order to graduate (Palloff and Pratt, 2007). Educators at all levels have acknowledged that our graduates will be facing a work environment that relies more and more on online tools and electronic communication. In order to succeed, our graduates need to become comfortable with this virtual work world. Having at least some online educational experience helps our learners better prepare

---

Hillary Kaplowitz, MS, is Instructional Designer, Faculty Technology Center, California State University, Northridge.

themselves for what awaits them once they enter the workforce (Palloff and Pratt, 2007; Reidling, 2004).

Advances in technology have also promoted this move toward more online instructional offerings. Computing devices have gotten smaller and more portable and seem to be everywhere. The advent of wireless connectivity allows people to "stay in touch" from just about anywhere. And reliance on these devices has increased the expectation that information should be immediately available whenever and wherever it is needed. So, it is not surprising that people want the convenience of the anytime/anywhere aspect that online instruction can offer.

MOVING TO THE ONLINE FORMAT: A CAUTIONARY TALE

Emerging technologies are transforming the web into a very interactive space that allows everyone to collaborate, create, publish, and share information (Ko and Rossen, 2010; Saeed, Yang, and Sinnappan, 2009), giving online instruction the potential for being extremely learner-centered. However, we must remain focused on the learner-centered principles of collaboration, participation, and responsibility as we develop our online instructional offerings. When we turn to technology as a way to reach out and deliver instruction to our learners, we must be careful to use that technology carefully and appropriately (Davis, 2009).

In the chapter on F2F, we discussed the tyranny of coverage. Asynchronous instructional offerings free us from the constraints of rigid time frames. But technology can be a seductive siren. Just because technology allows us to do something does not mean that we should do it. The decision to incorporate a particular type of technology into our instructional endeavors should be based on sound pedagogical principles (Marlow and Page, 2005; McLaren, 2009; Simonson and Schlosser, 2009). Does the technology help our learners reach the expected learning outcomes (ELOs) we have set for the instruction? Does it help to engage their interest and offer them ways in which they can interact with the material in order to construct new knowledge for themselves (Palloff and Pratt, 2007)? Furthermore, though we seem to have unlimited time for our instruction, remember that learners can absorb just so much at a "sitting" before they are overwhelmed by cognitive overload. So, even our online instruction should be offered in short, absorbable chunks.

We all have experienced the frustration of learning new technology whether it takes the form of software upgrades, new mobile devices, or even setting the climate control on a rental car. So we must also be cautious in the types of technology we choose to use, making sure our learners will not be overwhelmed by the technology itself. Remember what it was like to be a new-to-technology individual. How much time will it take to learn how to use the technology? How technologically savvy does the learner have to be? Are there special hardware or software needs? Keep in mind that our learners will probably vary in their familiarity and ease with technology. Try to accommodate those on the less technologically adept end of the spectrum by offering extra support as needed (McKeachie and Svinicki, 2006; Palloff and Pratt, 2007). The last thing we want is for our learners to become so intimidated and frustrated by the technology that the technology itself stands as an impediment to their learning.

This chapter will look at the various ways that online instruction can be created following learner-centered teaching (LCT) principles. We will examine the incorporation of technology and online delivery modes into full-length courses, and we will explore the possibility of using online instruction as an alternative delivery mode for the course-integrated one-shot guest appearances we often do for our classroom colleagues. Furthermore, technology offers the opportunity to develop "just in time" type tutorials and other online instructional material that people can refer to when they have a particular information-seeking need. So we will look at these stand-alone (not attached to any particular class or course) types of instruction as well. Because technology is an ever-moving target, this chapter will focus on the general principles of using technology in a learner-centered way rather than on specific types of technology. As with all teaching methods, we must concentrate on what we are trying to do first, and then look for the best ways to do it. As new technologies materialize, new opportunities for increasing the effectiveness of our instruction will be created. We must take advantage of anything that allows us to increase our effectiveness as learner-centered instructors in a digital world.

ADVANTAGES AND DRAWBACKS OF THE ONLINE FORMAT

Although advances in technology have opened up new avenues for reaching and teaching our learners, we must be cautious as we begin to explore these new possibilities. While online instruction has a great deal of potential, it is not without its issues. Just as in the F2F mode, we can use LCT practices to maximize the potential of this format while compensating for some of the problems inherent in this approach. Let's start with a look at the characteristics of online instruction and the advantages and drawbacks associated with both synchronous (in real time) and asynchronous (occurring anytime, anywhere) formats as depicted in Table 7.1.

Convenience and Flexibility

Online learning is often touted for its convenience and flexibility. Even synchronous (instructor and learners online at the same time) learning has its advantages over F2F modes because learners can connect to the session from their own homes and/or office computers or other electronic devices. Furthermore, learners

Table 7.1. Advantages and Drawbacks of the Online Format	
Advantages	**Drawbacks**
Flexibility—Learners, especially in an asynchronous format, can engage in learning activities when it fits into their own schedules.	It requires learners to be self-directed and motivated to learn on their own.
Convenience—Learners do not have to be physically present in a classroom at a specific time.	Learners may develop feelings of isolation and alienation due to lack of F2F contact.
Learners do not have to wait for a specific time and place to contact the instructor. They can complete assignments/worksheets and then submit them electronically. Feedback can be provided via the website or by e-mail without learners having to wait for a physical meeting with the instructor and/or physical return of a hard-copy submission.	If feedback is delayed, learners may become confused about how to proceed and could develop misconceptions and incorrect approaches to the material.
Learners can come from a wide geographic area, creating a diverse community of learners with a wide range of perspectives.	Time zone differences can become an issue, especially in synchronous instructional situations.
Contact time is expanded, which in turn allows for more in-depth examination of material.	Cognitive overload is still possible if too much material is addressed in a particular segment.
An asynchronous format allows learners to control their pace, to take longer to review resources, and to view things multiple times, which is especially appealing to reflective learners.	Active learners may miss the energy of the F2F format.
Learners who may feel uncomfortable speaking up in an F2F class are often more willing to share ideas in the online format. Participation is often required, thereby forcing reluctant learners to engage and get involved.	The fact that comments are available for all to see and may even be archived for future review can be intimidating to some learners.
Asynchronous discussion boards/forums allow for more peer-to-peer interaction than in F2F classes, where discussions are often cut short because of time constraints. Having more time to respond can result in richer, more thoughtful responses. In addition, everyone has an equal voice.	Asynchronous interactions lack the personal and immediate quality of exchanges between instructor and learners and among learners typical in F2F formats.
Instructors can select from a variety of materials, combining text, graphics, media, and various communication modes (e-mail, chat, discussion boards) to use those best suited for each learning task.	Both instructors and learners need to be comfortable with the various types of materials and modes used. Instructors must be willing to offer learners the support they might need, and learners must be willing to try new things.

(Continued)

Table 7.1. Advantages and Drawbacks of the Online Format *(Continued)*	
Advantages	**Drawbacks**
Use of multimedia formats can widen appeal to learners with a variety of learning styles.	Both instructor and learners must have the appropriate hardware and software to access and use the various multimedia formats.
Instructors can use the various technologies available to create material that offers learners more choice in and control over the material being examined.	Online teaching tends to be more labor intensive for instructors (in both the development and the delivery phases). Learners often comment that online learning takes longer than in the F2F setting.

can be distributed over wide geographic locales—although time zone issues do need to be taken into account when working in a synchronous mode. Although we can schedule multiple synchronous online sessions at various times to accommodate learners in different geographic locations, this can increase the instructor's time commitment as he or she needs to monitor these multiple exchanges (Palloff and Pratt, 2007).

The asynchronous format offers even more flexibility and convenience as learners can "sign onto" the instructional environment when it is most convenient for them to do so (Boyer, 2009). Learning, therefore, can be fit into an individual's busy schedule, allowing learners to better balance their learning, work, and life responsibilities (McCampbell, 2000; Palloff and Pratt, 2007; Rattanavijai and Sharma, 2003). So, online instruction allows us to accommodate our learners in a very learner-centered way by having our instruction delivered to them when they want it rather than making them come to us at a set time (De Roma and Nida, 2004; Miller and Mazur, 2009).

Furthermore, learners can collaborate online using a variety of document sharing and communication software. Collaborative groups can hold virtual meetings and discuss course-related issues and topics, work on case studies and real-world problems, and share their solutions with other groups (De Roma and Nida, 2004; Palloff and Pratt, 2007). Online interactions allow groups to have members who are geographically distant from each other, expanding the perspectives represented in the group (Dagli, 2003; Duffy and Kirkley, 2004b; Palloff and Pratt, 2007).

Motivation and Self-Direction

While flexibility and convenience are most often referred to as the biggest advantages of online instruction, the format does have a perceived negative side. Because learners are not required to make an appearance in a physical classroom, it is up to us to motivate them to attend our online offerings. Successful online learners need to be self-directed, but we are responsible for creating an environment that encourages them to join in the instruction and for showing them how participating in their own learning process will be beneficial to them and their fellow learners. One way to do this is through the use of authentic, real-life examples, projects, and assignments. The more learners can see how what they are learning has relevance to their own situations—both in work and in their own lives—the more they will be motivated to persevere in the learning and stay engaged with the material (Battalio, 2009; Park and Choi, 2009). Knowing what is important to our learners, which is another aspect of being learner-centered, helps us keep our instruction relevant to our learners.

Just as in the F2F format, we attract learners to our instruction by showing them that the instructional experience is worth their time and effort. We do this by how we communicate with our learners, the types of experiences we offer them, and the encouragement we give them as they interact with the material being addressed. Whether we are marketing our online instructional endeavors or interacting with those who have already joined us in the online environment, we want to create a situation in which learners want to participate in the instruction. We will return to this idea of creating a learner-centered atmosphere to encourage and support the self-directed online learner later in this chapter.

Isolation and Alienation

Because learners are not interacting with the instructor or each other in the same physical space, people involved in online instruction often report feeling isolated and alienated from the learning environment (Conrad and Donaldson, 2004; Ko and Rossen, 2010; Palloff and Pratt, 2007). Because much of LCT is based on the tenet that "we are all in this together," this lack of connectedness can be seen as a major deterrent to the online delivery mode. However, the dedicated learner-centered instructor can create an online environment that helps learners form virtual relationships with everyone involved.

Furthermore, the online learning community, being without geographic limits, can expand that community far beyond what might be possible in an F2F classroom. The opportunities for interacting with learners from a variety of backgrounds and experiences are vast, offering learners a chance to work with and learn from people with a wide range of perspectives.

Time Commitment

The convenience and flexibility of online instruction, especially in its asynchronous form, can also create an issue for the instructor. Because the instructional material is available 24/7, there is an assumption that instructors should also be available whenever the learners need them (Tomei, 2004). This is another reason why teaching online requires a bit more dedication and time commitment on the part of the instructor than F2F delivery—sometimes as much as three times as many hours per week in the full-length course (Palloff and Pratt, 2007; Tomei, 2004). If we ask learners to check online sites regularly in our full-length courses, then we must do so as well, and we must provide timely and constructive feedback as needed (Dykman and Davis, 2008; Ko and Rossen, 2010). We must be alert for any problems that might be surfacing in both the content and the usability of the online material. We must also monitor the site, especially if we are using any form of online discussions, to ensure everyone is participating at the appropriate level (Boyer, 2009). Our vigilance in monitoring our sites and regularly communicating with our learners goes a long way to compensate for the sense of isolation many online learners feel (Dykman and Davis, 2008; Palloff and Pratt, 2007). Keeping in touch with our learners this way adheres to LCT principles, creates the sense that we are out there and present even if they cannot see us, and helps to demonstrate our care and concern for learners as they interact with the material we are asking them to master. It is also important to set clear expectations for learners at the outset, such as providing them with guidelines on how to contact us and when they should expect our replies.

When working in the online environment, both instructors and learners often express the opinion that technology is both a blessing and a curse. Because teaching and learning in the online format is less familiar than the F2F one, both instructors and learners often find they have to spend a great deal of time conquering the technology before they can begin to engage in learning. This can be very frustrating for everyone concerned and often leads to learners (and sometimes instructors) giving up on the whole enterprise. Creating the material and making it available to learners electronically often requires instructors to develop a whole new body of skills—especially if they are working with course management software (CMS) or developing interactive webpages/tutorials.

Communication

Learners, too, often complain about how much longer it takes to accomplish a task in an online course than it would have in one that meets F2F, in part because much of the online experience is done through written comments. Committing thoughts to writing seems to be a far more labor-intensive task than just stating them aloud. Attention must be paid to grammar, spelling, and punctuation. Furthermore, people seem more concerned about making sense when their thoughts are made public in this written format (Pena-Shaff, Altman, and Stephenson, 2005). This has the potential to produce more well-developed and richer comments than the extemporaneous comments that occur in F2F situations. Although this all translates into more work for learners, in the end it has the benefit of producing deeper learning.

Language difficulties and cultural differences can also be exacerbated when communication is via the written word. Instructors must pay special attention to these issues and make sure that miscommunications do not occur because of a learner's lack of familiarity with the English language or cultural nuances in a Western-type educational system (Palloff and Pratt, 2007). Developing ground rules for all communications can go a long way to address this potential issue in advance, especially if learners are invited to be part of the creation of these ground rules.

It is important to clearly define expectations for writing style in the online environment. Some areas of the course may require scholarly writing, whereas in other areas informal writing and even abbreviations and slang common in text messaging and social networking is acceptable. Regardless of whether we are teaching full-length courses or creating stand-alone pieces or material to be used in course-integrated instruction, we must be familiar enough with all the potential learners in our environment to ensure that we do not include any language that might be offensive or difficult to understand for any segment of our user population. While this is also true for F2F encounters, the online environment can be more vulnerable to these types of problems that are often mitigated in an F2F setting through nonverbal communication as well as immediacy of response. So, it is important to review netiquette rules with learners and to stress that all learners need to respect one another's opinions.

Time on Task

The writing aspect is only one reason why online instruction seems to be more labor intensive than F2F endeavors. Online instruction does not have the same limitations of contact time as F2F instruction. So learners can, and do, spend more time on task. They can start and stop an assignment or activity; enter and leave a discussion; spend some extra time thinking before responding to questions.

The bottom line is that because there is a more open-ended quality to online instruction, learners can explore material at their own pace and in greater depth than is possible in the F2F format (Duffy and Kirkley, 2004a; Rattanavijai and Sharma, 2003). While they may complain about that and see it as a drawback, in the end this greater flexibility can result in a better, more effective learning experience. Furthermore, the very fact that learners can take control of their own learning in this fashion demonstrates LCT principles in action.

Privacy

The public nature of written communications, especially in the full-length online course, also raises issues of privacy. Administrators, for example, may have access to their comments. Furthermore, there is always the possibility that the course site, though password protected and restricted as it might be, will be vulnerable to security breaches. Learners should be made aware that their communications might not be completely secure and use good judgment in what they say—especially when communicating in the social networking arena (Davis, 2009; Ko and Rossen, 2010; Messner, 2009). If they feel something is confidential, learners should be directed to communicate with the instructor personally rather than post the information on the site. Assignments can be submitted to secure and private sections of the course site unless we want learners to view each other's work. Regardless of how learners communicate with us or submit their work, we and our institutions should respect that material posted and/or e-mailed is the intellectual property of the learner and is not to be used for other purposes without the learner's permission (Palloff and Pratt, 2007). These privacy issues can relate to both the stand-alone online and the course-integrated one-shot formats, especially if we are inviting learners to interact with us in some kind of social networking site format that is not within the CMS.

HOW ONLINE INSTRUCTION SUPPORTS LCT

Delivering our instruction online allows us to expand the types of material and modes we use to engage our learners. We can incorporate various levels of interactivity and expand our ways of communicating with our learners through the use of instant messaging, e-mail, social networking, asynchronous discussion boards, synchronous chat, video conferencing, interactive 3D virtual environments, and so forth. We can create lecture material and make it available through asynchronous podcasts or streaming videos. Or we can "meet" with our learners through synchronous video or web conferencing (Bauer, 2002; Ko and Rossen, 2010; Saeed, Yang, and Sinnappan, 2009). The possibilities are vast and are limited only by current technological advances, our willingness as instructors to use any of the technologies available to us, and our learners' abilities to access and/or interact with them.

In many ways online instruction has the potential of allowing us to be even more learner-centered than its F2F counterpart. Online instruction allows us to create an instructional situation that appeals to a broader range of learners. In addition to utilizing multiple modes of delivery (auditory, visual, or text), the online environment offers flexibility and convenience, thereby widening its appeal. Online environments can accommodate those who find it difficult to attend F2F classes because of their busy work and life commitments. Furthermore, learners and instructors can be geographically widespread and still come together in the online classroom.

Asynchronous formats are especially attractive to reflective learners who appreciate the freedom to spend as much time as they need on the material and the fact that they can move through the material at their own pace. In addition, online instructional offerings are often archived and so can be returned to if learners wish to review it or refresh their memories at a point in time when it is especially relevant to whatever task is currently at hand.

As already discussed, the online format also offers great appeal to the quiet learner who is reluctant to speak up in the F2F format but may be willing to share his or her thoughts in the more anonymous online setting (Battalio, 2009; Bauer and Anderson, 2000; Palloff and Pratt, 2007). Online formats, therefore, invite more voices into the conversation by providing space for those who are either uncomfortable with the fast pace of the F2F format or are reluctant to express themselves in the more visible and public arena of the in-person classroom. Moreover, the active learner has the option of working with the material as soon as it appears on the course site, while the more reflective learner is allowed to take his or her time before doing so. The online format, therefore, gives learners more choice in how and when they interact with the material and can provide multiple access points to the information with the instructor and with other learners—all of which supports the LCT approach.

SPECIAL CHALLENGES FOR LCT IN THE ONLINE FORMAT

As good as it is, online instruction is not without its issues. On the drawback side of the equation, some learners can end up being the "loudest" voice in both the synchronous and asynchronous modes. If everyone is interacting together in real time (synchronous), the fastest typist will get his or her ideas out there before anyone else, and those ideas may end up dominating the direction of the discussion. Even in the asynchronous mode, the spontaneous learner (as in those with the active learning style) may overwhelm the "conversation" through the sheer volume of messages posted. We need to take care, as we monitor both types of discussions, to maintain some sort of control over these "loudest" voices. Limiting the number of posts during a specific time period is one way to help level the playing field for all the learners. The spontaneous types will still be the first ones to post, but after a while the reflective types will join in (Palloff and Pratt, 2007). In the synchronous format, ground rules should be established on how to ask for attention (virtual hand raising) and then wait to be called on.

Accessibility and Design

Technology allows us to develop instruction that appeals to a far larger variety of learning styles, but it also can create barriers to that instruction if our learners are not familiar or comfortable with the technology being used to deliver the material. Remember that just because we might use a particular type of technology does not mean that our learners use it as well. Be careful and considerate when incorporating technology so that the capacity to use the technology does not end up interfering with learners' ability to engage in the learning experience

(Chernish et al., 2009; Palloff and Pratt, 2007). Remember that some users may not be able to access particular types of technology because they don't have the necessary software or hardware to do so. Furthermore, keep in mind that material should comply with federal standards such as Section 508, which deals with equal access to information for people with disabilities (GSA's IT Accessibility and Workforce [ITAW], 2011) and the Americans with Disabilities Act (U.S. Department of Justice, 2011). It is also important to find out what the requirements are in your specific situation. Very often there will be a department within your institution that deals with disability issues.

The principles of Universal Design for Learning (UDL) help instructors design their curriculum (online and F2F) so that it meets the needs of all learners (CAST, 2011). The three primary principles that guide UDL are very much in line with the LCT practices. Instructors who follow UDL guidelines provide multiple means of representation, action and expression, and engagement. Translated into practical terms, this means instructors should make sure their materials are presented in multiple modes to accommodate the various ways that people perceive and comprehend information. This includes offering options that appeal to people who prefer to learn through specific sensory modalities, as well as providing alternatives for those with sensory or learning disabilities. It also means paying attention to the language and symbols used, so they are understandable to all, as well as providing learners with a variety of ways to actively interact with the material in order to translate information into knowledge (CAST, 2011).

Creating a Sense of Community

Using LCT practices can go a long way to increase the effectiveness of online instructional endeavors. As in the case of F2F instruction, we need to set the tone and model the behavior that exemplifies LCT (Miller and Mazur, 2009). We start by creating a learner-centered atmosphere in which our learners can feel supported, safe, and connected (Dykman and Davis, 2008; Liu et al., 2009; Palloff and Pratt, 2007). While it is a bit more challenging to do so when we are not physically interacting with our learners, the judicious use of the technology available to us, along with timely communication and feedback, can create the feeling of community and a sense of belonging that should help to alleviate the sense of isolation and alienation that many online learners seem to experience (Boyer, 2009; McCombs and Vakili, 2005). Let's take a look at how we create this learner-centered atmosphere in our online efforts.

ATMOSPHERE—DESIGNING AN LCT ENVIRONMENT ONLINE

Although online education is a rapidly growing field, most learners are still more familiar with the F2F mode. As a result, learners often find it hard to adjust to the loss of personal contact. They miss the give and take of F2F interactions and feel isolated from both the instructor and their fellow learners (Duffy and Kirkley, 2004b; Palloff and Pratt, 2007). Creating a sense of community in the full-length online course can be challenging, but it is of crucial importance for online learning to succeed. We must strive to create a sense of belonging and connectedness among learners who may never meet each other in person. We build feelings of trust and mutual support through the ways in which we communicate with our learners, the language we use in our online materials, and by encouraging learner-to-learner exchanges—especially via collaborative group projects and discussion forums (Liu et al., 2009; Sorensen and Baylen, 2009). Most books on developing online instruction suggest using icebreakers at the beginning of a course so learners can get to know each other and to reinforce the idea that this will be a shared learning experience (Conrad and Donaldson, 2004; Ko and Rossen, 2010; Palloff and Pratt, 2007).

The learner-centered principles of collaboration, participation, and shared responsibility (CPR) for learning are every bit as important in the online environment as they are in the F2F one. We can use CPR as a way to create connections among learners and to reinforce the idea that we are all in this learning endeavor together. In the online instructional environment, CPR can go a long way to counter those negative feelings of isolation and alienation so common among online learners.

This sense of isolation and alienation can also affect the more stand-alone online offerings such as tutorials, podcasts, and online guides, especially those not connected to a particular course or class. Not only are learners being asked to operate in this more impersonal format, for the most part they are doing it on their own. Asynchronous stand-alone online offerings have the advantage of being available 24/7 and so can be accessed at the convenience of the learner. But learners must initiate the instruction themselves. So they need to be self-directed and motivated learners (Conrad and Donaldson, 2004; Ko and Rossen, 2010; Palloff and Pratt, 2007).

Finding ways to connect with our learners may be even more important in the stand-alone and course-integrated one-shot types of online instruction. When teaching full-length courses (F2F or online) we have the chance to build up relationships over time; but we have little or no time to form any kind of relationship with our learners in the more short-term encounters. Furthermore, in the asynchronous online mode we are unable to interact with our learners immediately, monitor their reactions to the material as they make them, or respond to their questions as they come up because learners and teacher are not all together at the same time. Even in the synchronous mode, the fact that you and your learners are not sharing the same physical space means you must take extra care to connect with them.

So, how do LCT principles help us to counter the seemingly impersonal aspect of stand-alone online instruction? One way is through the language we use in these offerings. We need to be as inclusive, friendly, and supportive in our language as we would be in our full-length course material. We also need to offer learners a reason for spending time in this online experience. In other words, we need to make it clear from the start "what's in it for them" if they complete the instruction. We can help create a sense of community in this opening segment by emphasizing that they are not alone in needing to learn this material. Many other people, just like them, also are struggling to grasp this information.

We can also take extra pains with the online instructional endeavors to create a learner-centered environment by knowing what is important to our learners and making sure our material includes relevant, authentic examples. Furthermore, offering learners a chance to interact with us, and perhaps other learners who share their interests and informational needs, can also help learners feel a bit more connected to us and to each other. Some instructors create opportunities for learners to submit questions or comments before, during, or after they have competed the learning experience and perhaps exchange ideas with other learners. At the very least, any type of online instructional material should include a way for learners to contact instructors if they need additional help. Reaching out to the learners in this way, as well as offering them ways to feel a part of a larger community, are all methods of applying LCT principles to online instructional experiences and will help overcome the drawbacks of these more impersonal instructional approaches.

Before we leave the topic of atmosphere, let's take a look at what we said about creating the learner-centered atmosphere in the F2F situation to see if there are any parallels with the online setting. We discussed setting the right tone and creating a warm, welcoming, inclusive, and supportive environment by how we:

- interact with them before they arrive,
- arrange the instructional space,
- greet them when they arrive,
- present ourselves during instruction, and
- interact with them during the instruction itself.

We need to be thinking along these same lines when we develop our online instruction. Here's how we do that.

Interact with Them Before They Arrive

Whether we will be interacting with our learners multiple times (as in term-long online courses), creating stand-alone material such as online tutorials for specific resources, or developing online versions of our course-integrated one-shot sessions, we should try to reach out to our learners before they "arrive" at the online instruction. In the term-long course situation, we can send a welcoming e-mail as soon as learners enroll in the course, post a welcome announcement for them on the course site, and/or direct them to your homepage where you describe your background, teaching style, and so forth. The point is that we want to let them know who we are and how we plan to interact with them before the course begins. This is also a good time to introduce LCT and stress the CPR aspects of this practice. Using a conversational tone in these messages helps to begin the community building necessary for successful instruction—especially in the online format.

Make the course material accessible well before the course begins so that learners can start to review how the course will run and what will be expected of them. Try to open up lines of communication early. The sooner we begin conversing with our learners the more they will feel connected to us and will start to view us as caring, supportive people instead of just faceless, formless cyber beings.

Arrange the Instructional Space

At first glance, this may seem irrelevant in the online environment; but we must remember that, although we are not moving furniture in a physical classroom, the ways in which we design the online space can either help to create the learner-centered atmosphere or act as a deterrent to it (Palloff and Pratt, 2007). We need to try to put ourselves in the learners' place and view the online material from their perspective. One way to ensure our materials follow learner-centered practices, and are understandable, usable, and appealing, is to ask people who are similar to those in the learner population to help vet the online material before releasing it for use. Remember that we will not be "on the spot" to help learners navigate the material. So make sure learners will be able to easily find what they need when they need it. The last thing we want is for our online material to be confusing or frustrating to use. Creating an activity to increase awareness of the structure of the instructional space can help alleviate many of these issues. A good strategy is to provide a tour of the site using a screencasting program to create a video that shows learners the different parts of the site. Adding a narrative commentary makes this approach appealing to auditory as well as visual learners. It can also be helpful to assign a first-week activity such as a scavenger hunt or quiz about the course site and syllabus to not only have the learners interact with the course site but also stress the importance of being able to navigate their learning space.

Greet Them When They Arrive

Again, on the surface this may not seem like something that applies in the online world. But it really goes along with the points we already made about making sure the online material is usable and has a warm, supportive, and welcoming tone. What will learners see when they first arrive at the online site? How will they be addressed? Is the language inclusive ("We will be doing this.") or formal ("Learners will do this.")? Remember that learners will be getting to know us primarily through the written word or perhaps via some kind of virtual video or audio representation. So we need to take special care to make our written and spoken words clear, friendly, and helpful.

Present Ourselves during Instruction

How will our learners perceive us in this nonphysical environment? Although it is harder to create a real presence in this virtual world, it is not impossible. The care and concern we have for our learners should be clear in everything we do— from the way we set up the course or create our stand-alone or course-integrated material to how we choose to interact with them. We need to try and make ourselves real to our learners. We can do this by participating in any icebreaker activity we assign. We should upload our own photo and complete our profile on the CMS as an example to others. We could even create a short welcome video. We must do whatever we can to help our learners get to know us.

We can also share what it felt like to be new to this material and/or to learning (and teaching) online. Including personal anecdotes such as these helps us connect to learners in a genuine and authentic fashion. Just as in the F2F format, we must endeavor to be honest, open, respectful, and empowering in all our interactions with our learners (Palloff and Pratt, 2007). And we must continue to reinforce the "we are all in this together" idea by downplaying our authority role and helping our learners view us as just one member of the learning community— albeit a fairly knowledgeable one (Conrad and Donaldson, 2004; McCombs and Vakili, 2005; Miller and Mazur, 2009). It may be more challenging to do this, operating as we are through technology rather than via our voices and our physical presence, but it is an even more critical element to creating a learner-centered atmosphere in this more virtual instructional world.

Interact with Them during the Instruction Itself

This has already been alluded to in previous sections, but just keep in mind that the language and tone we use to communicate with our learners is important not only when learners first arrive at the online site, but throughout our interactions with them. We have lots of opportunities to communicate with learners when we are involved in full-length courses and should use every opportunity to reinforce the learning community idea and the notion that we are there for them. This usually translates into being online at least once a day to make sure we can respond to learners' questions, comments, or concerns in a timely fashion.

When we are working in the more stand-alone and/or course-integrated one-shot online format, we also need to maintain a positive and welcoming tone. Although learners generally use these types of material more or less independently, including some way for learners to contact us, and possibly each other, via blogs or chat sessions deflects some of the sense of isolation associated with online instructional efforts.

The ways in which we provide feedback to our learners is also a vital part of LCT. Timely feedback is crucial in online settings, as it helps to combat feelings of isolation. We need to make sure our comments are constructive and are geared toward helping learners successfully attain the ELOs associated with the instruction. Constructive feedback goes beyond telling learners if their work is correct or incorrect. Our feedback should let learners know what was good about their correct responses, why their incorrect responses were wrong, how they can find out more about the topic, and what they need to do to improve their work.

While feedback is clearly part of the full-length course, it can also be incorporated into the more stand-alone and/or course-integrated one-shot material. Make sure that whatever form this feedback takes (comments or instant "scoring" as learners work through the material or actual "conversations" between us and our learners via e-mail or other online communication modes) maintains the warm, supportive, and inclusive tone representative of LCT.

HOW TO BUILD A LEARNER-CENTERED ONLINE EXPERIENCE

Now that we have a better understanding of the importance (and challenges) of creating a learner-centered atmosphere in our online instructional efforts, we must turn to the development of the actual material that will serve as our content. How we do this is reminiscent of the development process in the F2F setting. As always, we start with instructional goals and ELOs and then move on to how we will create a situation in which our learners can interact with the material to be learned in a way that will enable them to reach those intended ELOs. However, because we are using the online format, we must also examine the instructional technologies available to us and to our learners. We should be very selective and use only those technologies that really support learners' attainment of the ELOs. We want to choose technology that is familiar to most learners, that supports learning, and that does not act as a barrier to it. Learners will be relying on us to help them function in this online format, and they may need some technical support from us. So, making sure we have the skills to offer this support or know where to get help is extremely important. We can't just assume that our institution's IT department will be able to support the different instructional technologies chosen. In many institutions the faculty (and/or their teaching assistants) is the first line of support for learners. So we must be prepared (and able) to take responsibility for providing this technical assistance.

Once we have chosen the ways in which our learners will interact with the material and the technology that will support those interactions, we are ready to build the online environment for our full-length course, our stand-alone one-shot sessions, or the online versions of our course-integrated material). Many of the next steps will be similar for both the full-length and the single-session types of instruction, so let's take a look at each type in turn, beginning with the full-length course.

Full-Length Course

One of the most important elements in the online full-length course is the course syllabus. Learners will rely on the syllabus to find out what is expected of them during the course, to gather information about the various assignments associated with the course and the deadlines for these assignments, and to discover in what format communications between learners and the instructor and among learners will occur. The syllabus is the cornerstone for the course and as such must be as clear and as well-organized as possible (Dykman and Davis, 2008). Remember that online learners will be relying on what is written in the syllabus to help them navigate the logistics of the course. So, the online syllabus may have to be a bit more detailed than that of the F2F class. The syllabus includes everything learners need to know in order to be successful in the course. It should clearly explain course policies and communication methods. It should also provide learners with an easy way to contact us, usually in the form of an e-mail link (either your own or the internal CMS mail system) and/or telephone number, should they have any questions about the course and its requirements (Palloff and Pratt, 2007; Simonson, 2009). Some instructors set up a specific discussion forum where questions about the course can be addressed so that everyone can see the answers and thereby cut down on repetitive questions. When you use this type of forum, make sure to let learners know that this area is only for asking their course-related questions. Learners should be directed to send their private questions directly to us via e-mail.

The second key element in the online course is the weekly schedule. The schedule is a bird's-eye view of how the course will proceed. It should include the topic for each week, any relevant readings or links to appropriate sites, as well as a brief description of the activity learners will be engaged in, that is, online discussions, independent tutorials, collaborative projects, problem solving, listening to audio clips, viewing video presentations, or completing surveys or quizzes. The schedule should also note when assignments are due and how to submit these assignments. Including links to guidelines for assignments as well as directions on how to get to any resources learners need that week can be useful as well (Ko and Rossen, 2010; Palloff and Pratt, 2007).

Decisions about what activities the learners will engage in each week will depend on the topics and material being addressed, what technology we have available, and whether we are working synchronously, asynchronously, or a combination of both. Do we want to start the week with some formal presentation? If so, a short prerecorded video might be a nice way to begin the exploration of the topic. This could be followed by some kind of guided question-and-answer session either via synchronous chat or asynchronous discussion forums. Or we could present the learners with a problem to solve and ask them to work collaboratively, perhaps in small groups, to solve the problem and then have each group share its solutions electronically with the entire class—thus replicating the small group experiences of the F2F class (Conrad and Donaldson, 2004).

The most common format used in online instruction is the asynchronous discussion forum, which allows for the threading together of responses on the same topic (Ko and Rossen, 2010; Polin, 2004). These can be viewed as the online counterpart of the types of discussions typical in the F2F classroom. However, we can either initiate the discussion or ask learners (singly or in groups) to introduce the topic, again reinforcing the idea of a shared learning community in which the instructor is not the sole facilitator. Any discussion prompt should include questions or issues to be addressed during the discussion. A good prompt makes or breaks a discussion. So, the prompt should include thought-provoking, important, engaging questions that allow for multiple perspectives. Remember that the goal is to stimulate productive discussion among the learners. Learners are asked to read the prompt and then to post their comments on the topic. They are usually required to post a minimum number of responses to other learners' posts during the discussion. Posts must make substantive contributions to the current discussion or begin a new topic. Comments such as "I agree" or "Good idea" are not acceptable; for example, the person posting must expand on the idea, add new content or a new thought, or suggest additional resources on the topic. Some instructors require that learners post at least one or two discussion starters as well as a few responses to other learners' comments. Posting guidelines that include a rubric defining the expectations of a quality post should be set in advance as well as rules of behavior for the discussion (Conrad and Donaldson, 2004; Davis, 2009; Palloff and Pratt, 2007). Although we should keep our eye on the ebb and flow of the discussion to monitor participation levels and make sure that comments are submitted according to the established rules of behavior, it is probably a good idea to keep our ideas to ourselves until the discussion has drawn to a close. Research indicates that nothing shuts the discussion down faster than a comment from the instructor. Learners immediately feel that the instructor's ideas are the "right ones" and no longer engage in open and frank conversation (Palloff and Pratt, 2007; Polin, 2004). However, if the discussion seems to be winding down before its time, we can post a message that includes additional questions or issues that might recharge the discussion. And of course we should step in to correct any misconceptions, to provide any necessary information that will enhance the discussion, or to make sure the discussion remains on track.

The final development step is, of course, assessment. How will learners exhibit the attainment of the ELOs? Here is where the more public nature of the discussions can really help us. We can review posts to get an idea of how well each learner has grasped the topic. It is much easier to monitor discussions in the online format than in the F2F one where things are happening too fast for us to really record who is saying what (Bauer and Anderson, 2000). Furthermore, requiring participation in the online discussions helps to encourage everyone in the group (outspoken and reticent learners alike) to share their opinions and to really have a voice in the discussion.

The online format also encourages the inclusion of peer and self-assessment (Conrad and Donaldson, 2004; Palloff and Pratt, 2007). Learners can share documents and review each other's work. They can be offered opportunities to reflect upon the work and to post their reflections for others to see. Turning in assignments can also be streamlined in the online format. We can have our learners submit their papers and projects to us online rather than having to turn them in in person. We can send back our feedback on these assignments as well, thereby speeding up the entire process (Sorensen and Baylen, 2009).

Merely putting our syllabus, lecture notes, and schedule online does not create an LCT online experience (Palloff and Pratt, 2007). Just as we want to move beyond the passive, one-way communication mode in our F2F endeavors, we must look for ways to bring the LCT approach to our online endeavors. With a little creativity and some exploration of the opportunities technology affords us to present information, create collaboration, and perform assessments we can develop an online instructional offering that follows the CPR principles of LCT. Online formats allow learners to collaborate on assignments without having to travel to F2F meetings. They offer all kinds of options for active participation and give learners the opportunity to take responsibility for their own and their fellow learners' experiences through peer and self-assessment.

Stand-Alone or Course-Integrated One-Shot Sessions

But how do we bring these ideas into the more independent stand-alone and/or course-integrated one-shot online instructional settings? CPR principles can help us here as well. Just as in the full-length course, we should need to go beyond merely converting print handouts into computer-readable format and post them online. Although these types of resources may provide useful information for our learners, they do not constitute real instruction. What we want to develop are experiences where learners can interact with the material in an active, participatory fashion. We can design our offerings so that learners can have some control of how they move through the material, perhaps skipping sections that they already know or that are not relevant to them at that time and concentrating on sections that will be of most use. Giving learners control in this fashion allows them to take a bit more active role in and responsibility for their own learning. Additionally, because this material is online, learners have access to content they may want to review again later.

Although stand-alone and/or course-integrated one-shot online instructional material is usually intended for individual use, as mentioned earlier a degree of collaboration can be built into the experience by offering our learners access to discussion forums or other online communication formats where they can share their experiences and continue their exploration of the topic with their fellow learners and also with us.

Online tutorials and guides can be quite labor intensive to create, but they may well be worth the effort. If they are designed with care, these online instructional pieces may be able to be applied in a variety of settings. Material designed for a particular situation or course might be useful for other similar courses or could act as a stand-alone piece that learners could refer to even if they are not taking a particular course. Consider the time and effort involved as an investment that pays off because the content can be reused in other situations.

ELEMENTS OF LEARNER-CENTERED ONLINE INSTRUCTION

Regardless of whether we are creating a full-length course, a stand-alone piece, or material for use with a specific course or class, we need to think in terms similar to those discussed in the F2F chapter. We need to:

- start by getting their attention,
- end with a big finish, and
- decide what goes in between.

Online material needs to create interest from the start. Consider what would attract learners' attention. In other words, find a way to hook learners into the online offering. In full-length courses, we can devote some of the first week to creating this interest. In the more stand-alone and/or course-integrated material, we need to have some kind of interest-generating opening. These can be very similar to those used in the F2F setting, such as some kind of thought-provoking quote or video that highlights the value of the instruction. Or we can open with a series of research-related questions and say something like, "If you don't know how to answer these questions, we can help." Lots of standard instructional "hooks" can be translated into the online format with some creative thought and imagination.

Ending on an upbeat note may be even more important in the online environment than it is in the F2F one. We want our learners to leave the instruction feeling successful and confident in their newly acquired skills. So creating a way for them to reflect upon what they just learned and also to test their new knowledge is a crucial element of online instruction (Conrad and Donaldson, 2004). If we are using a CMS to provide instruction (in a full-length course or embedded in a classroom faculty's course site), we can use the quizzing and surveying tools provided. In the more stand-alone online format, survey tools such as those provided by *SurveyMonkey* (http://www.surveymonkey.com/) can be used for this purpose. Or we can create self-scoring quizzes using some type of specialized software that allows learners to send us their quizzes for review and feedback. Although that might be more labor intensive, it does open up lines of communication and also allows us to be very learner-centered in our feedback and support.

And of course we need to design the "what goes between" segments, that is, the various ways in which our learners will interact with the material to be learned. Again, many of the same ideas we discussed for F2F instruction are applicable in the online format. Use relevant, authentic, and meaningful examples that help learners become more involved and engaged and help them connect what they learned to their own lives (Conrad and Donaldson, 2004). Whether in the full-length course, the stand-alone piece, or the course-integrated one-shot session, include ways for learners to take an active role in the experience. Make sure learners are not just passively reading and clicking through the material. Obviously the instructor in a full-length course has lots of options for incorporating interactivity into the mix (discussion forum, chat, video/web conferencing, online surveys, quizzes, interactive 3D virtual environments, etc.), depending on the courseware being used. But we can create opportunities for active involvement in the stand-alone and/or one-shot online format as well. Interactive comprehensive checks can be interspersed between the more didactic information. Or learners can be directed to another window where they can actually try out some of the skills just reviewed in actual online resources. See the Explorations section at the end of this chapter for directions on how to find examples of engaging and interactive online information literacy instruction (ILI) material already developed by some of our ILI colleagues. If nothing else, these examples might serve as models when we want to create our own material.

SPECIAL CONSIDERATIONS FOR THE LEARNER-CENTERED ONLINE EXPERIENCE

One of the biggest issues about moving instruction online is the lack of familiarity with this format on the part of both the learner and the instructor. Learners are not always sure what is expected of them. Both instructors and learners need to have a basic competency level with whatever technology is being used to support instruction or the willingness to learn how to use the technology. Attracting learners to online offerings can be even more challenging than getting them to come to our F2F classes. And there is still the perception that online instruction is not as effective as F2F, an area subject to much research and discussion. Being learner-centered in our approach to online instruction can help us deal with these issues and can provide the support our learners may need to succeed in this somewhat unfamiliar and different learning environment. Let's look at some of the things we need to think about when designing our online offerings.

Technology Considerations

As learner-centered instructors, we should be particularly sensitive to access and usability issues when moving our instruction to the online format. Although online instruction offers many great opportunities to expand our reach and to free us from the time constraints associated with F2F instruction, we must make sure that the technology we are using will not be an impediment to our learners. We need to pick technology that will be familiar to most learners and that can be easily accessed and to incorporate UDL principles and address accessibility issues as discussed earlier.

We must be considerate of our learners' circumstances, especially if we require technology that has a cost associated with it. Consider the software and hardware. Try to avoid any type of technology that asks learners to download special programs or that needs very high-end equipment unless it is directly tied to the ELOs and is specifically stated in the requirements for the course. Connectivity can also be an issue. Although streaming video is a great way to create variety and appeal, learners will lose interest if the video takes a very long time to load. The overall rule of thumb is make sure technology supports instruction and is not an impediment to it. If learners have to spend considerable time figuring out how to access and navigate around in the online offering, they may very well give up and abandon the instruction altogether (Palloff and Pratt, 2007).

Marketing

When it comes to online instruction, our marketing must be even more informative than when we are promoting our F2F endeavors. Because many learners may be new to this type of instruction, it is important to include information about both the advantages of this format, and what will be expected from those who enroll in online courses. Emphasize how the online format allows learners to connect to and collaborate with a diverse range of people, thus enriching the educational experience (Liu et al., 2009). While our marketing can stress the convenience of not having to come to campus and the "do it on your own time" flexibility associated with asynchronous offerings, learners must also be alerted to the more self-directed nature of this type of experience. Learners must be willing to take responsibility for checking the course site, posting and reading messages, submitting assignments online, finding ways to work collaboratively on group projects, and organizing their own time in a much more active way than in the F2F class. Giving potential learners a "heads-up" before they enroll in an online course helps to prevent learners from becoming overwhelmed and/or unable to cope with this less familiar format. We can even provide an online learner readiness quiz so that learners can self-assess their abilities in this regard. Many institutions already have them, or we can develop our own (Cerro Coso Community College, 2011; MiraCosta, 2011; Sierra College, 2011).

Marketing our stand-alone online offerings is even more challenging, because we must show learners why they should spend their time on this material. Stress that online offerings have the advantage that learners do not have to come to the library at a specific time and date—the material can be completed at the learners' convenience, exactly when the learners need to do so—and that learners will have access to librarians to answer their questions even after they are done.

Value-Added Aspects

As mentioned earlier in this chapter, online instruction seems to take more time for both the learner and the instructor than F2F classes. Therefore, we need to be very up front about this with our learners and emphasize the plus side of the online format. We should stress the convenience and flexibility of this format and remind learners that in the F2F situation they would be spending time sitting in a physical classroom. Another plus is that while F2F instruction can be very fast paced, causing some learners to get lost in the shuffle, in the online setting learners can often have the option to move through the material at their own pace. And online instruction offers us the opportunity to connect with our learners in a more personal, direct, and very learner-centered way. Of course, this does mean that our time commitments as instructors might increase because of the more individualized nature of our interactions with our learners.

Effectiveness

Although online instruction is increasing by leaps and bounds, it is still developing as an educational mode. So questions abound about the effectiveness of this format, and many educators doubt that the same quality of learning can occur in the online format as in the F2F classroom. Studies comparing the effectiveness of online versus F2F formats are beginning to appear in the research literature. These research findings seem to indicate that the formats can be equally effective, especially if they are well designed with learner-centered principles in mind (Chernish et al., 2009; Lohr, 2009; U.S. Department of Education, 2010). More research is needed in this area, but the results should prove helpful to those who wish to find the best way to move their instruction online.

Moving the ILI One-Shot Session Online

Technology offers us alternative ways to deal with the one-shot sessions still common on our college and university campuses. We can use technology to augment our F2F sessions, or we might even be able to replace our F2F guest appearance with an online instructional experience. We can expand our F2F contact time by directing learners to online material either before our meeting with them—to get them ready for our instruction—or providing them with material they can refer to after the session for review and follow-up questions. See the section "Think outside the F2F Box" in Chapter 6 for more on this idea.

We can also offer one-shot instruction without ever going to the classroom. If the classroom instructor has a course site (and a great many do), we could ask to post instructional material on that site. Or we could provide links back to instructional material on our own or the library's site. Finally, we might look at the material we tend to present in the F2F format and see if any of it could be transformed into an online equivalent. We could then suggest that our classroom colleagues direct learners to this online instructional material. It would be even better if they agree to make completing this material a course requirement, because learners often skip optional or nongraded assignments. This approach should appeal to those classroom instructors who, as we are aware, are often reluctant to give up time during their busy course for a visit from the librarian. Providing this type of course-integrated online support might be a wonderful way to increase our instructional reach.

FINAL REMARKS

Online instruction can be every bit as learner-centered as the more familiar F2F format. In fact, it has the potential of increasing the learner-centered quotient in many ways. One important way is by giving learners more control over and responsibility for their learning. Asynchronous offerings allow learners flexibility and convenience. We also can appeal to learners with a variety of styles by incorporating sound, animation, video, and lots and lots of interactivity. E-mail, chat, video/web conferencing, online discussions, blogs, wikis, and whatever else might be coming along in the future will let us interact and communicate with our learners in ways never before possible. Although online instruction is often criticized for being cold and impersonal, technology now allows us to be in touch with learners in new and exciting ways. Proper use of technology can help us create a dynamic, warm, and productive online learning community.

Adhering to learner-centered principles as we consider our online instructional options and create our ILI offerings can go a long way to counter the negative issues associated with online learning. As in all aspects of instruction, pedagogy should come first. If we apply the same sound pedagogical principles to our online instruction as we do to our F2F endeavors, and remain focused on being learner-centered in our approach, online ILI can be every bit as effective as, if not more effective than, our F2F sessions, and they can offer us ways to reach out to a wider audience than ever before.

REFLECTIONS

1. Put yourself in the online learner's shoes by enrolling in an online class or course. Think about what it feels like to be an online learner. Ask yourself the following:
   a. Does this type of learning appeal to you? Why or why not?
   b. What would make it more appealing?
   c. Do you think this was an effective way to learn the material? Why or why not?
   d. What do you think could be done to make the online material more effective?

   Keep this experience in mind when you are developing online instruction. Remember how you felt in this somewhat less familiar format, and try to create a welcoming and supportive atmosphere in your own online offerings.

2. Find an F2F class or course that you have taught for some time. Could this class or course be transformed into an online offering? Develop a mock-up of what this online class or course would look like. Do you think creating this online alternative would be a feasible and effective approach?

3. Review an F2F class you currently teach. Are there ways that you could use technology to augment the instruction? Is there material available on your library website that might be useful? Can you find already developed online tutorials that might support this instruction? Can you come up with new ideas for using technology to supplement your F2F offering?

4. Finally, think about some ILI that you have always wanted to offer but have not been able to obtain support for offering an F2F version. Ask yourself the following questions:
   a. Could you think of an online alternative?
   b. Are there tutorials or other online ILI material that are already available and might be useful to you? Or would you have to create something new?
   c. In either case, do you think that online ILI would appeal to your classroom partners and/or your community of learners?
   d. Would you need special expertise and/or technology to create this online instruction?

    e. If you were to go ahead with this idea, do you have the administrative and financial support needed to take on the project?

    f. Are there grants available either locally or from national organizations that might help you make this happen?

Be creative in your thinking, and explore all your options. You might find yourself inspired to follow up on your ideas to create new ways to offer ILI to your learners.

EXPLORATIONS

Books

Conrad, Rita Marie, and J. Ana Donaldson. 2004. *Engaging the Online Learner*. San Francisco: Jossey-Bass.

> Don't be put off by the older publication date. This book is full of great ideas for turning online instruction into a dynamic and engaging experience. It will spark ideas for both the full-term course and the more stand-alone and/or one-shot online instructional endeavor.

Ko, Susan, and Steve Rossen. 2010. *Teaching Online: A Practical Guide*. 3rd ed. New York: Routledge.

> Now in its third edition, this book is viewed by many as the premier resource about online instruction and is full of practical advice for developing online instruction. Though intended for those teaching full-length courses, many of the tips and examples can be used in the stand-alone and/or one-shot endeavors as well.

Orellana, Anymir, Terry Hudgins, and Michael Simonson, eds. 2009. *The Perfect Online Course: Best Practices for Designing and Teaching*. Charlotte, NC: Information Age Publishers.

> This collection of articles highlights all aspects of online instruction, including how to make online instruction more interactive, encourage and support the self-directed learner, build online communities, and create a person-centered (or learner-centered) atmosphere.

Palloff, Rena M., and Keith Pratt. 2007. *Building Online Learning Communities: Effective Strategies for the Virtual Classroom*. 2nd ed. San Francisco: Jossey-Bass.

> This book is another of the "must reads" for those who wish to develop effective and engaging online instruction. This second edition combines all the excellent aspects of the first with more timely discussions of technology. It is very learner-centered in focus with tips and advice that can be applied to both the full-length course and the stand-alone and/or one-shot types of instruction.

Repositories for Online ILI Tutorials

ALA. ACRL. Instruction Section. 2010. *PRIMO: Peer-Reviewed Instructional Materials Online.* Accessed December 3. http://www.ala.org/ala/mgrps/divs/acrl/about/sections/is/projpubs/primo/index.cfm.

This is an excellent site for quality ILI tutorials that can be incorporated into instructional efforts or can serve as a model for the creation of new online endeavors.

A.N.T.S.: ANimated Tutorial Sharing Project. 2010. *About ANTS.* COPPUL: The Council of Prairie and Pacific University Libraries. Accessed December 3. http://ants.wetpaint.com/?t=anon.

This is an excellent site for quality ILI tutorials that can be incorporated into instructional efforts or can serve as a model for the creation of new online endeavors.

REFERENCES

Battalio, John. 2009. "Interaction Online: A Reevaluation." In *The Perfect Online Course,* edited by Anymir Orellana, Terry Hudgins, and Michael Simonson, 443–462. Charlotte, NC: Information Age Publishing.

Bauer, John F. 2002. "Assessing Student Work from Chatrooms and Bulletin Boards." *New Directions for Teaching and Learning,* no. 91: 31–36.

Bauer, John F., and Rebecca S. Anderson. 2000. "Evaluating Students' Written Performance in the Online Classroom." *New Directions for Teaching and Learning* 2000, no. 84: 65–71.

Boyer, Naomi R. 2009. "The Learning Contract Process: Scaffolding for Building Social, Self-Directed Learning." In *The Perfect Online Course,* edited by Anymir Orellana, Terry Hudgins, and Michael Simonson, 401–422. Charlotte, NC: Information Age Publishing.

CAST. 2011. *Universal Design for Learning Guidelines Version 2.0.* Universal Design for Learning Center. http://www.udlcenter.org/aboutudl/udlguidelines.

Cerro Coso Community College. 2011. *Online Student Skills Quiz.* Cerro Coso Community College. http://www.cerrocoso.edu/studentservices/survey1.asp.

Chernish, William N., Agnes L. DeFranco, James R. Linder, and Kim E. Dooley. 2009. "Does It Matter? Analyzing the Results of Three Different Learning Delivery Methods." In *The Perfect Online Course,* edited by Anymir Orellana, Terry Hudgins, and Michael Simonson, 23–35. Charlotte, NC: Information Age Publishing.

Conrad, Rita Marie, and J. Ana Donaldson. 2004. *Engaging the Online Learner.* San Francisco: Jossey-Bass.

Dagli, Arif. 2003. Faculty and Student Perceptions and Experiences on Interaction in Web-Based Learning. In *Information Technology and Organization: Trends, Issues and Solutions,* edited by Khosrow-Pour Mehdi, 1173–1174. Hershey, PA: Idea Group Publishing.

Davis, Barbara Gross. 2009. *Tools for Teaching.* 2nd ed. San Francisco: Jossey-Bass.

De Roma, Virginia, and Steve Nida. 2004. "A Focus on 'Hands-On,' Learner-Centered Technology at the Citadel." *TechTrends* 48, no. 5: 39–43.

Duffy, Thomas M., and Jamie R. Kirkley. 2004a. "Introduction: Theory and Practice in Distance Education. "In *Learner-Centered Theory and Practice in Distance Education*, edited by Thomas M. Duffy and Jamie R. Kirkley, 3–13. Mahwah, NJ: Lawrence Erlbaum.

———. 2004b. "Learning Theory and Pedagogy Applied in Distance Learning: The Case of Cardean University." In *Learner-Centered Theory and Practice in Distance Education*, edited by Thomas M. Duffy and Jamie R. Kirkley, 107–141. Mahwah, NJ: Lawrence Erlbaum.

Dykman, Charlene A., and Charles K. Davis. 2008. "Online Education Forum: Part Two—Teaching Online Versus Teaching Conventionally." *Journal of Information Systems Education* 19, no. 2: 157–164.

Fox, Megan. 2007. "The Mobile Age." In *Information Tomorrow: Reflections on Technology and the Future of Public and Academic Libraries*, edited by Rachel S. Gordon, 3–18. Medford, NJ: Informtion Today.

GSA's IT Accessibility and Workforce (ITAW). 2011. *Section 508*. ITAW. http://www.section 508.gov/index.cfm.

Ko, Susan, and Steve Rossen. 2010. *Teaching Online: A Practical Guide*. 3rd ed. New York: Routledge.

Liu, Xiaojing, et al. 2009. "Does Sense of Community Matter?" In *The Perfect Online Course*, edited by Anymir Orellana, Terry Hudgins, and Michael Simonson, 521–543. Charlotte, NC: Information Age Publishing.

Lohr, Steve. 2009. "Study Finds that Online Education Beats the Classroom." In *Bits* (blog). *New York Times*. August 19. http://bits.blogs.nytimes.com/2009/08/19/study-finds-that-online-education-beats-the-classroom/.

Marlow, Bruce A., and Marilyn L. Page. 2005. *Creating the Constructivist Classroom*. Thousand Oaks, CA: Corwin Press.

McCampbell, Bill. 2000. "Toys or Tools? Online Bulletin Boards and Chat Rooms." *Principal Leadership* 1, no. 3: 73–74.

McCombs, Barbara L., and Donna Vakili. 2005. "A Learner-Centered Framework for E-learning." *Teachers College Record* 107, no. 8: 1582–1600.

McKeachie, Wilbert J., and Marilla Svinicki. 2006. *McKeachie's Teaching Tips*. 12th ed. Boston: Houghton-Mifflin.

McLaren, Angelene C. 2009. "Designing Effective E-learning: Guidelines for Practitioners." In *The Perfect Online Course*, edited by Anymir Orellana, Terry Hudgins, and Michael Simonson, 229–245. Charlotte, NC: Information Age Publishing.

Messner, Kate. 2009. "Making a Case for Twitter in the Classroom." *School Library Journal*. http://www.schoollibraryjournal.com/article/CA6708199.html.

Miller, Christopher, and Joan M. Mazur. 2009. "Toward a Person-Centered Model of Instruction: Can an Emphasis on the Personal Enhance Instruction in Cyberspace?" In *The Perfect Online Course*, edited by Anymir Orellana, Terry L. Hudgins, and Michael Simonson, 275–296. Charlotte, NC: Information Age Publishing.

MiraCosta College. 2011. *Test Your Potential as an Online Student*. Mira Costa College. Accessed May 29. http://www.miracosta.cc.ca.us/Instruction/DistanceEducation/quiz.aspx.

Palloff, Rena M., and Keith Pratt. 2007. *Building Online Learning Communities: Effective Strategies for the Virtual Classroom*. 2nd ed. San Francisco: Jossey-Bass.

Park, Ji-Hye, and Hee Jan Choi. 2009. "Facters Influencing Adult Learners' Decisions to Drop Out or Persist in Online Learning." *Educational Technology and Society* 12, no. 4: 207–217.

Pena-Shaff, Judith, William Altman, and Hugh Stephenson. 2005. "Asynchronous Online Discussion as a Tool for Learning: Students' Attitudes, Expectations, and Perceptions." *Journal of Interactive Learning Research* 16, no. 4: 409–430.

Polin, Linda. 2004. "Learning in Dialogue with a Practicing Community." In *Learner-Centered Theory and Practice in Distance Education*, edited by Thomas M. Duffy and Jamie R. Kirkley, 17–48. Mahwah, NJ: Lawrence Erlbaum.

Rattanavijai, Chayan, and Sushil K. Sharma. 2003. "Learning Outcomes in Web-Based Synchronous and Asynchronous Learning Environments: A Comparative Analysis." In *Information Technology and Organization: Trends, Issues and Solutions*, edited by Khosrow-Pour Mehdi, 1070–1071. Hershey, PA: Idea Group Publishing.

Reidling, Ann Marlow. 2004. *Learning to Learn: A Guide to Becoming Information Literate in the 21st Century*. 2nd ed. New York: Neal-Schuman.

Saeed, Nauman, Yun Yang, and Suku Sinnappan. 2009. "Emerging Web Technologies in Higher Education: A Case of Incorporating Blogs, Podcasts, and Social Bookmarking in a Web Programming Course Based on Students' Learning Styles Preferences." *Educational Technology and Society* 12, no. 4: 98–109.

Sierra College. 2011. *Online Student Readiness Quiz*. Sierra College. Accessed May 29. http://lrc.sierra.cc.ca.us/dl/survey/OL-student-assess.html.

Simonson, Michael. 2009. "Designing the Perfect Online Course." In *The Perfect Online Course*, edited by Anymir Orellana, Terry Hudgins, and Michael Simonson, 547–550. Charlotte, NC: Information Age Publishing.

Simonson, Michael, and Charles Schlosser. 2009. "We Need a Plan." In *The Perfect Online Course*, edited by Anymir Orellana, Terry Hudgins, and Michael Simonson, 3–21. Charlotte, NC: Information Age Publishing.

Sorensen, Christine K., and Danio M. Baylen. 2009. "Learning Online: Adapting the Seven Principles of Good Practice to a Web-Based Instructional Environment." In *The Perfect Online Course*, edited by Anymir Orellana, Terry Hudgins, and Michael Simonson, 60–86. Charlotte, NC: Information Age Publishing.

Tomei, Lawrence. 2004. "The Impact of Online Teaching on Faculty Load." *International Journal of Instructional Technology and Distance Learning* 1, no. 1. http://www.itdl.org/journal/Jan_04/article04.htm.

U.S. Department of Education, Office of Planning, Evaluation, and Policy Development. 2010. *Evaluation of Evidence-Based Practices in Online Learning: A Meta-analysis and Review of Online Learning Studies*. Washington, DC: U.S. Department of Education.

U.S. Department of Justice. 2011. *ADA Home Page: Information and Technical Assistance on the Americans with Disabilites Act*. U.S. Department of Justice. Last updated August 31. http://www.usdoj.gov/crt/ada/.

Chapter 8

Creating the Blended Learner-Centered Experience— A Case Study in Transformation

With Hillary Kaplowitz

Things do not get better by being left alone.

—Winston Churchill

As you can see from the previous two chapters, face-to-face (F2F) and online instruction each has its own set of advantages and drawbacks. One way to make the most of the two delivery modes while minimizing the drawbacks of each is to use what is commonly referred to as a "blended" or "hybrid" approach. Blended/hybrid instruction uses a mix of traditional teaching methods and computer-based remote learning (Bliuc, Goodyear, and Ellis, 2007; Donnelly, 2006; Graham, 2006). This approach takes advantage of the flexibility and convenience offered by online learning, allowing learners to have much more control over their own learning (Georgouli, Skalkidis, and Guerreiro, 2008; Goode et al., 2007) while still maintaining the interactive and interpersonal aspects of the F2F format. The combination of F2F instructional elements with online ones can help to minimize feelings of alienation and isolation often associated with online learning and allows learners to interact with each other and with the instructor in a more immediate and personal way (El Mansour and Munpinga, 2007). A careful mix of online and F2F elements can offer learners the best of both experiences and creates more opportunities for learners to find aspects of the instruction that matches their preferred learning style (Ko and Rossen, 2010; Palloff and Pratt, 2007).

Hillary Kaplowitz, MS, is Instructional Designer, Faculty Technology Center, California State University, Northridge.

We have already addressed the advantages and drawbacks of the two delivery methods in Chapters 6 and 7. The blended/hybrid approach gives us the opportunity (or capability) of combining the best of both F2F and online learning while compensating for some of the drawbacks of each—as long as we apply good instructional design principles. Because some of the course is taught in the F2F format, personal relationships and a sense of community can begin to develop. However, by making effective use of the tools and activities within a course management system (CMS), contact time can be greatly expanded and an enhanced sense of community and shared responsibility can result (Palloff and Pratt, 2007; Rovai and Jordan, 2004). Furthermore, learners can be given more control over their own learning as they interact virtually with the material, the instructor, and each other as it fits into their personal schedules (Dalsgaard and Godsk, 2007; MacDonald, 2006; Young, 2002).

Although many instructors have access to a CMS, they frequently view it merely as a way to distribute information such as the weekly class schedule and a list of assigned readings. However, most CMSs offer interactive features that could support a more blended learning environment, allowing F2F seat time to be replaced by online activities. Discussion boards can be used to extend examination of a topic first discussed in the F2F setting. Or, conversely, an online discussion could be reviewed and summarized in a subsequent F2F meeting. Assignments can be submitted by posting them to the course site, thus allowing work to be reviewed by both the instructor and other learners as appropriate. Furthermore, links to supplemental material can be included so that learners can expand and enrich their understanding of the material to be learned. F2F sessions can then be used for in-depth examination of the material, for practice in applying that material, and for community-building experiences.

Using a blended/hybrid approach allows the instructor to determine the best way to deliver information in order to maximize learner potential (Bodie, Powers, and Fitch-Hauser, 2006). By relegating the logistical activities to the online space (announcements and assignment distribution, for example), instructors not only increase contact time but also can shift the quality of F2F contact to higher level processing activities such as analysis, synthesis, and evaluation. Furthermore, reticent learners who might not be willing to contribute in an F2F setting are given the opportunity to be heard in the various communication features available in the online arena. Finally, by providing multiple vehicles for learning, blended instruction supports many different learning styles (Boyer, 2009; Goode et al., 2007; Sorensen and Baylen, 2009).

CHANGING MY WAYS

Having discovered all the advantages of using a blended format, I began to give some serious thought to adopting that mode of delivery for my own instruction—

specifically for a full-term course I teach at the UCLA Information Studies department called "Information Literacy Instruction: Theory and Technique." The idea of moving to a blended format for my own teaching both intrigued and terrified me. But I felt that a blended format offered the best experience for my learners. And having embraced the learner-centered approach for my teaching, I felt that I had to conquer my fears and make the effort to turn my course into one that better addressed the needs of all my learners.

The following is an account of my personal journey from teaching in a totally F2F format to a blended one in which F2F sessions comprise approximately 30 percent of the learners' instructional experience. The remaining roughly 70 percent of the course occurs in an asynchronous online format. I had no real experience in online learning as either a learner or a teacher when I embarked on this journey. However, as CMSs began to be developed to support instruction, I started to see how using these systems could have a positive impact on my teaching practice. So I started what was a sometimes painful journey toward a more blended approach. I began with the smallest of steps, and, as I became more comfortable with each stage, I made more changes until I reached the current fully blended incarnation of the course that I now use.

Change can be scary, especially when dealing with new technology. Moving slowly worked for me. I have never been interested in technology for technology's sake and so approached this transformation with a somewhat skeptical attitude. But I soon discovered that using a learner-centered teaching (LCT) approach allowed me to make decisions about which of the two formats to use at particular points in the course based on sound pedagogical principles. Many aspects of the course could easily move to the online format, while others really seemed more suitable for the F2F interaction. For example, while discussions could clearly be moderated in the online format, I felt that my learners, who were after all taking the course to find out how to teach, needed to experience the F2F format as well. I could model various types of LCT approaches during the F2F session as well as give learners an opportunity to try some of these approaches out for themselves. Furthermore, they could also get the chance to practice their own teaching skills in the F2F setting.

The transition from traditional F2F to the blended approach did not happen overnight. It took years for me to get to the place I am now. But I am very glad I made this journey. I truly believe that my current blended version of the course provides these future information literacy instruction (ILI) librarians with the best learning experience possible and gives them a chance to familiarize themselves with F2F and online delivery modes of instruction—both as the learners and the teachers.

I should also mention that I could not have made this journey without the assistance of Hillary Kaplowitz, upon whose insight and instructional design expertise I relied every step of the way. She was an invaluable source of information as well as someone with whom I could discuss my ideas and who could provide reality checks when I was about to go astray with my ideas. I strongly urge you to find similar support as you move into the blended/hybrid delivery mode for your classes and courses.

Look into resources available to you at your institution for instructional design and technology support. Or find a colleague who has already made this transition and might be able to give you some valuable insights about the experience. Ask them for suggestions and to provide feedback on your work. Just finding someone else who is at your level but interested in exploring together would be useful.

Here, then, is my story.

THE STARTING POINT

IS 448 (Information Literacy Instruction: Theory and Technique) was developed by my fellow UCLA librarian Esther Grassian and me in 1989 for the UCLA graduate information studies program as a traditional F2F offering. Esther and I alternated teaching this class for over 20 years and continue to teach it today. IS 448 is a graduate-level course whose goal is for learners to be able to identify and analyze ILI needs, design and implement appropriate instruction, assess the results of instruction, and revise as needed. The course, taught over a ten-week period, meets weekly for three and a half hours.

Traditionally the course had been taught through a combination of lectures, discussions, and guest speakers. In later years the adoption of the CMS Moodle

Course expected learning outcomes (ELOs) are:

Learners will be able to:

1. Make preliminary assessments based on theories learned in class to determine the:
   - Intended audience
   - Instructional needs of that audience
   - Goals and outcomes for the proposed instruction
   - Appropriate methodology for reaching those goals and outcomes
   - Recommended course of action
2. Plan and administer an instructional program by:
   - Developing an instructional approach
   - Communicating with administrators via written memos and proposals
   - Implementing the plan
   - Assessing, revising, and updating the plan as needed
3. Apply relevant educational, psychological, and instructional design theories to develop appropriate instructional programs and design supporting materials as needed.

at UCLA allowed for the incorporation of online teaching and learning tools to supplement the F2F meetings. Moodle, which stands for Modular Object-Oriented Dynamic Learning Environment, is open source software designed to support a social constructionist framework of education (Moodle Corporation, 2011).

The major assignment for the class is a case study. Learners choose from 12 to 15 different cases—set in a variety of library environments. Teams of two or four learners collaborate to develop an ILI proposal that addresses the situation described in the case. This proposal is developed over the course of the entire ten weeks—in three stages:

1. One-page "Memo to an Administrator"
2. Draft proposal
3. Final revised proposal including sample outlines, examples of support material, and a 10- to 15-item bibliography

A second assignment, the "Observation Report," requires learners to critique either in-person or virtual ILI and comment on the instructional effectiveness of the offerings. Participation both during F2F meetings and in a later version of the course on the course's online activities is also factored into the learner's final grade.

Practice teaching is another requirement for this class. Each learner prepares a seven- to ten-minute instructional session on any topic of interest. Topics do not have to relate to libraries or information literacy. Learners typically choose to teach about their hobbies or an athletic or leisure pursuit. This assignment is not graded. However, learners receive written feedback from all of their fellow learners at the completion of their presentation.

Experience with group or team teaching is another part of the IS 448 experience. When the course was entirely F2F, learners were asked to form teams around one of four or five specific topics, such as assessment, distance learning, active learning, and teaching in a diverse world. The teams were then assigned a designated time slot during the term in which to present their topic in any way they wished. The teams assigned advance readings to prepare their fellow learners for the session and then led the F2F instruction on the designated date.

As can be seen from the description of the class and its assignments, IS 448 had always been taught from the authentic, active learning perspective. As learners work on a real-world instructional case study, they must reflect on and pull together everything they have learned during the course in order to develop a solution for their case. The three-part nature of the assignment allows for extensive instructor formative feedback during the course itself and summative feedback once the final product is turned in. The individual presentation and the team project assignment both rely on peer-to-peer evaluation and feedback. Questions, comments, and discussions have always been encouraged both during F2F meetings and on the course site. Furthermore, most in-class sessions have included one or more active learning experiences. However, as I learned more about online instruction and CMS capabilities, I felt that an overall revamping of the course to include more online opportunities for learning could enhance the LCT aspects of the experience for everyone—teacher and learners alike. Because IS 448 is at its heart a course that is intended to prepare future librarians to teach information literacy in all delivery modes, it seemed important that these instruction librarians in training should have both online and F2F experiences during the course.

MOVING TO THE LCT/BLENDED APPROACH— THE TRANSFORMATION OF IS 448

Moving to the blended/hybrid format happened over a number of years and was not entirely planned. In fact, at the beginning it sort of just snuck up on me. It happened in stages and is an ever-evolving, ongoing process. Here's how it all evolved.

Step One: F2F Using CMS to Distribute Material

My first introduction to online teaching came when my institution adopted a new initiative that would require all teaching faculty to include an online component to their courses. The Information Studies department had adopted Moodle as its CMS and urged faculty to create course webpages.

As with most new-to-online-teaching instructors, my first reaction was panic. My second one was to look for help. So I made contact with the department's website coordinator and set up a meeting. He very kindly spent quite a bit of time with me helping me understand what the CMS could do (and at that early stage of development, not do) and how I could use it. He also offered to create my first course site himself with materials I supplied.

So, my first attempt at using a CMS was pretty much to just create a repository of course materials such as the syllabus (general information, assignments, grading, etc.), copies of course materials (i.e., the case studies that would serve as the basis for the major course assignment), a week-by-week schedule (with topics, readings, and assignments for each class meeting), and my contact information. In other words, I basically built a static, read-only course site that allowed me to distribute my materials virtually and offered learners access to them anywhere and at any time they needed them. This was certainly a move in the right direction but not exactly a step that took full advantage of the online delivery mode offered by a CMS.

Step Two: F2F Using CMS Features

Having the first step under my belt, I decided that the next time I taught I would incorporate more of the CMS features into my instruction. So, in addition to mounting all my course material, I decided to change the team-led instruction assignment from an F2F to a virtual experience. Teams were still formed around topics of interest, but, instead of presenting the material in class, each team was asked to lead an online discussion of the topic during a specific week during the term. So interactions for this assignment made use of Moodle's online discussion feature. I monitored these discussions but did not actively participate during the discussion itself to avoid overwhelming or dominating the discussion (Ko and Rossen, 2010; Palloff and Pratt, 2007). Of course, I did step in as needed, especially if the discussion seemed to be going off topic, to address any misconceptions, or to answer questions that required my expert knowledge.

While I thought this online discussion element was a positive change, I wanted to challenge my learners to try more than online discussions as an approach to online teaching. So the next time I taught I changed this assignment somewhat. This time the teams had to create a virtual learning experience. They could do anything they liked (lead discussions, create a webpage, post a PowerPoint presentation), but the mode of delivery had to be online. Teams were also required to plan an assessment task for the F2F meeting following their virtual presentation.

Both the online discussion and the virtual instruction team projects were peer graded—with each team member receiving a grade from his or her teammates. Those grades were averaged to calculate an individual's grade for the assignment in order to avoid the typical group work problem in which all learners may not do their fair share. If this were the case, their teammates would give them a lower grade, which would then result in a lower grade for the assignment.

These types of assignments began to add more online elements to my course. Typically when you do that, you should reduce the amount of F2F contact required for the course. However, I was still reluctant to let go of my F2F contact with the learners. All I was willing to do was give them one full week off and end one session at the midpoint break. Basically the learners were taking about 85 percent of the previous F2F course and spending an additional 30–40 percent of their time online. In an entirely F2F course, learners are expected to do approximately two to three hours of outside class work (including assignments, readings, studying, etc.) for every hour spent in the classroom. So for my course, if F2F would meet three and a half hours per week for ten weeks, they should be spending about 1,050 hours working on course assignments outside of the classroom over the ten-week-long quarter. I was essentially asking them to still do that while adding a considerable amount of online work on top. So the net result was that I overloaded the learners with more work than was really fair for the term and the number of credits. My learners were quite gracious and supportive of my experiments, however, and said that although the course was a lot of work, they really profited by the experiences—especially the chance to work in both the online and F2F format.

Step Three: First Blended Version

Thus inspired by my baby steps into the online teaching world, I decided to take the leap and create a true blend. I knew from my experiences with the overloaded courses that I really had to find a better balance between the online and the F2F elements of the course. My goal was a 70–30 split, with the bulk of the course-work taking place online. So I started looking for ways to replace traditionally F2F activities with online ones and to use more of the capabilities for collaborative learning offered by a CMS. Good instructional design, of course, always starts with outcomes. So I reviewed the overall course outcomes as well as the specific out-comes for each of the week's session to see what seemed most appropriate for an F2F session and which elements could be transformed into online ones. In reflecting upon the topics and associated activities I had included in the completely F2F offerings of the course, I concluded that, to adhere to LCT principles, the three F2F sessions in the blended version should offer learners opportunities to practice and apply what they were learning in a shared learning community environment.

The first F2F class was devoted to building the foundation for the course. See Table 8.1 for a summary of the activities included in that session.

In addition to the activities described in Table 8.1, I reviewed the course site with the class to make sure everyone was comfortable with its format and organization.

Table 8.1. Face-to-Face Session 1		
Goal: To introduce students to course content, assignments, expectations, the philosophy of learner-centered teaching, "hot topics" in ILI, and the case study method.		
Activity	**Purpose**	**Format**
Icebreaker	• To reinforce concept of a learning community.	• Learners complete Individual Profile forms. • They then exchange forms with a partner. • Members of individual pairs introduce each other to the rest of the class.
Brainstorming "hot topics"	• To give learners more responsibility for the course content. • To highlight current ILI "hot topics."	• Learners form small groups to discuss possible topics for course's online discussions. • Each group nominates three to five topics. • The entire class ranks the topics. • The highest-ranking topics become topics for online discussions.
Simulated case study	• To help learners begin to think about how to approach the case study assignment.	• Learners form small groups to discuss a sample case study. • Groups are asked to answer three questions: What do we know? What do we need to know? Who do we ask? • Groups share results.

I also introduced the concept of a Grading Contract. Although the case study assignment represented the bulk of the course grade, the learners were allowed to allocate point values to each of the remaining assignments. This allowed learners to have a more active, participatory role in their own learning—thus further supporting the learner-centered nature of the course. Grading contracts were due by the second week in the term.

For the second F2F, I decided to concentrate on the topics that seemed most difficult for the learners to grasp and that would benefit from some extra hands-on practice. I chose to concentrate on Marketing, Planning, and the Psychology of Learning for this session. These topics were also the ones that offered the best options for collaborative, participatory activities. See Table 8.2 for the activities included in this second F2F meeting.

Table 8.2. Face-to-Face Session 2		
Goals:		
➤ To highlight and discuss different points of views about information literacy.		
➤ To show the importance of outreach and marketing as an aspect of ILI.		
➤ To tie the principles of LCT to ILI.		
➤ To help learners understand the relationship between outcomes and assessment in the planning process.		
➤ To familiarize learners with the principles associated with the three major theories of learning and how to apply these principles to ILI.		
➤ To familiarize learners with the principles associated with the three major theories of learning and how to apply these principles to ILI.		
➤ To introduce the learners to the concept of learning styles and how to apply this concept to ILI.		
Activity	**Purpose**	**Format**
The Selling of ILI	• To give learners the opportunity to formulate their ideas regarding the value of ILI. • To allow learners to demonstrate their understanding of how different stakeholders view ILI. • To help learners develop "talking points" for selling ILI to different stakeholders. • To give learners practice in developing marketing strategies for selling ILI to various stakeholders.	• The room is set up to resemble a conference on "Marketing Your Product: The Selling of ILI." • The class is divided into groups. • Each group is asked to create a marketing presentation for one of four stakeholder groups (administrators, collaborators/partners, colleagues, learners) using arts and crafts materials available in the room. • Each group presents its material to the rest of the class.
		(Continued)

	Table 8.2. Face-to-Face Session 2 *(Continued)*	
Activity	**Purpose**	**Format**
Think/Pair/ Share	• To give learners the opportunity to apply the principles of LCT to ILI practices.	• Learners spend about two minutes to come up with ideas of how to make ILI more learner-centered. • Learners spend the next five to seven minutes exchanging ideas with a partner. • Pairs share their ideas with the entire class.
The "Teaching Tripod" Small Group Activity	• To help learners practice how to tie outcomes to assessments in the planning process.	• Learners work in groups of three to five learners to complete a worksheet. • The task is to select one of the goals listed on the sheet and to come up with one or two expected learning outcomes (ELOs) for the goal. • Groups share ideas with the entire class. • Groups are then asked to come up with assessment ideas for each of the ELOs. • Groups share ideas with the entire class.
Empty Outline	• To encourage learners to review their assigned readings about the three major theories of learning. • To give learners the opportunity to articulate their understanding of these theories in their own words.	• Learners are divided into three groups (Doing, Thinking, Feeling) and are asked to indicate what theory of learning is associated with their group's name, key figures linked to the theory, and some principles related to it. • Groups present their ideas to the rest of the class.
Jigsaw	• To give learners an opportunity to apply psychological learning theory to ILI practice.	• Learners in Empty Outline groups are instructed to count off 1, 2, 3. • Learners regroup with all 1s in one group, all 2s in a second group, and all 3s in a third group. • Each new group now has representatives from each of the three theories discussed in the Empty Outline segment. • Groups are asked to design ILI that incorporates principles of all three theories of learning. • Groups report back to the entire class.
One-Minute Paper	• To allow learners to reflect upon and sum up what they learned from the entire session.	• Learners are asked to respond orally to two questions: "What are one or two things you learned from today's session?" and "What are one or two things you would still like to know?" • The instructor records the responses on the board.

The activities-based nature of this class meeting further demonstrated the use of nontraditional types of instructional approaches and illustrated how large quantities of material could be addressed without resorting to lengthy lecture-type presentations. These activities not only allowed learners to take more responsibility for their own and their classmates' learning, but they also offered a rich basis for in-depth discussions on these very important topics.

The "What Stuck?" Game—A Variation on the One-Minute Paper Activity

In later offerings of this course, I transformed the One-Minute Paper exercise into a competition called the "What Stuck?" game. Learners returned to their original teams, and the teams were given five minutes to come up with as many things as they could about what had transpired during the entire session and write them on flip-chart paper. Teams could list concepts/topics/ideas, teaching methods and techniques, assessments opportunities, and so on. The members of the winning team each got a prize, and everyone else received a smaller gift as well. The result was an incredibly enthusiastic review of the material and an even livelier end to the day's activities. It also offered me an even better (and sometimes surprising) view of what the learners had thought was valuable about the day.

The entire day was, therefore, an example of meta-teaching. Not only did we address some very important topics, but the learners also experienced a variety of LCT methods that they would hopefully want to incorporate into their own future instructional endeavors.

That left the third F2F for the learners to do their own individual presentations. As in the previous offerings of the course, I wanted to give learners the opportunity to practice F2F teaching in the safe and supportive environment we had created for our learning community. See Table 8.3 for details of this class meeting.

Table 8.3. Face-to-Face Session 3		
Goal: To provide learners with actual teaching experience.		
Activity	**Purpose**	**Format**
Individual presentations	• To give learners the opportunity to plan and deliver a brief instructional segment. • To help learners become more confident and comfortable with F2F teaching. • To help learners develop ways of dealing with stage fright. • To help learners improve their stage presence (use of voice and body, ways of involving learners, etc.).	• Each learner is allocated five to ten minutes (depending on class size) to lead instruction. • Topics do not have to be related to ILI. • Other learners offer written feedback after each presentation.

As in the previous versions of the course, I encouraged learners to teach something that they were interested in, such as a hobby or outside-of-school activity. My reasons for this were that I wanted learners to know what it feels like to teach something they felt passionate about and to remember that feeling and take it into their ILI endeavors. If a teacher feels passionate about the material and teaches from his or her authentic self, that passion will show and will spread to and infect the learners (Brookfield, 1990, 1995). As before, the presenters got written feedback from all members of the audience to help them evaluate their experience. Feedback was confidential and for the presenter's eyes only. To further support the idea that in a learning community members learn from each other, I did not review this material, thereby maintaining the confidential nature of the material.

Learners were allowed to decide whether to present in either the morning or the afternoon portion of the day. They were not required to attend the entire day but were welcome to do so if they wished to offer support to and learn from their fellow learners. This allowed learners the option of reducing their contact time for that last day to two and half hours versus the five hours of the other two sessions.

So that took care of the F2F meetings. The next step was to figure out how to translate the remaining material. Clearly I could substitute some of the in-class discussions with online versions. The team-led instruction from the F2F version was turned into leading online discussions on topics chosen by the class during the first F2F session. I also made a change in how these team-led discussions were evaluated. In previous versions of the course, members of the leading team provided me with feedback via e-mail regarding their assessments of their colleagues' contributions to the team effort. While I was happy with the idea that team members evaluated each other, I also thought that the effectiveness of the discussion should also be evaluated. So learners who were not on the leading team were also required to provide feedback using the free online survey tool *SurveyMonkey* (http://www.surveymonkey.com/) on what they thought about the discussion itself—what they learned, the leaders' role in the discussion, what they still wanted to know about the topic, and so on. I used the results of both sets of surveys (peer evaluations within the team and learners' evaluation of the team's efforts) to compute the grades for this assignment.

That was a fairly easy transition, but what about some of the other activities? One big challenge was the guest visits that had been a big part of all my F2F sessions. So I again went back to why I had decided to include these visits in earlier versions of the course. The original purpose of those sessions was twofold, to expose my learners to ILI in a variety of environments and to provide learners with contacts in the various types of libraries. With this in mind, I added a new assignment in which learners would interview an information literacy librarian and share their reports on the course site. I also continued the Observation

Report assignment that I had used previously in which learners observed F2F and/or web-based instruction and submitted a report on what they learned from the observations. In the previous 100 percent F2F versions of the course, these Observation Reports were turned in to me, and I set aside part of the final class meeting for learners to exchange their impressions of the observations. For the blended version, this sharing took place on the course site instead. These reports were no longer turned in to me but were posted to the site instead. So, learners had two opportunities—the Interview and the Observation Reports—to learn about ILI from their own as well as their fellow learners' experiences. To ensure that everyone read at least a few of their colleagues' reports, I facilitated online discussions exploring the differences and similarities in ILI from different perspectives that learners had discovered from the two assignments.

That took care of most of the online components of the course, but I wanted to do one more thing to help support the learning community idea. So I added an element of peer review to the Case Study assignment. This team-based assignment was accomplished in three stages—the Memo to an Administrator, the Draft Proposal, and the Final Proposal. Only the Final Proposal received a grade. In the past, I was the only person to read these papers. But the CMS offered an opportunity for further sharing (Palloff and Pratt, 2007), so I decided to have the first stage—the Memo to an Administrator—posted to the course site. I then added a new, graded assignment—the Memo Critique. Each learner was assigned one memo to review and critique. These critiques were then posted to the course site as well. This additional assignment gave learners the opportunity to find out how other teams were working on their cases, gave learners practice in providing constructive criticism, and offered each team additional feedback beyond that which I provided as the instructor. I was very pleased by the thoughtful and professional way my learners critiqued their assigned memos, and I am sure that the teams appreciated the additional help.

Finally, I wanted to build more reflection into the course as well as give learners a real opportunity to comment on and make suggestions about how the course was going. The first online activity was an Opening Reflection in which learners expressed what they expected from the course and listed their personal learning outcomes. One of the final online activities was a Closing Reflection in which learners could look back on the course to consider how well (if?) those outcomes were accomplished. Although Reflections can be set so that they are private (viewable only by the student who posted the reflection and the instructor), I chose to have both of these Reflections posted to the course site for everyone in the course to read. Although learners were not required to discuss the Reflections, they often commented on each other's ideas. The Reflections helped all the learners not only to identify their own individual thoughts but also to see how those thoughts fit in with those of others in the community. In later versions of the course, I reversed this public Reflections posting idea and made them private instead. I thought learners would be more comfortable with that approach.

In keeping with the "we are all in it together" principle of LCT, I also wanted to offer learners an opportunity to help fine-tune the course. So I created a Mid-Point Survey on *SurveyMonkey* to gather input about how learners felt the course was meeting their needs. I wanted to learn what they thought about the balance between online and F2F instruction, solicit suggestions on ways to improve the course site, and gather some preliminary feedback about the various course assignments and activities. These surveys provided valuable insight into the course and opened lines of communication about aspects of the course that learners felt needed improving. Although some changes could not be made midstream in the course, I endeavored to address concerns and made some adjustments, particularly to the layout of the course site, based on the results of this survey.

I also created a Final Feedback Survey on *SurveyMonkey* so that I could gather additional information from my learners. Although the university does provide learners with a standard course evaluation form, I felt this form would not be specific enough to suit my needs. The results of this Final Feedback Survey were extremely helpful as a way for me to reflect on what went well and what could use some rethinking for any future blended offerings of my course.

Although there were some learning curve issues as both the learners and I had to get used to the online mode of instruction, all in all this first incarnation went better than I had expected. The university-required student evaluations as well as the results of surveys that I developed for my own purposes all indicated that my learners were satisfied with the blended version and felt it offered them a broader experience because it allowed them to see what it was like to learn (and to teach) in both the F2F and online modes.

Step Four: Second Blended Version

My first foray into blended instruction sold me on the idea. I could really see how this combination of online and F2F delivery modes took advantage of the best of both while compensating for some of the drawbacks of each. The F2F sessions countered the feelings of alienation often felt by online learners and helped set a more personal tone for the course. Learners got to know each other and me on that first day, and the idea of us all being members of a community of learners was established by that day's activities and the various collaborative assignments that ran through the course. On the other hand, contact time was greatly expanded through the use of online discussions and document sharing. Furthermore, because of the asynchronous nature of the online components, learners had more freedom to work on their assignments and participate in discussions as best fit their own schedules. So, I was pretty satisfied with the changes I had made, and I was ready to try it again.

However, I was still struggling with the workload issue. So, this time around, I decided to lead the online discussions myself, thus losing the element of peer evaluations from the course. Because I felt this was a valuable experience for learners to have, I decided to make a change in how the Case Study assignment was graded. As mentioned earlier, any team project is subject to the equity of workload issue. That is, not all members of the team may do an equal amount of the work. In the past, I had given everyone on the team the same grade on the Case Study assignment. But, given that this assignment represented the major part of the course grade, I thought it might be fairer to let learners offer some feedback on whether or not they felt everyone made an equally valuable contribution. So, using the model I had previously used for peer evaluations of team-led discussions, learners were now required to turn in evaluations of each member of their team at the same time that the final (and graded) proposal was due. I used these feedback forms (which I had e-mailed directly to me) to compute individual final grades on this assignment. Each person's grade, therefore, was a combination of both the content grade, which I provided, and the group process—computed from the feedback forms. I felt this approach offered a better opportunity for learners to participate in and take responsibility for the learning experience both for themselves and for their teammates.

To build a bit more flexibility into this second offering of the course, I created an off-site option for the third F2F session. Learners still had to do an individual presentation, but they could choose to do their presentation at a site other than our classroom during that last F2F meeting. The catch was that they had to find someone to not only observe their presentation but also to submit a report to me commenting on the work. I required that learners who were taking this option notify me well in advance so that I could contact the observer to verify that he or she was willing to observe the student and then to report on that observation. A little under a quarter of the learners in this second incarnation took this option. These learners were excused from that last F2F meeting, although they were invited to attend if they wished to do so. Because we had fewer than the full class scheduled to present that day, we all decided to hold class just during the morning segment. So, again, learners had to attend that last F2F for only two and half hours rather than the five hours (plus lunch) scheduled for the other two F2F sessions.

While I did reduce the required F2F contact time by offering the off-site and half-day options, I did add one more assignment. Although one of the purposes of the Individual Presentation was to get some experience in the actual act of F2F teaching, I also wanted to get learners to put some thought into the instructional development process and to do some postinstruction reflection. So I added a short paper in which learners were required to specify the ELOs for their presentation and to comment on whether or not the ELOs were accomplished, how they knew if the ELOs were accomplished (that is, what assessments they used), what they felt went well during the presentation, and what they might improve for the next time. I felt this paper encouraged learners to get into the habit of both carefully developing their instruction ahead of time and reflecting on their experiences after the fact. I led an optional online discussion the last week of the term to give learners the opportunity to share what they felt they had learned from the Individual Presentation experience and anything else they wished to discuss from the entire course. To compensate for this additional assignment, I dropped one of the online discussions. So, learners now were given the opportunity to share their experiences on both the Interview and the Observation Report assignments during the same discussion.

The rest of the course remained the same as the first blended version, and again postcourse evaluations indicated that learners were satisfied with the experience. While many learners in both blended versions expressed the desire to have more F2F sessions, stating that they enjoyed the in-person interactions with their fellow learners and with me, the chance to get immediate feedback as they tried their hands at applying the material during in-class exercises, and the opportunity to watch me model a variety of teaching techniques, they did acknowledge that the blended version provided more options and allowed them to learn about both modes of instruction.

Moving Forward

Although I am firmly committed to the blended instruction idea, I still felt I had a lot to learn about creating the best, most balanced blend. After reflecting on my learners' and my experiences with both blended versions, I still had the feeling that the workload continued to be a bit too heavy. Based on these reflections, I have come up with a few new ideas for the course, which I am testing out in my most current offering of the course:

1. I have dropped the Grading Contract and replaced it with what I am referring to as the Learner's Choice option, which is now worth 15 percent of the grade. Learners choose from four different assignments—the Interview Report, the Observation Report, a Book Report, or a Current Trends in Research Report (a review of journal literature for the past three to five years). Learners are also allowed to select one of two due dates for turning in these reports. Here is my rationale for this new approach. All four options are effective ways to learn more about teaching, but each approaches the topic in different ways. By giving learners a choice between four different types of assignments, I am allowing them to select the type of assignment that most appeals to them and so should increase their interest in the work. The two different due dates also allow learners to have a bit more control over their workload for the term. And the net

result is one less assignment, because they no longer have to do both the Interview and the Observation Report.

2. The second change is a return to the team-led online instruction assignment. Having reduced the number of assignments by using the Learner's Choice options, I could reinstate this valuable learning experience. While we still brainstorm topics for online discussions on day one, I took over leading those discussions. Teams were now tasked with selecting a topic from specific chapters in the textbook and coming up with a way to present that topic online to the rest of the class. Format was entirely up to the team. It could still be an online discussion, but it did not have to be. I also decided that the teams would remain the same for both the case study project and the team-led activities in order to address a recurring complaint from previous classes that being on two different teams for the same class was complicated and confusing. Each case study team was randomly assigned to a week during the term during which they led instruction on their selected topic. The same elements of peer grading and learner feedback surveys using *SurveyMonkey* remained in place for this assignment.

So far these changes seem to be going well. I especially like giving learners the opportunity to develop online instruction without any restrictions on how they will do so. I also am finding the Learners' Choice assignments fascinating. Although each type of report is somewhat different, all the reports are being written in a thoughtful and insightful manner. All these reports have been posted to the course site, allowing learners the opportunity to share in their fellow learners' experiences. The follow-up online discussion of these reports gave everyone the chance to explore what they all had learned about teaching and to compare and contrast their various experiences.

I have also made the last optional online discussion an "Anything Goes" discussion, allowing learners to bring up anything they like from the topics and activities from the entire course. While I generally stay out of online discussions until the very end to avoid dominating the activity, I take a more active role in this discussion both because it is the last one in the term and because it gives me a chance to further interact with the learners about course topics. This final discussion also serves as a capstone or final wrap-up for the course. Although participation in this discussion is optional, everyone has access to the material even if they do not personally add their thoughts to the discussion.

BABY STEPS

This is the story of my journey so far. As you can see, I did not embark on this journey willingly or by choice. The decision to add online elements to my course was the result of an administrative edict. I am not sure when or even if I would have turned to the online format as a way to supplement my F2F offerings without that outside push. But I am very grateful for that push because it forced me to reconsider my course in a very different light.

Furthermore, the more I read about LCT, the more I realized that if I really wanted to be a learner-centered teacher I would need to put my personal preference for F2F instruction aside and offer more format options to my learners. The wonderful thing about the blended delivery mode is that it includes something for everyone. For those of us who come from an F2F background—both as learners and as teachers—it offers the advantage of being able to keep at least some of our preferred F2F contact. And we can ease into the blended approach by moving slowly toward incorporating more and more online material into our courses over time.

I urge you to do what I did—take baby steps. Examine what you teach, whether it is a full-term course or a single one-shot workshop, and look for places where incorporating an online component can not only enrich the instruction but also offer extended contact time and provide learners with more options related to their personal learning style. Do what we do when we want to update our F2F sessions. Add just one new thing at a time. See how that goes. If it works, keep it in. If it doesn't, reflect on why it did not work and see what can be done to improve it for the next time. If you keep trying new things each and every time you teach, you may wake up one day to discover that all those baby steps led you to the creation of a blended class or course.

FINAL REMARKS

The transition from a completely F2F format to a blended one has been challenging and exciting for me. The most difficult aspect was letting go of the F2F components. I love the in-person contact and did not have any previous personal experience with being either a teacher or a learner in an online environment prior to making this transition. But taking the plunge helped me to stretch myself in a variety of ways and pushed me to determine how best to accomplish each of my course's learning outcomes. It also made me put my money where my mouth is in terms of being learner-centered. Not everyone likes to learn (or to teach) in the same way—F2F or online. Nor is either mode the best approach for every topic. So, creating the blend made me reconsider why something should be taught F2F while other things would benefit from the online approach.

I truly believe that the blended format enriched the course. The fact that we meet only three times during the term with the bulk of the course online meant a more flexible and convenient experience for the learners. Those who preferred F2F interactions got a taste of that, while those who might be more reflective and less likely to speak up in an in-person class were given the time to reflect upon topics and have their voices heard during the online components of the class. Requiring the learners to share their documents via the course site also created a richer, more collaborative learning environment. Learners were given the opportunity to benefit by their fellow learners' experiences and were challenged to not only read each other's reports but to discuss and, in the case of the Memo Critique, assess them as well.

The public nature of the online discussions and the fact that these discussions are archived allowed me to monitor learning in a very different way than in a complete F2F setting. F2F discussions move quickly, and it is often difficult for the instructor to keep track of who is contributing and what each person is saying. But online discussions, whether the learners are addressing a specific topic or exchanging ideas about one of the course assignments, are there for me to review and to gain insight into what my learners are getting from all these experiences. And learners are able to profit by more than their own experiences and reports, thus further reinforcing the idea of a shared learning community. The blended format seems to be truly a learner-centered one by offering a variety of opportunities to collaborate, participate, and take responsibility not only for one's own learning but also for that of every member of the community as well.

REFLECTIONS

1. What is holding you back from moving to the blended format? Identify what you feel would be challenging for you. What might some of the barriers be that could potentially stand in your way of moving to the blended format?

2. Now look for resources that would help you overcome these challenges and barriers. Identify people in your environment who could support you as you move into the blended format. Meet with these people and discuss your concerns. Find out exactly what these resource people can do to help you move to the blended format.

3. Try your hand at adding some online components to one of your F2F one-shot workshops. Use something familiar to you. See if you can get your potential learners to fill out an online survey in advance of your meeting with them. Or e-mail them a welcoming message. Ask if you can lead an online discussion on the faculty's course site or just be added to the faculty's own discussions. Participate in those discussions as appropriate. You can also use either the survey or the e-mail approach to get some follow-up information about what learners got out of the instruction. Once you become comfortable with these online elements, look for other ways to supplement your F2F offerings through online components.

4. Do the same thing for your full-term online courses. Because you probably will have access to a CMS for these courses, you will have a menu of options/features from which to choose. If this is your first experience using a CMS, choose something that does not require a big learning curve on your part.

   a. Start by posting your handouts and course materials and using the course site as a means of communicating with your learners. Posting answers to learners' questions on the site means that everyone who has the question will have access to the same answer. If one person has the questions, you can be pretty sure others will have it as well.

   b. The next element to add would be the online discussion forums. Substitute an online discussion for one of your in-class sessions and cancel the F2F meeting. As you get more comfortable in the online mode, you will be able to drop more of the F2F meetings in favor of other types of CMS-supported activities.

   c. You can meet with your learners in real time via chat or video conferencing software. You can create online mini-lectures with video and/or screencasting that you post on your site as resource material for your learners. And, of course, you can add links to pertinent and reputable online material available locally and/or beyond the confines of your own institution. Keep experimenting with different types of online components and various features of your CMS with the goal of moving more and more into the blended mode of delivery.

EXPLORATIONS

Anderson, Karen, and Frances A. May. 2010. "Does the Method of Instruction Matter? An Experimental Examination of Information Literacy Instruction in the Online, Blended, and Face-to-Face Classrooms." *Journal of Academic Librarianship* 36, no. 6: 495–500.

> This article addresses the topic of mode of delivery as it relates to ILI and includes an excellent literature review. Interestingly, the results of this study indicate that the method of instruction did not influence students' retention of information literacy skills.

Bell, Steven J., and John D. Shank. 2011. *Blended Librarian.* http://blended librarian.org/.

> Created by Steven Bell and John D. Shank, the originators of the term "blended librarian," this website is designed to provide basic information about blended librarianship and to provide information about the Blended Librarians Online Learning Community. It is a great way to find out more

about this topic and offers a variety of resources to help you become more familiar with the ideas underlying being a blended librarian.

Chernish, William N., Agnes L. DeFranco, James R. Linder, and Kim E. Dooley. 2009. "Does It Matter? Analyzing the Results of Three Different Learning Delivery Methods." In *The Perfect Online Course*, edited by Anymir Orellana, Terry Hudgins, and Michael Simonson, 23–35. Charlotte, NC: Information Age Publishing.

> This is a comprehensive examination of the advantages and drawbacks of a variety of instructional delivery methods.

Georgouli, Katerina, Ilias Skalkidis, and Pedro Guerreiro. 2008. "A Framework for Adopting LMS to Introduce E-learning in a Traditional Course." *Educational Technology and Society* 11, no. 2: 227–240.

> This is an excellent resource for turning the traditional F2F class into a blended one. It identifies the steps to take as you make the transition and offers tips and hints on how to slowly move toward your goal of truly blended instruction.

Ko, Susan, and Steve Rossen. 2010. *Teaching Online: A Practical Guide.* 3rd ed. New York: Routledge.

> Chapter 13 of this book concentrates on teaching in web-enhanced and blended formats. It offers excellent, practical advice about how to avoid pitfalls and increase the effectiveness of these delivery modes.

Shank, John D., and Steven J. Bell. 2007. "Librarianship and Technology and Instructional Design = Blended Librarian." In *Information Tomorrow: Reflections on Technology and the Future of Public and Academic Libraries*, edited by Rachel S. Gordon, 173–191. Medford, NJ: Information Today.

> This article ties the concepts of instructional design, technology, and librarianship together in an accessible and readable fashion. It emphasizes what we need to know about all three fields if we are to remain relevant in today's instructional world.

REFERENCES

Bliuc, Ana Maria, Peter Goodyear, and Robert A. Ellis. 2007. "Research Focus and Methodological Choices in Studies into Students' Experiences of Blended Learning in Higher Education." *Internet and Higher Education* 10, no. 4: 231–244.

Bodie, Graham D., William G. Powers, and Margaret Fitch-Hauser. 2006. "Chunking, Priming, and Active Learning: Toward an Innovative and Blended Approach to Teaching Communication-Related Skills." *Interactive Learning Environments* 14, no. 2: 119–135.

Boyer, Naomi R. 2009. "The Learning Contract Process: Scaffolding for Building Social, Self-Directed Learning." In *The Perfect Online Course*, edited by Anymir Orellana,

Terry Hudgins, and Michael Simonson, 401–422. Charlotte, NC: Information Age Publishing.

Brookfield, Stephen D. 1990. *The Skillful Teacher: On Technique, Trust and Responsiveness in the Classroom.* San Francisco: Jossey-Bass.

Brookfield, Stephen. 1995. *Becoming a Critically Reflective Teacher.* 1st ed. The Jossey-Bass Higher & Adult Education Series. San Francisco: Jossey-Bass.

Dalsgaard, Christian, and Mikkel Godsk. 2007. "Transforming Traditional Lectures into Problem-Based Blended Learning: Challenges and Experiences." *Journal of Open and Distance Learning* 22, no. 1: 29–42.

Donnelly, Roisin. 2006. "Blended Problem-Based Learning for Teacher Education: Lessons Learned." *Learning, Media and Technology* 31, no. 2: 93–116.

El Mansour, Bassou, and Davison M. Munpinga. 2007. "Students' Positive and Negative Experiences in Hybrid and Online Classes." *College Student Journal* 41, no. 1: 242–248.

Georgouli, Katerina, Ilias Skalkidis, and Pedro Guerreiro. 2008. "A Framework for Adopting LMS to Introduce E-learning in a Traditional Course." *Educational Technology and Society* 11, no. 2: 227–240.

Goode, Sigi, Robert A. Willis, James R. Wolf, and Albert L. Harris. 2007. "Enhancing IS Education with Flexible Technology and Learning." *Journal of Information Studies Education* 18, no. 3: 297–302.

Graham, Charles R. 2006. "Blended Learning Systems: Definition, Current Trends, and Future Directions." In *Handbook of Blended Learning: Global Perspectives, Local Designs*, edited by Curtis J. Bonk and Charles R. Graham, 3–21. San Francisco: Pfeiffer.

Ko, Susan, and Steve Rossen. 2010. *Teaching Online: A Practical Guide.* 3rd ed. New York: Routledge.

MacDonald, Janet. 2006. *Blended Learning and Online Tutoring: A Good Practice Guide.* Burlington, VT: Gower.

Moodle Corporation. 2011. "About Moodle." Moodle. Last modified August 8. http:// docs.moodle.org/en/About_Moodle.

Palloff, Rena M., and Keith Pratt. 2007. *Building Online Learning Communities: Effective Strategies for the Virtual Classroom.* 2nd ed. San Francisco: Jossey-Bass.

Rovai, Alfred P., and Hope M. Jordan. 2004. "Blended Learning and Sense of Community: A Comparative Analysis with Traditional and Fully Online Graduate Courses." *International Review of Research in Open and Distance Learning* 5, no. 2: 1–13.

Sorensen, Christine K., and Danio M. Baylen. 2009. "Learning Online: Adapting the Seven Principles of Good Practice to a Web-Based Instructional Environment." In *The Perfect Online Course*, edited by Anymir Orellana, Terry Hudgins, and Michael Simonson, 60–86. Charlotte, NC: Information Age Publishing.

Young, Jeffrey R. 2002. "Hybrid Teaching Seeks to End the Divide Between Traditional and Online Instruction." *Chronicle of Higher Education* 48, no. 28: 33.

Chapter 9

Learner-Centered Teaching in Action—Vignettes from the Field

Tell me and I will forget, show me and I may not remember, involve me and I will understand.

—Native American proverb

Having explored the various aspects of learner-centered teaching (LCT) presented in this book, you may be thinking, "This is a great idea, but I am not sure I can actually do it." You might be a little fearful of the apparent chaotic nature of LCT and are worried about turning control of the session over to your learners. And you could have reservations about how time-consuming active, participatory techniques seem to be. In this chapter a number of frontline, practicing information literacy librarians will illustrate how LCT can and is being done in information literacy instruction (ILI).

I want to express my deep, heartfelt gratitude to these wonderful people who were so generous with their ideas and so devoted to the LCT cause that they wanted to share their experiences with you. These professionals have dedicated themselves to transforming their ILI into experiences that turn their learners from passive recipients into active participants. All of them express the notion that teaching in a learner-centered fashion is worth the effort because it results in more engaging and effective instruction that learners can apply to new situations. In other words, these learner-centered instructors work hard to create the type of instruction that helps the people with whom they work become effective and confident lifelong learners.

The contributors to this chapter come from a wide variety of library settings. Some vignettes describe ILI for very young children. Two of the vignettes are set in the public library settings, while others describe ILI in a variety of academic settings—from community colleges to universities. Next comes a set of vignettes from librarians who work with a very specialized set of learners—those who are involved in the fashion, graphics, interior design, and entertainment industries; medicine; or pharmacy. The chapter closes with a vignette that illustrates what can happen when librarians reach out to learners who are not necessarily part of their institution's primary audience.

While you may not find a vignette that matches up exactly with your own institutional setting, I am sure that the ideas will resonate with you anyway. So read these vignettes (presented in the contributors' own voices) with an eye toward how you might adapt them for use with your own learners. After all, the information literacy principles being highlighted should be applicable in any library setting. One of the most inspiring ideas I ever encountered was Virginia Rankin's work on teaching critical thinking to middle school students (Rankin, 1988). I completely changed my approach to teaching after listening to her present her ideas at an ALA conference and then reading her published material back in the late 1980s. You never really know when something you encounter will inspire you. So, sit back, put your feet up, and enjoy the following examples of LCT in the real world of ILI.

FROM THE SCHOOL LIBRARY PERSPECTIVE

Vignette 1: Starting Them Young

Contributor: Christa Harker, Librarian, James Bowie Elementary (Richardson ISD, Texas).

Type of institution: K–6 public elementary school.

Instructional situation and audience: First-grade students. Teacher/librarian collaborative research project conducted in the library. Project integrates science curriculum, problem-solving skills, and information literacy skills.

Overall instructional goal of session: Through research of a variety of animals, students discover patterns in nature that lead toward conclusions about form and function in an animal's structure; for example, how an animal moves is related to its body shape, number of legs, whether it has wings, and so forth.

Expected learning outcome for learner-centered example being described: Students will be able to use discovered patterns in form and function of animals to create their own original, made-up animal that would "make sense" in nature; for example, its body type would help dictate how the original animal would be able to move.

Learner-centered example: Students each research a different animal, paying special attention to its body shape, legs, wings, mouth shape, teeth, food, and so forth. They compile their information on a large class chart. In a teacher-led discussion, they begin to determine certain patterns in nature related to form and function. Typically, the students discover many patterns. In a discussion about movement and body shape, students determine such patterns as:

- Animals must have wings to fly, but not all animals with wings can fly.
- Animals with no legs usually move by slithering or swimming.
- Animals with legs usually are able to move by running and/or walking.
- Many animals with larger back legs and very small front legs are good at jumping and hopping.

Students take these patterns and use them to create new, original animals. Their new animals must follow the discovered patterns in order to "make sense" in nature. Using the example described, the students decide the form and shape of their new animal and determine how their new animal will move.

Reasons for choosing this learner-centered approach for your teaching: First-grade students are highly motivated and curious, and they especially enjoy the opportunity to create something new. This project allows them to take many research skills they have learned throughout the year (note taking, online database usage, nonfiction book usage) and combine those skills into a new product while using higher-level thinking and problem-solving skills.

Joan's musings: *Many people question whether young children are capable of learning information literacy skills. This vignette shows that if we match the material to the age level of our audience, we can create an effective ILI session that will get even children as young as first-grade students started on the road to becoming lifelong learners.*

Vignette 2: Appealing to All Their Senses

Note: *This work was developed while Ms. Hartford was a student in my UCLA ILI course in 2010.*

Contributor: Stevie Lemons Hartford, expected Master's in Library and Information Studies June 2011, University of California–Los Angeles. Intention is to become a school librarian in a K–5 setting.

Type of institution: Developed for a school library setting.

Instructional situation and audience: This lesson is intended for third-grade learners during one 30-minute library class visit. The chief component, the rehearsal of a song, would be introduced in this instructional session and practiced during each subsequent library visit for a couple of weeks.

Overall instructional goal of session: The goal of this information literacy lesson is for third-grade students to understand the nonfiction organization in school libraries using the Dewey Decimal System and to apply these categories to their reading interests and to the layout of the physical space.

Expected learning outcome for learner-centered example being described:

1. Learners will be able to sing along with a recorded song that attributes nonfiction classification to Melvil Dewey and highlights topics that can be found in each hundred's block.

2. Learners will be able to stand beside the nonfiction shelving section that matches their reading interests.

Learner-centered example: This lesson uses an original "Dewey Decimal Song" written by myself and recorded and produced by my husband, Corey Hartford. The song can be found at http://www.LemonsWedge.com/DeweySong. Prior to instruction, learners should have been taught the difference between fiction and nonfiction as well as the basic layout of the library. Before beginning, pre-teaching challenging words and vocabulary must occur. Provide a copy of the lyrics to every student, and display it on a projector. Encourage children to identify tough words and collaboratively arrive at meanings while you facilitate.

One of the strengths of this lesson is its differentiation for various learning styles. Ask students who are auditory learners to close their eyes and listen to the song. Kinesthetic learners should trace each hundred's number with their finger on their desk as it is sung. A slide show containing visual images representing the categories for visual learners is presented on the projector in time with the sound recording. This song is a difficult sing-along because it is not set to a familiar tune; however, this keeps it from being too "kiddie." This song will still appeal to fourth and fifth graders as you revisit the Dewey Decimal System each year as part of a spiraling information literacy curriculum. Because of the song's complexity, allow students to join in singing as they feel comfortable and plan to conduct a sing-along for multiple library visits in a row. Keep each new session fresh with changes, such as pointing to the shelving area at the correct point in the song, ladies versus gents verses, or singing in funny voices.

These are the song's lyrics (for music and visuals, visit http://www.Lemons Wedge.com/DeweySong):

Well, there was a man who wrangled books
Gave chaos and mayhem dirty looks
He grouped by subject on his shelves
So people could find books for themselves
And his name . . . (ah ha!)
His name was Melvil Dewey. (Dewey!)

Yeah, his system is still in use today
Dewey Decimal numbers will lead the way
All minds that are alert and keen
Can learn what the numbers mean

All thanks... (Thanks to whom?)
Thanks to Melvil Dewey. (Dewey!)

Well, in the **000s** you'll find generalities:
Computers, encyclopedias, and abnormalities.
And the 100s are about your thoughts and feelings.
Philosophy, psychology, and ghosts are its dealings.

While **200s** cover Greek and Roman mythology,
The world's religions and its surrounding theology.
While the **300s** include the social sciences,
Holidays, careers, and yes those government alliances.

400s have languages, and dictionaries for specifics,
Also Spanish, sign language, and Egyptian hieroglyphics.
And Science is in **500s** along with math,
Experiments, astronomy, and nature's wrath.

Well **600s** is for your science that's applied,
Inventions, and cooking, and buildings side by side
700s contain the arts,
With your crafts, your games, and your music as parts.

Well **800s** offer jokes, poetry, and plays,
All supporting a literature craze.
900s contain history and geography,
Events of the world and its topography.

By hundred groups the books were sorted
Nonfiction searching was better supported
The Dewey Decimal System spread like wild fire
All the librarians could not help but admire
And to the rock star, lift a lighter
For his name... was Melvil Dewey. (Dewey!)

Visual on-the-spot assessment will inform your pacing. If students are struggling with the lyrics, split the students into small groups to help each other. When this first outcome has been met and all students have at least heard the Dewey Decimal Song more than once and attempted to read it aloud or sing it, it is time for the second stage of the lesson.

On their printed lyrics sheet, students will write numbers 1, 2, and 3 beside the book categories that most interest them. Together the class and librarian will review the locations of the various hundreds' blocks within the library. Students will relate their preference selections to the physical locations within the library. In a calm and orderly manner, students will stand up and walk to the shelves representing their third, second, and first favorite types of non-fiction books. This active learning activity provides you with feedback about student understanding of various subjects being shelved together in different locations and provides them with real-world practice for their next library check-out visit.

Reasons for choosing this learner-centered approach for your teaching: I believe in both learner-centered teaching and active learning, because the students interact with the material more deeply. A Dewey Decimal lesson could consist of the librarian droning on with little interaction among learners. It would certainly take less time to plan, but what would the students take away? They would think of information literacy as boring and groan about going to the library. This song presents a challenge and will get stuck in their heads. I would not be a bit surprised to hear it outside the library during carpool. Hopefully, the students will leave with a better understanding of library organization and an increased fondness for library instructional sessions.

Joan's musings: *This very creative approach reinforces the idea that people of all ages can be reached with our ILI and adds the idea of trying to appeal to a variety of learning styles as well. The "sing-along" aspect makes the instruction both interactive and fun. Who says ILI has to be dull and boring?*

FROM THE PUBLIC LIBRARY PERSPECTIVE

Vignette 3: Getting Them Involved

Contributor: Jerry Dear, Librarian/Information Strategist, San Francisco Public Library, Main Branch, Magazines & Newspapers Center.

Type of institution: Public library.

Instructional situation and audience: "Power Googling: Searching Smarter and Faster," a 1.5-hour workshop, introduces some advanced search features of the Google search engine. Through a combination of PowerPoint slides, live web demonstrations, interactive discussions, and a short practice exercise, participants learn how to use Google more effectively and efficiently. Learners comprise a heterogenous group of individuals—mainly adults ranging from college level students to senior citizens. In this setup, only the instructor has access to a computer, while the audience follows along on a projector screen.

Overall instructional goal of session: This "Power Googling" workshop enables learners to familiarize themselves with specialized features of the Google search engine beyond the basic search box. They learn to utilize advanced search strategies to construct more precise search statements, generate relevant search results, and thus search smarter and faster.

Expected learning outcome for learner-centered example being described: After instruction participants will be able to:

- Navigate Google menus to find specialized search features.
- Identify how to access Google's advanced search screens.
- Construct search statements by using Google operators and advanced search strategies.
- Interpret search results after applying Google operators.
- Customize search results to suit particular information needs.

Learner-centered example: Teaching the average web surfer how to search for information with Google can be a challenging task, given that most people already presume they know how to "Google" practically any topic. Hence, in my "Power Googling" workshop, I aim to teach public library users how to access advanced and often hidden features in this popular search engine to maximize their web researching experience.

Audience members range from college students to savvy web searchers and senior citizens, so I often start by asking how many of them use Google. Not surprisingly, nearly 90 percent of the learners respond affirmatively, so I then inform them that my workshop focuses on using advanced search techniques beyond merely entering random keywords into a search box. Next, I present the agenda and begin with a couple of questions: What is a URL? What is an operator? By introducing these technical terms from the outset, I encourage the audience to define in their own words the terminology that will be used throughout the workshop. As a warm-up exercise, I pull up the Google search engine and ask the audience if they already use the advanced search screen. This question yields fewer responses, at which point I ask if someone can demonstrate how to access this screen. My underlining goals thus center on establishing a focused agenda, defining technical jargon, and guiding the audience to navigate Google's various menus and search screens.

As the lesson continues, I highlight screenshots of Google search statements accompanied by actual search results and from there invite the audience to guess what might be happening. For instance, I might enter **allintitle:"san francisco earthquake" filetype:ppt** into the search box, but, instead of explaining how special operators like **allintitle** and **filetype** affect the search results, I challenge the audience to discover these functions independently. From the screenshots, they eventually conclude that the phrase "San Francisco earthquake" appears in the titles of webpages within PowerPoint presentations. Throughout this continuous lecture/demonstration/question/discussion technique, the audience members share a collective learning experience.

Midway into the lecture/demonstration, I switch gears and pass out a practice exercise in which the audience members formulate their own search statements. Collaboration is encouraged, and, after a few minutes, I activate the advanced search screen and ask them to tell me which search boxes and drop-down menus to fill out. Using this mini-activity as a springboard, I then demonstrate how Google's advanced search screen enables them to construct complex search statements. In the remaining time, I introduce additional Google operators designed to retrieve ready-reference information, such as finding stock quotes, applying measurement conversions, performing mathematical calculations, and finding similar websites.

Overall, throughout this workshop, I employ an inductive approach to showcase the inner workings of Google's search mechanism, run targeted searches, and invite the audience to share their observations and, from this exchange, identify unique search strategies. Instead of lecturing for an hour, I use slides to dialogue with the audience, experiment with examples gathered from their input, and clarify lingering questions. Most important, employing a variety of lecture/demonstrations punctuated by questions and discussions reinforces understanding and retention, thereby solidifying the collective learning experience.

Reasons for choosing this learner-centered approach for your teaching: When teaching my "Power Googling" workshop, especially in a setting where learners lack computers, I strive to hold their attention, given that the workshop runs for over an hour. LCT engages the audience and piques their curiosity and interest, so I aim to keep them motivated and focused at every stage of the lesson. In the process of asking questions and dialoguing with them, I am better equipped to foster an interactive discussion, thereby transforming what might be a dry, passive lecture into a stimulating and more meaningful, active learning experience.

Joan's musings: *This is a great example of how we can use learner-centered techniques to get our learners involved even if we aren't set up for hands-on practice with actual computers. Incorporating lively question-and-answer exchanges and giving learners the chance to try and figure some things out for themselves get the learners involved and thinking. Plus allowing them to "discover" some of the content on their own helps them develop metacognitive abilities and transferrable skills. These learners have not only learned the content of this workshop, they also have learned what to do when they encounter new resources in the future.*

Vignette 4: Going with the Flow

Contributor: James Sherman, Librarian II, Los Angeles Public Library (LAPL).

Type of institution: Public library.

Instructional situation and audience: Adult computer comfort classes, seven students on a Saturday afternoon.

Overall instructional goal of session: Getting an e-mail account and learning how to use it.

Expected learning outcome for learner-centered example being described: After instruction, learners will be able to:

1. Create an e-mail account.
2. Send e-mail messages.
3. Check their messages.
4. Reply to messages.

Learner-centered example: In 2006, I started a series of adult-level computer classes at the Mark Twain Branch in South Los Angeles. As a guide, I used LAPL's training scripts. These scripts are designed to help trainers introduce the patron to concepts and skills and then are paced to allow the patrons to try the concepts and skills themselves, with the encouragement of the instructor. Given the short time frame of the class and the amount of material to be covered in order for the class to be worthwhile, this approach was always a challenge.

My anecdote concerns one class in particular, which was focused on getting an e-mail account. When the patrons showed up, it soon became apparent that the incredible variety of abilities made the challenging model less tenable. Some already had an e-mail account and wanted to learn about more advanced topics, such as how to deal with spam, while others had never used a mouse before. I had to diverge precipitously from the script and encouraged patrons with more experience to help those with less experience, as I went to each person to answer specific questions. I had been interested in peer-to-peer ILI in library school; I just had no idea that I would first use it on the fly.

This improvisation allowed me to address what the particular student wanted the most help with. In turn for the help that the highly skilled patrons provided their peers, I promised more specialized, one-on-one help later, after the workshop. I offered this either immediately afterward in one case, or later, even at slow times at the reference desk. At that time, I focused on what *they* wanted to do. While these improvisations were unofficial, they had at least the possibility of being flexible to the patron needs. Most of the real work, though, happened one on one, outside of the planned time frame of the class.

Although there was no evaluation of this class, it was apparent that this was not completely successful because not every patron wanted to help their fellow patron. There was one participant in particular (out of seven who took the class) who left in a dissatisfied mood, angry that the class was a waste of her time. She wanted to learn, not teach, she said, which reminded me that the only time I feel like I really understand things is when I teach. To be fair, the patron never signed up to teach. However, the other patrons seemed to have little trouble with this, and in some sense the informality was helpful in establishing rapport. It should be noted that, for the patrons who had little to no experience, a quick introduction to the mouse does not make for a competent mouse user.

Finally, regarding a peer-to-peer model in a public library setting, a certain level of attentiveness would be required, as there are no restrictions on who can enter the library and take the class.

Reasons for choosing this learner-centered approach for your teaching: Although this was an improvisation born of necessity, it did lead me to consider a pitfall in the traditional instruction method (teacher/pupil) that enforces the idea of the librarian as know-it-all helping the supplicant. Being a facilitator in a peer-to-peer situation can create a more flexible learning environment in both the instructional setting and the library as a whole, in which patrons ultimately feel more comfortable about continuing to learn.

Joan's musings: *This is a great example of flexibility and responding to our learners' needs even when they turn out to be different from what we had expected. While it is always tempting to just go with what has been prepared, responsive, learner-centered teachers have the courage to throw out their original plan when faced with the fact that it is not going to work with the particular group they are facing. As can be seen from this vignette, not all learners are happy with a more learner-centered approach. But they may find, when thinking back on their experience, that teaching someone else actually helped them refine their own skills. Teaching should not be a popularity contest. We do what we think is best for the circumstances with which we are presented. While our learners may not completely understand the approach we are taking, our job is to create the best learning environment we can. Using a learner-centered approach often means taking chances, making on-the-spot adjustments, and being flexible and responsive to the needs of our learners—with the end goal of learning in mind.*

FROM THE ACADEMIC LIBRARY PERSPECTIVE—PART ONE: COMMUNITY COLLEGES

Vignette 5: Reflecting on Doing Research

Contributors: April Cunningham, Library Instruction Coordinator, Saddleback College, Mission Viejo, California; and Allison Carr, Social Sciences Librarian, California State University San Marcos.

Type of institution: The following instruction has been offered both at a two-year public community college and a four-year public university.

Instructional situation and audience: Saddleback College is a suburban community college in Orange County, California. The librarians teach a series of eight workshops that we repeat throughout the semester. Tailored orientations are conducted when professors request more focused instruction after students have attended workshops. The library's credit courses have been included in learning communities and the honors program and they are among the classes that fulfill the information competency general education requirement.

California State University San Marcos (CSUSM) is a public university with almost 10,000 students. CSUSM is primarily an undergraduate, commuter campus, with a few master's programs. Information literacy is integrated throughout the lower and upper division curriculum, in the general education program and major courses. Additionally, the librarians participate in a two-week research module in the first-year experience course, General Education Lifelong Learning, during which students learn the basics of college research, including the research process.

Overall instructional goal of session: Students learn about Carol Kuhlthau's Information Search Process (Kuhlthau, 1993) (renamed Research Process in our example) to use as a framework for college-level research. This framework puts academic research into a context they can easily understand and use to complete each of their college research assignments.

Expected learning outcome for learner-centered example being described: Students will be able to:

1. Describe how research is a cognitive and affective process, not merely information retrieval.
2. Summarize the difference between an appropriate research process in high school and in college.
3. Reflect on and revise their own research process based on the new model they've learned.

Learner-centered example: Kuhlthau's Information Search Process is versatile enough to use in many different instructional situations, including reference, multisession orientations, and research assignments in our own credit courses. This example focuses on introducing the model and represents the most common way that we incorporate it into one-shot workshops and orientations.

We use Kuhlthau's model of the research process for a few reasons. Students appreciate that the model is not our idealized version of how research has to be done, but, instead, it is based on high school and college students' own descriptions of how they approached research. The model also acknowledges the common feelings that students are likely to experience at each stage. To prepare students to consider the research process as something more than a Google search, the librarian asks students to think about research papers they have had and how they felt when they realized that the paper required outside research. Students uniformly report that they have never been taught a research process before, and most consider their own research process messy and somewhat out of control. By talking about the feelings (which are often negative) that accompany the early stages of research, the librarian validates students' experiences, and students can put their feelings in context. The connection of tasks with feelings and emotions keeps this model descriptive rather than proscriptive, inviting students to look for similarities and differences between their own experiences and the experiences described in the model.

When taught in freshman courses, we also use the model to invite students to discuss the differences between research in high school and research in college. Through our work with students as well as composition instructors, we have found that the biggest difference between high school and college research is how the topic is chosen. In high school writing, students are expected to answer a question that their teacher thinks is important. In order to do this, students form the habit of reading to find the right answer. In contrast, we offer students our definition of college-level research in which the goal is to create a good question and support it with appropriate evidence. Once a student has identified her research question, then she can start her focused research, but until then the reading and research she is doing can all be considered part of the search for an interesting question. This can also help the students begin to understand the difference between the reporting they did in their papers in high school and the analysis they are asked to do in college.

Understanding the structure and purposes of the research they are being asked to do empowers students to make decisions that match their values and goals. When the research process is treated, instead, as something that students are expected to pick up through trial and error, students may make decisions out of desperation, frustration, or misunderstanding. By having an explicit model against which to compare their experiences and assumptions, students can use the distinction between assignments asking for reporting or analysis when they are trying to interpret their professors' instructions. They can also decide to use different reading strategies when they are in the question-posing or question-answering phases of their research. Additionally, students can make informed decisions about the types of sources to use at each stage of the process.

In multisession orientations or credit courses in information literacy, we can observe students applying the principles throughout the research process when they mine background sources for research questions and access a variety of sources for evidence to answer the question they have posed. In brief interventions, like the one shot, we observe the early stages of new understanding and self-awareness by making space for students to critique the model. Questions about what the model may be missing, when it might make sense to approach research in a different way, and whether or not the model is still valid in the age of the Internet spur conversations among students. By using a brief assessment tool, such as a One-Minute Paper or "3-2-1" assessment, we gather students' initial reactions to the model and ask how they might use the model for future research assignments. Many students react positively, expressing interest in this new framework, which can help them succeed in their college research assignments.

For more information and materials, please visit http://public.csusm.edu/acarr/scilworks/.

Reasons for choosing this learner-centered approach for your teaching: Metacognition is essential to solving ill-structured problems, like research assignments, where students are posing their own questions and therefore have to create their own parameters for defining the problem and its appropriate solutions. Students can be taught to become aware of and strengthen their metacognition when they critique models of the task they are trying to accomplish. Modeling is particularly important for a complex process without one right answer, like college research, because an effective model communicates to the learner what standards she can set for her performance and how she will know if she is meeting her goals.

Joan's musings: *According to the American Library Association, an information-literate person is someone who has learned how to learn. This vignette offers an example of how to incorporate "thinking about thinking" or metacognition into an ILI endeavor. Not only do learners gain some experience in looking for information, they are also encouraged to reflect on how they feel about doing research. They learn that others share many of the negative feelings they are experiencing. Furthermore, learners are given the opportunity to think about the research process itself. As a result, learners gain valuable insight into their own research process—insights that can help them in their future information-seeking endeavors.*

Vignette 6: Making It Fun

Contributor: Cinthya Ippoliti, Library Division Chair, Paradise Valley Community College, Phoenix, Arizona.

Type of institution: Community college.

Instructional situation and audience: This session typically takes place with undergraduate students who have to write an argumentative research paper on a variety of self-selected topics as part of an introductory English course.

Overall instructional goal of session: The goal of the session is to get students started in structuring their argument, breaking down their topic into keywords, and searching our databases for scholarly resources.

Expected learning outcome for learner-centered example being described: At the end of this class, students will be able to:

1. Break down a topic into specific concepts and keywords.
2. Create effective search queries.
3. Select the appropriate resources needed to complete the research.

Learner-centered example: First, I would like to discuss the larger context in which this session fits in order to explain the rationale behind our methodology, which will also reflect the learning-centered practices we employ. We've adapted what we're calling an ILab model whereby students take a pretest at the beginning of our time with them to gauge their knowledge in the three main areas of information literacy competency (determining an information need, accessing information effectively, evaluating quality of information). We then see the students for at least two sessions during which we tailor our activities to meet the areas of need that the pretest indicated. I will be describing one of these sessions in more detail. Between sessions, students fill out a variety of handouts based on the course content and assignment that allow us to provide individualized feedback. We end by administering a posttest to determine the increase of proficiency in the areas covered. This model has worked very well, and the comments from our students have been overwhelmingly positive—they feel better prepared to tackle research assignments, more confident in their abilities to use scholarly resources, and believe the time was well spent and did not detract from the other competencies in the course. In addition, test scores have gone up an average of 20 percent across each semester.

Building on the general trends we've examined across the three years we've been working with this model, students consistently have problems in two areas:

1. effectively understanding and using Boolean operators to create search queries; and

2. being able to distinguish between credible, quality resources and those of less quality, especially on the Internet.

We've therefore focused our instruction to tackle these two outcomes. Following is a description of the first session designed to assist students in identifying keywords and crafting effective search queries.

Students are asked to come to class with some possible topic ideas. I typically begin the session by asking how many students have a topic in mind. From those who raise their hand, I ask someone to volunteer their idea, and I write that broad subject on the board to increase immediate buy-in to the research process. I've found that students are more likely to be engaged if it's their topic or their friends' topic being discussed. I ask the entire class to brainstorm together what possible arguments can be made from the initial idea and write them on the board. So, for example, if the student says something like the economy, we might end up breaking up that broad subject into things like jobs, housing, health care, and so forth. I then ask students to form small groups and write on giant Post-it notes what their specific research question might be based on our shared topic. A potential research question might be:

> Should the government bail out homeowners who can afford to pay
> their mortgages but whose homes have lost a large amount of value?

I walk around as each group discusses its question and offer suggestions. At the end of the allotted time, I have students post their questions around the room for all to see, and we have another quick discussion.

I then return to the board and briefly explain how to break up their research question into keywords and apply Boolean operators. But because we know students have a difficult time with this aspect of doing research, I have each person write one of the keywords on an 8 × 11–inch card. I also pre-make cards with Quotes (to represent phrase searching), AND, and OR. I tell each student to stand up, find a partner with another keyword and a Boolean card, create a physical search string, and then write the search string on the board. This part of the session almost always results in lively discussion and laughter as students move around the room and discover the wide variety of possible combinations. We then analyze the search strings they created, and I offer additional suggestions for improving them. (This portion of the session is based on an activity designed by PVCC library faculty Kandice Mickelsen).

As a final step, I demonstrate how to apply the string they just created in searching the databases. This is followed by hands-on time with their *own* topic as they fill out the handout that they will turn in to me for additional feedback. Figure 9.1 (p. 216) shows a snippet of this handout.

Reasons for choosing this learner-centered approach for your teaching:

1. Everyone learns differently. Kinesthetic learners like moving around, visual learners enjoy the cards, and those who are more linear thinkers feel the handout keeps them organized.

2. Assessment is built in. From our pre- and posttests to the qualitative feedback each student gets, we have a pretty good idea of what we should focus on, and we can assist each person in finding information.

3. We can scaffold the learning process. Instead of throwing all of these concepts at students in one (usually insufficient) session and hope something sticks, we pause at key points to reinforce and build on the previous session's concepts, raising the odds that students will understand the information and be able to apply it in the future.

Joan's musings: *Nothing bores learners more than being made to sit through something they already know. This vignette illustrates the importance of doing some kind of preliminary needs assessment so that instruction can be tailored to learners' specific needs. Customizing instruction in this way illustrates the learner-centered nature of our teaching by demonstrating our desire to make the instruction relevant to our learners. Furthermore, incorporating a more "physical" way to learn about Boolean operators adds to the liveliness and fun of the session. I doubt if anyone falls asleep during this session!*

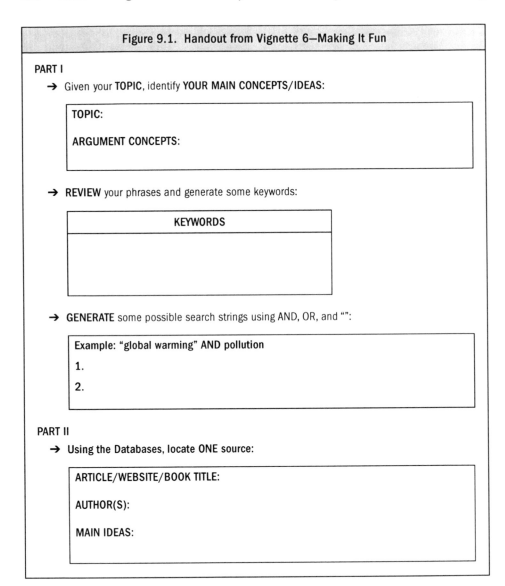

Figure 9.1. Handout from Vignette 6—Making It Fun

PART I
→ Given your **TOPIC**, identify **YOUR MAIN CONCEPTS/IDEAS**:

> TOPIC:
>
> ARGUMENT CONCEPTS:

→ **REVIEW** your phrases and generate some keywords:

> KEYWORDS

→ **GENERATE** some possible search strings using AND, OR, and "":

> Example: "global warming" AND pollution
> 1.
> 2.

PART II
→ Using the Databases, locate ONE source:

> ARTICLE/WEBSITE/BOOK TITLE:
>
> AUTHOR(S):
>
> MAIN IDEAS:

FROM THE ACADEMIC LIBRARY PERSPECTIVE—PART TWO: COLLEGES AND UNIVERSITIES

Vignette 7: On-the-Spot Needs Assessments

Contributor: Jacqui Grallo, Reference and Instructional Technology Librarian, California State University Monterey Bay (CSUMB).

Type of institution: University.

Instructional situation and audience: I will discuss a two-hour (one-shot) ILI session with upper-division undergraduate students in HCOM 389, Otter Realm Workshop. HCOM stands for "Human Communication," a highly interdisciplinary major at CSUMB, and *The Otter Realm* is the student newspaper. The students work on feature news stories and are asked to synthesize primary sources and information that lends their stories local significance. Most students have participated in one or more instruction sessions focused on the more typical applications of information literacy (e.g., research papers and presentations) but have limited experience using library resources to support journalistic endeavors.

Overall instructional goal of session: The goal is for each student, with support from *The Otter Realm* advisor and editor-in-chief, the librarian, and the online course guide, to actively explore library and Internet resources and to find human, print, and online sources to support original, locally oriented reporting.

Expected learning outcome for learner-centered example being described: Students will be able to find, for their next feature story, at least one of each of the following:

1. a credible, authoritative human source to interview;
2. a quote or paraphrase to be properly attributed from a print or online primary source; and
3. a fact or statistic that gives the story local significance.

Learner-centered example: A key learning outcome of HCOM 389, Otter Realm Workshop, is a well-developed ability to carry out research in the manner of a journalist or investigative reporter. Students are challenged to identify and pursue a unique angle on their topic of interest, often from a local perspective.

A planning meeting with the faculty advisor for *The Otter Realm* revealed reluctance on the part of student reporters to seek out primary sources (other than their peers) to create a truly original story. So, the advisor and I decided to focus the instruction session on using the web to identify credible, authoritative human sources to interview and on using library resources and the web to find facts and statistics to give a story local significance. The ultimate goal was for students to develop a sense of how to make a unique contribution to *The Otter Realm* readers' understanding of a given issue as opposed to simply re-reporting what is already in the news. As every librarian knows, understanding the nature of primary sources is a challenge for many undergraduate students. Students writing for *The Otter Realm* must not only understand primary sources but also be able to find, evaluate, and integrate them.

To point students to examples of appropriate resources for researching news stories, I created an online research guide using the open source research guides tool Library a la Carte (LALC). Most of the tabbed sections of the guide contained links to resources with which students could actively engage during the session, but two sections were designed to elicit information from the students. A few days before the session, the advisor and I sent the students a link to the guide and asked them to use the comments module (similar to the comments feature of popular blogging software) on the first section of the guide to post in their own words the topic of the feature story they were working on. This allowed me to design a preassessment tool comprising questions based on students' actual work. The idea here was for students to have an authentic problem-solving experience with a real reward rather than simply going through the motions of a hypothetical, contrived exercise. The purpose of the preassessment was to evaluate students' comprehension of the concept of primary and secondary sources as well as their ability to apply that understanding to practical situations in the specific context of their work for *The Otter Realm*. I designed the preassessment using *SurveyMonkey* (http://try.surveymonkey.com) and used the multimedia widget feature of LALC to embed it in the second section of the guide. I directed them to the guide as students walked into the computer lab at the beginning of the session and asked them to complete the preassessment. When everyone was finished, I displayed the results of the preassessment (instantly available by logging into *SurveyMonkey* on the instructor's computer) via a data projector for the class to see. Thus, we were able to discuss, in a manner akin to discussion that often follows the use of student response systems (i.e., clickers), the concept of primary sources in light of students' anonymous answers and in the context of an actual in-progress story.

For example, one student was writing about civil behavior in the classroom. A multiple-choice question presented a sample source—the memoir *Teacher Man* by Frank McCourt—and then asked students to decide whether the source was primary or secondary or whether not enough information was given to make a decision. The results of the preassessment revealed that the class was evenly split among the three choices. This led to some spirited discussion about why students answered the way they did, without identifying any answer or individual as "wrong" while offering the students the opportunity to learn from one another. Another question listed examples of possible sources for a student's piece on the use of soy products in the campus dining commons and asked students in a "check all that apply" fashion to indicate which they thought were likely to be useful for writing a meaningful story. Students' answers varied widely, so we were able to engage in another discussion about not only why students would or would not use a particular source but also how a source might contribute to an original piece with local significance. Another question asked students about how to properly attribute sources and served as a jumping-off point for a rich conversation about plagiarism.

Reasons for choosing this learner-centered approach in your teaching: I chose this transparent approach to preassessment because I wanted students to be aware of what they knew and didn't know about doing research in the specific context of writing feature stories for *The Otter Realm.* My hope was that beginning the session by giving students a voice, and having them tell me what they already knew, would set the tone as learner-centered and help the students understand the value of their time spent in the instruction session. Furthermore, I wanted to use the results of the preassessment to initiate conversations wherein students could learn from one another.

Joan's musings: *This vignette is a prime example of giving learners a voice in their own learning. Allowing learners to discover for themselves what they know and what they need to know is a great way to get their attention, and allows the instructor to structure the instruction so that it meets the learners' real needs. Furthermore, the use of a freely available resource such as* SurveyMonkey *allows for the type of polling activities usually associated with audience response devices (clickers) but eliminates the need to purchase equipment or learn how to use the program associated with these devices. The creative use of this surveying tool establishes the learner-centered mind-set from the very beginning of the session and invites learners to be active partners in the learning enterprise.*

Vignette 8: Collaborative Learning in Action

Contributor: Trudi E. Jacobson, Head of User Education Programs, University at Albany, New York, SUNY.

Type of institution: University.

Instructional situation and audience: One-credit information literacy course. Information literacy is one of the UAlbany general education program requirements for undergraduates. Courses are taught in a variety of departments (Women's Studies, Communication, East Asian Studies, etc.). Librarians have been teaching information literacy courses since the requirement was established in 2000. While the requirement is aimed at lower-level undergraduates, many of the students in our sections are juniors and seniors.

Overall instructional goal of session: Abbreviated course goals: To create higher student engagement in the course, increase level of students' responsibility for their learning, and increase appreciation of course topics and applicability to lifelong information seeking endeavors.

Expected learning outcome for learner-centered example being described: After completing this course, learners will be able to:

1. Describe their information need.
2. Locate resources that will address that need.

3. Develop effective and efficient search strategies for those resources.
4. Critically assess and evaluate the information they find and the sources in which it appears.
5. Discuss a wide range of ethical and social issues connected with accessing and using information.

Learner-centered example: Team-based learning (TBL), based on the work of Larry Michaelsen at the University of Oklahoma in the late 1970s, is being used by instructors of courses in a wide range of disciplines. I found no record in the literature of its implementation in an information literacy course, but highly structured components and best practice examples from other fields made it seem feasible to employ it in my one-credit course. TBL includes a readiness assurance component, which includes assigned readings and readiness assessment tests (RATs), application exercises for each instructional unit, and peer assessment within the permanent teams that are formed on the first day of class (Michaelsen, Knight, and Fink, 2004).

The reading assignments provide students with the key concepts and issues connected to each unit of the course (such as database searching, finding and evaluating web resources, and information ethics). Before any material connected to the unit is raised in class, students first take an individual RAT and then the same test as a team, using an immediate feedback assessment technique. The discussions within the teams as they work through the challenging multiple-choice questions on the RAT show both the level of their preparation and their engagement with the topic. Notable changes in the classroom environment include students taking responsibility for their own learning and treating the course material more seriously.

While I have always had individual and group discovery activities in my course, the TBL model's application exercises are structured somewhat differently. They are intended to contribute to both team cohesiveness and the friendly spirit of competition engendered by the team RATs, as well as to extend students' knowledge of the topic through team discussion. Ideally, each team works on the same carefully designed problems, and teams report their results simultaneously. This works for some of my exercises, but in others, each team has a different example that it then has to present to the rest of the class.

Not only does the students' increased preparation make them better able to tackle the application exercise problems, but their cohesiveness as a team enables them to produce more sophisticated work. I recently asked teams to select three critical pieces of advice, and one warning, for students who are new to database searching. Teams wrote their responses on sticky flip-chart paper, which they mounted on the wall. The teams then perused the other sheets, selected one item from another team's selections that they found particularly important, and explained why in the ensuing discussion. After the resulting conversation, one student said he thought that the collective advice was so important that it should be made available to students who don't take the course. This was a wonderful suggestion, one that reflected both pride in the work of the teams and the importance of the material. The sheets were then hung in high-traffic points around the library. This is just one example of the significant changes connected to student learning that have resulted from using TBL.

Another key element of TBL is peer assessment. In courses longer than the seven weeks available to me, there might be opportunities to engage in both formative and summative assessments. I use only summative. Students have a set number of points to divide unevenly—they are not allowed to give each team member the same number of points, forcing distinctions in contributions to the team—and also provide comments on each team member's strengths and areas to work on. While the knowledge that this form of assessment will count for 5 percent of the grade encourages some students in their teamwork, my feeling is that many students become strong team members for other reasons entirely, based on the steadily increasing cohesiveness of the team and students' respect for the contributions of other team members.

Now that I have used TBL for six sections of the course, I cannot imagine teaching a credit-bearing undergraduate course without it. While I've always loved teaching with strong active learning components, TBL raises the bar. Now many of my students are fully engaged learners, relying on themselves and their teams much more than on me. The energy level in the room has increased. I encourage other librarians who teach courses to consider using TBL as a learner-centered approach. A good resource is the extensive TBL website (http://teambasedlearning .apsc.ubc.ca/?page_id=7), which includes a link to an electronic discussion list focused on the practical aspects of teaching with TBL.

Reasons for choosing this learner-centered approach for your teaching: I've been teaching this course at least three times a year for ten years, and I wanted to shake things up, for the benefit of both my students and me. The teaching center on campus has been promoting team-based learning, and the outcomes reported by those who are using it are impressive. The higher-level undergraduates who typically take my class have the ability to do more advanced work, and asking them to come to class already prepared, and then to engage in more complex application exercises within their teams, offers an opportunity to challenge them.

Joan's musings: *This is a great example of how collaborative learning benefits everyone involved. Asking learners to share perspectives, discuss ideas, and bring it all together into one cohesive whole creates a richer learning experience and mimics how problems tend to be solved in the real world. As the cognitive psychologists were fond of saying, "The whole is greater than the sum of its parts." Plus the collaborative nature of this learning experience* *creates a strong sense of shared responsibility for all members of the team. Each member takes pride in the accomplishments of the entire team and celebrates the contributions of each member. These learners are really "in it together," and their goal is for everyone on the team to succeed at the task at hand.*

Vignette 9: Getting Out of the Classroom

Contributors: Pearl Ly, Library Faculty for the Natural Sciences, California State University San Marcos (CSUSM); and Allison Carr, Library Faculty for the Social Sciences, CSUSM.

Type of institution: Four-year public university.

Instructional situation and audience: CSUSM is a medium-sized, public university with 9,500 students. CSUSM is primarily an undergraduate, commuter campus and serves many nontraditional students, including first-generation, minority, veterans, and returning students. Information literacy is infused throughout the lower- and upper-division curriculums.

At CSUSM, all instruction librarians teach a two-week library research module as part of a semester-long first-year experience course, General Education Lifelong Learning (GEL) 101. It estimated that 75 to 80 percent of all incoming freshmen take GEL 101, and there is evidence that students who complete this course within their first year have higher retention rates than those who do not.

The "Research Module" is designed for students to learn basic information literacy skills in order to complete their GEL 101 research assignment. Students are introduced to college-level research expectations, information sources, and information evaluation and to the ethical use of information.

Overall instructional goal of session: Students complete a library scavenger hunt in order to learn about basic library services, study spaces, and locating library materials within the physical building. Students answer questions about places and items in the library and provide "proof of completion" with cell phone pictures.

Expected learning outcome for learner-centered example being described: After the library scavenger hunt, students will be able to:

1. Identify specific locations in the library's physical layout in order to alleviate library anxiety.
2. Articulate where to get help in the library in order to complete research assignments.
3. Demonstrate use of the library catalog in order to locate books, periodicals, and films on the shelf.

Learner-centered example: The library scavenger hunt activity was designed to address the lack of understanding students have about physical library space. In instruction sessions, many librarians demonstrate how to use online library catalogs to find an item record and then describe how to find it on the shelf. Librarians also review the variety of library services available to students and describe where to find them in the building. Students rarely take time outside of the classroom to see the location of the services or materials until they need them, which may be too late, adding to library anxiety. We encounter many of these students at their point of need at the reference desk. Despite exposure to library instruction at CSUSM, many students have not entered the library stacks and do not feel confident doing so. The scavenger hunt is a learner-centered activity to get students out of the classroom and into the physical library, providing an opportunity to learn about the variety of services, spaces, and materials.

For this activity, the class is given a set amount of time to complete the hunt, which varies between 20 and 40 minutes, and are divided into groups of four students. Each group is given a map and a worksheet with library locations and instructions. Groups must visit each library location and stay together in their groups during the activity. To better facilitate collaboration, each group member has an assigned role. The leader is in charge of the group, ensuring that the group completes the hunt, stays on task, and returns to the classroom on time. The navigator is in charge of the map and ensures that the group gets to each location. The recorder takes notes and fills in the worksheet. The photographer takes photographs with a cell phone camera at appropriate locations.

Groups visit areas of the library that support student learning and practice finding items commonly needed for research assignments. To learn about library services and where to get help, students visit highly used service desks, such as Circulation, Reference, Media Library, and the Student Technology Help Desk. Students use the library catalog to find the call numbers of a book, magazine, and DVD and must locate the items on the shelf. There are stops to highlight quiet, active, and group-study spaces the library offers. Students either have to answer a question about, or take a photograph of, the item or location to demonstrate their learning.

A benefit of the scavenger hunt activity is that it allows students the opportunity to take charge of their learning in a reflective environment. After returning to the classroom at the designated time, groups review their pictures and worksheet with the librarian. Once all students have returned, the activity is processed as a class and students get answers to the questions they were unsuccessful in answering. Outside of the classroom, students with library anxiety are often afraid or embarrassed to ask for help or do not know where to get assistance. For example, students may visit the library needing to find a book for an assignment. If they are unable to find it in the library catalog or on the shelf, they may ask for help or leave the library and go to a more comfortable place such as a local bookstore to find their item. By contrast, if students are unable to find an item on the shelf during the scavenger hunt, they return to the classroom, describe their challenges, and get immediate help from a librarian. After this activity, students may be more likely to seek help in the library for future questions.

Feedback from students has been overwhelmingly positive, and many list the scavenger hunt as their favorite activity in the two-week GEL Research Module. They enjoy exploring the library in groups and express interest in the new things they learned about the library. Students have remarked surprise at being able to check out movies from the Media Library and are pleased to find a cozy study space in the library's Reading Room. Also, students have offered suggestions on how to improve the scavenger hunt and make it more meaningful. For example, one student remarked that answering a question about a location, instead of just visiting it, might make students pay more attention. Utilizing student and classroom faculty input, this activity was revised and is now used by all CSUSM instruction librarians in GEL 101 classes.

More information about scavenger hunt design, setup, and instructional materials is available at http://public.csusm.edu/acarr/scavenger/index.html.

Reasons for choosing this learner-centered approach for your teaching: By devoting classroom time for library scavenger hunts, students experience the physical library on their own. Students teach themselves how to locate library items and become familiar with places to get help. Students are placed in groups with assigned roles to keep each other on task, ensure participation, and feel more comfortable exploring the library. Students enjoy using technology, i.e., cell phones, during the scavenger hunt to document their learning. When "learning how to find library items" is presented in a fun way, students are more likely to internalize and use the information they learned and the physical library layout.

Joan's musings: *This is another example of the advantages of active versus passive learning experiences. We often take it for granted that if we describe the library layout and even show and/or distribute maps that highlight where various services and materials can be located in the library, our learners can take that information out into the real world and apply it to the actual physical layout. Anyone who has tried to navigate their way around by just using a map can attest that it is not always that easy. This vignette not only gets the students out of the classroom and actively exploring the library, it brings everyone back together to reflect on and share their experiences under the guidance of the librarian. Think of the time this exercise saves these learners when they actually need to do library research. Having to go to the library no longer is something to be feared. These students know their way around and can proceed to the important stuff of finding the information they need.*

Vignette 10: I'd Rather Do It Myself!

Contributor: Christina Mayberry, Science and Engineering Librarian, California State University, Northridge, Oviatt Library.

Type of institution: University.

Instructional situation and audience: Many of the instructors for the undergraduate courses are interested in having their students learn how to evaluate sources. Sometimes the instructors have specifically asked for this topic, and other times I include it in the session because it is very important. The library's website has a section of its online research strategies guide that is dedicated to evaluating sources (http://library.csun.edu/guides/subject-guide/11-Step-3-Evaluating-Sources?tab=43). Instead of just showing the students the section and briefly reviewing it, I like to have the students perform an evaluation exercise so that they can practice using the criteria provided in the online guide.

Overall instructional goal of session: The goal of the instruction session is to teach students about finding sources, evaluating sources, and citing sources relevant to the subject area for their course or for a specific assignment(s) in their course.

Expected learning outcome for learner-centered example being described: Students will be able to:

1. Apply criteria for evaluating sources provided in an online library guide by selecting a website within a specific domain.
2. Determine whether or not the selected website qualifies as an appropriate source to use for an assignment in their course.

Learner-centered example: Students work together in pairs or groups depending on the size of the class, the configuration of the classroom, and the availability of a computer for each student. The class is divided into four groups so that each quarter of the class searches for and selects a website on a topic related to its course from a particular domain, such as .gov, .edu, .com, or .org. A list of websites from which to choose is generated by performing an advanced search in Google (http://www.google.com/advanced_search) in the "Search within a site or domain" box for one of the four domains. The students are asked to use the evaluation criteria provided in the online library guide (http://library.csun .edu/Guides/ResearchStrategies/EvaluatingInternetResources) to determine whether or not they think the selected website would be appropriate to use for an assignment in their course (or the specific one on which they are currently working). Because each category has multiple pairs or groups, I ask one pair or group to volunteer to tell the class what website they selected and walk the class through the evaluation process and their determination of its credibility. If the students have difficulty with any criteria (often the author is tricky), I will ask questions and offer tips as to how they might figure it out. Sometimes students do not always volunteer, but I have found that walking around the classroom while the students are performing the exercise often helps. I also suggest that they take notes either on paper or on the computer to help them while they work through the evaluation criteria.

Reasons for choosing this learner-centered approach for your teaching: I have found that students learn more when they can practice what they learn before they have to apply it to an actual assignment. Students also seem to ask more and better questions when they have to work through the application of concepts taught in class while the instructor is available to them. This exercise also shows students what online resources are available in their subject area in different domains, which they might not have discovered on their own.

Joan's musings: *We generally remember more about material that we have explored for ourselves than we do if someone just tells us about it. Being learner-centered means letting go and allowing the learners to explore on their own. While it may be a bit more chaotic a format and requires the instructor to be flexible and ready for just about anything to happen, the net result for our learners is that they gain more insight into whatever is being addressed and are better able to apply this newly acquired knowledge to new situations they may encounter in the future.*

Vignette 11: Setting Your Learners Free

Contributor: Tiffini Travis, Director of Information Literacy and Outreach Services, California State University, Long Beach.

Type of institution: University.

Instructional situation and audience: This vignette applies to a typical college-level library instruction session in a hands-on lab. However, it can be applied to any instructional situation. For the purpose of this example, we will say this is a class of college freshmen and sophomores who are conducting academic research for the first time. This session is for a three- to five-page research paper on a pre-determined topic. The students are at-risk and enrolled in the Educational Opportunity Program (EOP 100 program). This will be their only organized visit to the library for this course. They need to find five sources on an issue related to their college major. They determine the issue themselves. Some but not all have selected their topics.

Overall instructional goal of session:
- Participants will utilize appropriate research databases.
- Participants will analyze advanced features and functionality of a database.

- Participants will apply these skills across platforms regardless of interface design.

Expected learning outcome for learner-centered example being described: This activity is learner-centered as it uses a discovery method of instruction to motivate students to use the library databases. Students will be able to:

1. Determine their specific information need.
2. Select the database they feel best suits the need.
3. Evaluate articles to see which sources best satisfy that need.

Learner-centered example: A general discussion with accompanying slides (embedded in the LibGuide page: http://csulb.libguides.com/outreach) starts the session. As the discussion continues, students think about who would likely care about their topic, how to connect terms with AND, and the differences between scholarly and popular sources. Students are asked to reflect on their majors and answer the question: What do you want to be when you grow up?

Based on their answers, each student writes down the following:

- What their major is.
- What they want to be when they grow up.
- What is a topic/issue that interests them about their profession.
- What are some keywords and synonyms to search for that topic.
- Which databases by topic relate to their topic.

They are then allowed to search in the databases they have selected and find relevant articles. Because this is a learner-centered approach, there is *no demo of the databases.* This allows students to mix and match terms on their own and gives me the ability to roam the room and monitor progress. For students with more difficult topics I can spend more time helping with brainstorming or modifying search terms. I also try to encourage peer-to-peer learning by encouraging students to ask each other questions if they get lost or can't find a feature of the database.

After students have search results on the screen, I ask them to find one article that says "Full Text" and then to find one article that is not full text so they can learn to use SFX linking. They dissect the records by finding where the "cite" option is and how to e-mail/download the full text. If they do not have all the features, there are additional slides in the presentation that they view on their own. Again, nothing is demonstrated during this part of the session.

Reasons for choosing this learner-centered approach for your teaching: After years of doing the dog and pony show (librarian models, student follows), I realized that the purpose of our instruction should be intuitive problem-based activities that have the students learn while they are doing. This creates a more meaningful approach to library instruction for the students and for me as well. Letting loose the binds that I held onto as a new librarian gave my students the chance to grow and learn at their own level. The result has been an increased confidence level for the students and less emphasis on me as the teacher.

Joan's musings: *Here again we see an example of another instruction librarian who embraced the idea of "letting go" and allowing learners to try things out for themselves. She moved from being the "sage on the stage" to the "guide on the side" with the express purpose of offering her learners a better, more effective instructional experience. Adopting LCT sometimes feels like an enormous leap into the unknown. But, as this vignette illustrates, taking the leap results in a more engaging, interactive, participatory, and effective learning experience for everyone concerned.*

FROM THE SPECIAL LIBRARY PERSPECTIVE

Vignette 12: Catching Learners' Attention

Contributor: Lucy Bellamy, Head Librarian, Fashion Institute of Design & Merchandising, California.

Type of institution: Private college "dedicated to educating students for the Fashion, Graphics, Interior Design, and Entertainment Industries" (http://fidm .edu/about/index.html).

Instructional situation and audience: Undergraduate English Composition and Critical Thinking research skills instruction presentation.

Overall instructional goal of session: Instructors typically request that staff provide a general overview of specific online databases, such as EBSCO*host*, Lexis-Nexis, and/or ProQuest, as a means to direct students away from using Google or Wikipedia as sources for their research papers.

Expected learning outcome for learner-centered example being described: After instruction students will be able to select quality, authoritative resources to meet their information needs.

Learner-centered example: Promoting the online subscription services is particularly challenging, as many students have been "Google-ized" by the fast and numerous results retrieved with very simple searches. Our students are typical of the "millennial" generation for whom the ease (and speed) of the Internet is too intoxicating to overcome when it comes to academic research. An attempt to "detoxify" students from the free web requires that staff create instruction presentations using examples to which students can relate. One successful outcome involved an instruction session where the historical newspaper database ProQuest was required as a resource for a Critical Thinking class. The instructor provided very general guidelines regarding subjects for staff to use during the in-class demonstration of topics, such as recycling, gun control, and global warming.

In the past, students would sit passively while staff "inform," "deliver," and/or "teach" the available resources for their projects. In an effort to change the audience from passive to active, we work with instructors prior to most class presentations to not only discuss objectives but also learning outcomes for the assignment. Our goal is to develop a list of topics that would not only attract students' attention but also provide them with an interesting way to use this and other resources available to them for their projects (current and future). One such example involved the film *Changeling*, which featured an actress students admire, Angelina Jolie. The film is a dramatized account of a kidnapping that took place in Los Angeles, California, during the late 1920s and carried on through the early 1940s. I developed a search strategy using ProQuest to demonstrate how to compare the "Hollywood truth" of the film illustrating the event(s) and the accounting detailed in the *Los Angeles Times* newspaper published during the time. This example opened the doors—so to speak—for students to think of and volunteer other such events featured in recent films (e.g., *Titanic, Evita, Zodiac,* and *Milk*) to compare the news account (using other newspapers in the database, such as the *New York Times, Washington Post,* and *San Francisco Chronicle*) against the Hollywood version of the event.

Reasons for choosing this learner-centered approach for your teaching: Our students are of the generation where books are not (unfortunately) the format of choice for research. Using online subscription services are a more attractive option, because it mirrors their experience with the Internet. Developing research strategies, which use events/topics of interest to students, and using library resources to conduct research on them—such as an historical newspaper database like ProQuest—allows students to see library staff more as interested research partners than as archaic library drones.

Joan's musings: *An important aspect of being learner-centered is to be knowledgeable about our learners. This allows us to select examples that will capture their attention and help us get them involved with the material. Using a fairly recent movie as a starting point is a great way to do that. Plus the movie used in this example is set in Los Angeles, another way to make the material real to the learners. Rather than just telling the learners about how to do research in a newspaper database, this contributor let the learners see how they could compare movie "truth" to the real thing.*

Vignette 13: Taking Responsibility

Contributor: Emily Brennan, Information Services Librarian, University of Southern California (USC) Norris Medical Library.

Type of institution: The USC Norris Medical Library serves the faculty, students, and staff of the Schools of Medicine and Pharmacy; the Division of Biokinesiology and Physical Therapy and Division of Occupational Therapy; and surrounding hospitals.

Instructional situation and audience: This library session teaches third-year School of Medicine graduate students in their Family Medicine Clerkship rotation about Evidence-Based Medicine (EBM) concepts and resources. This session is taught to a new group of 25 students every six weeks.

Overall instructional goal of session: At the end of this session, students will understand the five steps of EBM, particularly step one (create a searchable clinical question) and step two (acquire information and evidence). Regarding step two of the EBM process, students will learn how to best select the most appropriate resource, as well as how to search each resource effectively.

Expected learning outcome for learner-centered example being described: Students will be able to categorize EBM resources by type, choose the appropriate resource, and effectively search each resource in order to find treatment recommendations.

Learner-centered example: This clerkship session teaches students about EBM concepts and resources. I spend the first ten minutes providing background information, such as how to access the Family Medicine subject guide, steps of EBM, and the Evidence Resources pyramid (Haynes, 2001). This portion of the class is interactive, with students providing answers aloud. The Evidence Resources pyramid is divided into four sections, with each section being a different resource category (i.e., summaries, synopses, syntheses, studies). I provide a description of each category (e.g., synopses is critically appraised journal articles) and discuss when to use each category of resources. I then give the students 25 minutes to complete an in-class exercise. They are encouraged to work in pairs and to consult their classmates as well.

The first part of the exercise provides a list of seven EBM resources. The students must match each resource to the appropriate category on the pyramid (Figure 9.2). At this time, the students have their browsers open to the Family Medicine subject guide. The resources are categorized by type in this guide, although the categories are not named the same as on the class exercise. For example, some resources on the Family Medicine guide are in the category named "Journal Club," while those same resources would be in the "Synopses" category in the class exercise. That said, students should be able to match each resource to the appropriate category on the pyramid by reading the category descriptions in the Family Medicine subject guide. This activity requires the students to actively think about which resources belong to which category, as well as when they would use each type of resource.

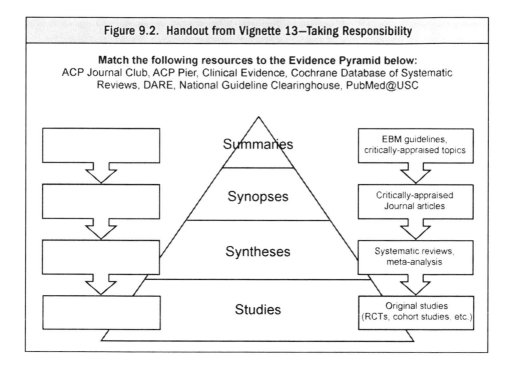

Figure 9.2. Handout from Vignette 13–Taking Responsibility

Match the following resources to the Evidence Pyramid below:
ACP Journal Club, ACP Pier, Clinical Evidence, Cochrane Database of Systematic Reviews, DARE, National Guideline Clearinghouse, PubMed@USC

The second part of the exercise asks the students to explore the specified resources in order to answer a given clinical question. They are asked to explore one resource from each of the four categories and to describe the treatment recommendation provided in each resource. As the students are researching, I walk around to answer questions. Because they have not yet received a demo of the resources, they often encounter difficulty and ask many questions.

The third part of the exercise asks the students to provide a final treatment recommendation for their patient based on their findings in the four resources they searched. This requires them to critically appraise conflicting recommendations and to weigh the level of evidence provided by each resource before providing a final recommendation.

Once they have completed the exercise, I ask for volunteers to demo their search techniques in front of the class. I provide necessary background information, search tips, and other valuable commentary for each resource.

Reasons for choosing this learner-centered approach for your teaching: I chose to use this learner-centered approach because requiring the students to actively take responsibility for their own learning increases their level of interest, as well as their comprehension and retention of information. Furthermore, after they encounter trouble while searching the databases, they are more apt to listen to advice by classmates who were successful in their searching techniques.

Joan's musings: *This librarian really said it all in her reasons for choosing this format for her instruction. It fits all the CPR principles of learner-centered teaching. Learners are encouraged to work collaboratively in a very active/participatory manner and are asked to take responsibility for their own and their fellow students' learning. Furthermore, as they work directly with the material, they discover some of the limitations of their own knowledge and are primed to learn more.*

Vignette 14: Making It Real

Contributor: Amy Chatfield, Information Services Librarian, University of Southern California (USC) Norris Medical Library—liaison to the USC School of Pharmacy.

Type of institution: The Norris Medical Library is an academic health sciences library serving graduate and professional students, staff, and faculty.

Instructional situation and audience: My situation focuses on Pharmacy residents. Residents hold a PharmD from an accredited school. The highly selective residency program enrolls approximately 35 people a year and includes four components: work in a clinical practice setting, attendance at a weekly didactic session, instruction to PharmD candidates, and completion of a research project of the residents' choice. Most didactic sessions in the residency program are presented as lectures, and most PharmD curriculum is also lecture based. I provided a 1.5-hour didactic session eight weeks into the residency program and chose to make my session a hands-on computer class focused on the PubMed database. At the time of teaching, I had been a pharmacy librarian for about a month and was still learning about residents' clinical duties and their information needs.

Overall instructional goal of session: The goal is for residents to gain advanced searching skills in PubMed.

Expected learning outcome for learner-centered example being described: At the end of the session, residents will be able to:

1. Identify keywords and concepts from a clinical scenario.
2. Create a controlled vocabulary search in PubMed.
3. Select relevant articles from a list of search results.

Learner-centered example: The class began with a brief demonstration of the Medical Subject Headings (MeSH) database (the controlled vocabulary used in PubMed). The demonstration gave me a chance to discuss "normal results" for a search ("if there are 20 million citations in PubMed, retrieving 200 citations in a search is actually a very good, narrow search") and describe the advanced searching skills residents were being asked to acquire.

A guided worksheet was used for the bulk of the session, but this could be done without any written aids. I find that the pharmacy program enrollees really enjoy getting handouts in class, so I try to fulfill this when reasonable. The worksheet began by asking residents to consider their past two months of clinical practice and remember a time when they had a question or unfulfilled information need. They were then asked to write the clinical scenario that brought about this question. The worksheet also included some "canned" scenarios that residents could use if they could not recall a personal scenario. The worksheet then continued using the resident-written scenario as a guide and asked residents to identify main concepts in their scenarios, locate MeSH headings (and subheadings) that best covered those concepts, and search PubMed for research articles.

Most residents chose to work in pairs or small groups. About half the residents used their own searches, and half used the sample scenarios. If I do this exercise again, I would not provide the sample scenarios. The residents who created their own scenarios had more difficulty locating appropriate MeSH headings, but an easier time when narrowing or expanding a search and selecting relevant items from a list of results. Residents who used canned scenarios had the opposite experience: it was easy to find MeSH headings (perhaps because of leading language in the scenarios that pointed them toward appropriate headings), but they had major problems with conceiving of ways to narrow or expand their search and select relevant articles. This made sense, and, given my learning outcomes for the class, I thought insisting that residents use their own scenario will provide more relevant learning opportunities. Also, because residents are notoriously short on time, using a real-life example helped to make the required didactic session less onerous. While they had to be there for 1.5 hours, at least they were spending the majority of that time looking for an answer to their real-life clinical question.

This approach required more effort on my part as a teacher. Because everyone in the class was working on a different topic—and topics generated by residents included both direct patient care questions as well as questions about pharmacy regulations and economics of the pharmaceutical industry—I had to shift mental gears frequently to appropriately help residents overcome difficulties with searching for their personalized topics.

Reasons for choosing this learner-centered approach for your teaching: I wanted the session to better mirror residents' actual experiences with information seeking. I have noticed that much information-related education provided to health sciences students focuses on "best cases"—search examples are chosen to provide a reasonable amount of results and permit the educator to point out specific aspects of a database. In real-life health care settings, there are few "best cases." I see health sciences students becoming frustrated with searching when they encounter an overwhelming or underwhelming amount of research evidence.

This approach permits residents to research a novel problem that they are personally invested in and have immediate assistance to help avoid frustration.

Joan's musings: *Once again we see that knowing our audience and what is important to them is key to effective, learner-centered instruction. Not only did the exercise focus on an important resource for these learners, it also allowed them to make good use of their time during the instruction by working on a real-life question. As the contributor pointed out, residents are very busy people and want to make the most of their time. Working on their own questions during the ILI session allowed them to learn the concepts of effective PubMed searching and at the same time moved them toward a solution to their questions.*

FROM THE PARTNERSHIP AND OUTREACH PERSPECTIVE

Vignette 15: Fostering Inquiry through Shared Media

Contributor: Kristen Mastel, Outreach & Instruction Librarian, University of Minnesota.

Type of institution: Research university.

Instructional situation and audience: At the University of Minnesota we have a Summer Youth Program for 5- to 15-year-olds. The day programs combine physical activity with learning experiences in a research setting. This particular project started with a group of students in the animal science camps ages 9–11 focusing on raptors, veterinary care, and wildlife in nature. The University of Minnesota Raptor Center provided the Summer Youth Program with a set of cameras. This reflection exercise is used after various activities throughout the program and as a way for students to collaborate and collectively discuss topics at a deeper level.

Overall instructional goal of session: The students will acquire the skills to identify animals and processes during the day with supportive documentation and express this knowledge through media.

Expected learning outcome for learner-centered example being described: A digital camera will be used to document daily camp animal science interaction and activities. Additionally:

1. Students will be able to identify the animals and processes they witnessed or interacted with using credible resources in order to provide background information on the day's activities to nonparticipants.
2. Youth will be able to use VoiceThread in order to transform gathered media and comment using video, voice, and text.

Learner-centered example: Each day at camp, participants document their activities through the use of photographs and movies on a digital camera, whether it is at the raptor center learning about owls or seeing a horse receiving a routine checkup at the equine center. In the library's lab students are able to review their images and video. In the digital collaborative space of VoiceThread students are able to group their photos and videos into themes. After the themes have been established with the assistance of the summer camp leader and librarian, the students, in groups of three to four, are asked to review the media and pose questions on VoiceThread regarding the subject matter. (We try to not focus on photography quality, as this is not the focus of the camp, but we do hope that through reviewing others' images and tips through the week students become more proficient with their cameras.) The students then begin to research supportive documentation for each theme and its questions.

For example, after reviewing some images of a horse's height measurements a student commented on VoiceThread, "What is a hand?" This brought students to discuss what a credible resource is with direction by the librarian. Encyclopedias and statewide databases are often used in researching a question. Many of the students have used these resources in their elementary school media center; however, occasionally the librarian does a brief instruction on the resources available to them. More often, though the librarian leads them to the resource and lets the students play and discover on their own. Students respond to the posed question with an answer either visually with another image (in this instance they found a diagram), text including a link whenever possible, or verbally with a video or voice recording.

After the session the librarian and camp instructor review the activity's VoiceThread, and they supply comments on the students' interactions, discoveries, and thoughts. Students are encouraged to review the VoiceThread with their parents at the completion of each camp day, time permitting. This serves as a digital archive of the camp, though temporary, as we have no intention of preserving the content for long-term use for legal and ethical reasons. It should be acknowledged that the students sign a media waiver at the beginning of camp permitting internal use of the images.

Reasons for choosing this learner-centered approach for your teaching: In partnering with the Summer Youth Camp we discovered the need to document the activities in the camps and provide to students an outlet for further dialogue. The educational VoiceThread license proved to be an easily accessible option, as it required no special equipment or plug-ins but has much versatility. The question-and-answer discussion in VoiceThread was a natural fit, as it addressed the issue of the camp leaders often being asked the 5 Ws throughout a day. Rather than having an authoritative answering approach we wanted to foster investigation and inquiry, and this activity begins that conversation.

Joan's musings: *Today's learners are very technologically adept and are accustomed to sharing information using a variety of electronic devices. Using VoiceThread, a web-based* *collaborative tool, learners can share their images and make comments about all the images being posted, thus putting the instruction into a format that is more like the way they share information in their real lives. Rather than forcing the learners into our mold, this instruction accommodates the ways in which learners interact and learn on a daily basis. Furthermore, this is an interactive and fun way for the learners to share their information with each other and the instructor.*

FINAL REMARKS

I hope you enjoyed this glimpse into the types of LCT that are going on in the real world of ILI. You may have noticed that some of the vignettes were coauthored. The experiences described in those vignettes are a result of teamwork—in both the development and the delivery of the instruction. That is actually a great way to get started with LCT. Trying something new and different can be scary, especially in the beginning. Teaming up with a colleague can help you find the courage to take that first leap into the new and, for you, untested waters of LCT. You get someone with whom to share the work and support you during the process. You can bounce ideas off of each other and have someone with whom to do the all-important reality checks before you try anything out. The extra brainpower and the additional set of eyes and hands can only improve your end product.

LCT can be labor intensive at the delivery stage as well. So, team teaching, especially when you are trying out a new LCT technique, can be really helpful. LCT activities tend to be quite challenging, especially in larger groups. With so much going on at the same time, it can be hard to pay attention to all the learners/groups. Even experienced learner-centered teachers like the extra help. They often recruit "rovers" (colleagues, staff, or even student workers) to assist during hands-on activities. These rovers give you extra eyes to monitor what is going on. They can help learners who might get lost during the exercise, need extra help completing the task, or have any kind of question or problem during the class. Another benefit to recruiting rovers is that it is a good way to spread the word about LCT to other instruction librarians. Your rovers may find the session to be so much fun and effective that they will be moved to try an LCT technique in their own sessions.

It seems clear there is a lot of LCT going on in the world of ILI. Librarians from elementary school all the way up through college, specialized institutions of higher education, and professional schools are transforming their instruction to include more collaboration, participation, and sharing responsibility for learning with their learners. I hope you have found these vignettes both interesting and thought provoking and that they have inspired you to try some LCT of your own.

REFERENCES

Haynes, R. Brian. 2001. "Of Studies, Syntheses, Synopses, and Systems: The '4S' Evolution of Services for Finding Current Best Evidence." *ACP Journal Club* 134, no. 2: A11–A13.

Kuhlthau, Carol Collier. 1993. *Seeking Meaning: A Process Approach to Library and Information Services, Information Management, Policy, and Services.* Norwood, NJ: Ablex.

Michaelsen, Larry K., Arletta B. Knight, and L. Dee Fink. 2004. *Team-Based Learning: A Transformative Use of Small Groups in College Teaching.* Sterling, VA: Stylus.

Rankin, Virginia. 1988. "One Route to Critical Thinking." *School Library Journal* 34, no. 1: 28–31.

Part IV

Summing It All Up

Chapter 10

Where Do We Go from Here?

Be not afraid of going slowly; be only afraid of standing still.

—Chinese Proverb

We have reached the end of the road for this particular exploration into the wonders of learner-centered teaching (LCT). I hope you found the material presented intriguing and inspiring. Now it is your turn to start your journey. And, of course, mine is not over. As any good teacher will tell you, although our goal is effective instruction, we never quite get there. We need to continuously reflect honestly on what we have done with an eye to making it better (Brookfield, 1995; McCombs, 2003; McCombs and Miller, 2007). And we keep looking for new and exciting ways to engage and empower learners through our information literacy instruction (ILI) efforts. So, as you begin your own journey, here are a few travel tips.

START SMALL

Don't try to change everything about your teaching all at once. Do what I did when I transformed my face-to-face (F2F) course into a blended one. Take baby steps. Pick one aspect of your teaching that you would like to make more learner-centered. Do you want to incorporate more learner involvement? Find something that you tend to present in a formal, lecture-like manner and see if you can come up with a way to have the learners interact with the material in some collaborative, participatory way instead. It is okay for you to change just five minutes of your instruction the first time around. The important thing is to start somewhere. And then reflect on the change. See if you think it worked. If so, keep it in. If not, try to determine how to make it better. Keep working on that small segment until you are comfortable with it, and then try to add a bit more. As time goes on, you may find that you have shifted the balance in your instruction from a teacher-centered, lecture approach to a more learner-centered one.

Don't forget to look at your online material with the goal of making it more learner-centered as well. Think about how adding online material to your F2F offerings might help you make the material available and accessible to the learners. Take a look at the Reflections sections that are at the ends of the chapters in this book. Each of them includes some suggestions about how to become more learner-centered in your teaching practice. Try some of these suggestions out. You will probably like some better than others. The point is to try. As the quote that started this chapter off says, we don't get anywhere by standing still.

TEAM TEACH

Trying something new can be a bit intimidating. This is especially true for LCT, because so much of it requires us to let go of our traditional "in charge of everything" role. But it is not quite as scary if we have help. Team teaching is a wonderful way to test the waters, take those baby steps, and have someone to lean on while you do so. Find someone who already teaches from the learner-centered perspective. Offer your assistance. You might start out by just being a rover in someone else's class. You can observe LCT in action and get a better idea of how it works. After that, you might ask to do a little of the LCT yourself. Or find someone who is interested in LCT but has not tried it in practice yet. See if working together gives both of you more incentive (and courage) to try some LCT approaches out. In the spirit of two heads are better than one, even a pair of novice learner-centered teachers can begin to transform their instruction by working together on the process.

Team teaching offers you a safety net. You don't have to carry the weight of the entire instruction yourself. You share the responsibility and the work with your partner. And you have someone with whom to debrief and discuss what, if any, improvements could be made for the future.

BECOME A CRITICAL OBSERVER

We can learn an awful lot from watching other people teach. Anytime you attend a presentation or participate in instruction (F2F or online) or training of any kind (synchronous or asynchronous) set aside a small part of your brain to reflect on what the presenter/teacher is doing. Was there something he or she did that you found particularly effective? What made it effective? Do you think you might like to incorporate that method, technique, or approach in your own teaching? Also try to identify things that you thought were not quite to your taste. Why did you find those things less effective? What do you think could be done to improve them? If you modified these techniques or methods somewhat, could you then use them in your own instructional endeavors (Cruickshank, Jenkins, and Metcalf, 2009; Grassian and Kaplowitz, 2009)?

Good presenters and teachers inspire us and provide us with engaging and innovative instructional ideas. But don't discount the less effective people we encounter. If you can identify what went wrong and figure out how to fix it, you have gained something valuable from that less than effective situation.

SHARE YOUR IDEAS

Seek out other ILI librarians and pool knowledge, tips, and techniques. Join local, regional, national, and international groups that are involved in ILI. Instruction librarians tend to be a very generous and gregarious group of people. They love to talk about their teaching ideas and to hear about what others are doing. Take advantage of this wonderful trait. You will be amazed at the ideas that are sparked by these conversations with other ILI devotees.

SEEK OUT NEW INFORMATION

More and more books and articles are being published every day on LCT. Break out of your librarianship box and look for material in instructional design, instructional technology, pedagogy, and psychology. And do the same when thinking about the professional conferences you want to attend. While ILI topics are often featured at our own professional conferences, remember that we are interested in improving our instructional techniques. So broaden your horizons and mingle with people in other disciplines who are also devoted to instructional effectiveness and excellence. As an added bonus, these nonlibrarian conferences give us a chance to interact with faculty and other professionals with whom we might wish to collaborate at some time in the future.

RECHARGE YOUR BATTERIES

Use all these ideas as a way to continue to learn and grow as an ILI librarian. Even the most dedicated among us can get a bit bored when teaching the same material over and over again, year after year. If we don't do something to shake things up once in a while, we can begin to dread having to teach that "Fill in the blank" class one more time. With enough repetitions, we can begin to feel as if we are on autopilot, and that loss of enthusiasm will show. It's not that we no longer care about the topic. It's just that we are tired of teaching it.

So, take baby steps; team teach; be a critical observer; share your ideas; and seek out new knowledge. Get inspired to try something new. Recharge your instructional batteries. Become reenergized about your role as an ILI librarian. And use these activities to keep reminding yourself why you love being a teaching librarian.

TECHNOLOGY AND THE FUTURE OF ILI

Even as someone who loves the F2F mode, I have to say that the future of ILI is bound up with technology. And my experiences with the blended format taught me the value that technology (if used judiciously and appropriately) can add to any instructional endeavor. Technology is not only here to stay, it is also forever morphing. Just as we get used to one type of technology, another one comes along with the potential of once again changing and hopefully enhancing our teaching efforts.

Before computers, before the Internet, research was print bound and was by necessity done with resources contained within the four walls of our library buildings. So we taught our learners how to make the most of the materials they had physical access to. Furthermore, as our learners became more familiar with these resources, we encouraged them to develop critical thinking skills and information-seeking strategies that we hoped were transferrable to new situations. Our goal was to equip our learners with the ability to use whatever materials they encounter in the future, that is, to be lifelong learners.

The advent of technology and widespread availability of computers changed all that. It blew out the walls of our libraries and allowed our learners to explore an entire world of information. Although the right to use some licensed resources is often restricted to particular authorized people, our learners still have access to much more than any physical library building could realistically hold. The world is truly our information playground.

So, we had to add "how to use technology" to the list of things we felt needed to be shared with our learners. In this technologically dependent, information-rich world, our learners first must learn to walk (become technologically literate) before they can run (use this technology to search for information). The decisions we now have to make about what we include under the heading ILI becomes much more complex and complicated. Once again we are faced with the dilemma—so much to teach, so little time to teach it.

Keeping an eye on emerging technologies is a hard job but an important one. We need to learn enough about each so that we can answer the following questions:

1. Will it last?
2. How are our learners using it?
3. Do we need to teach it?
4. If yes, how do we learn how to use it?
5. Can it help us expand our reach and enhance and enrich our instructional endeavors?

The answers to these questions help us determine where to expend our efforts, which technologies to incorporate into our instruction, and how to direct our own continuing technology-related education.

Each new generation of learners grows up in a different technologically enhanced world. It behooves us as ILI librarians to familiarize ourselves with what our learners are using in their daily lives to communicate with each other and to connect with the world and its plethora of information resources. New technology provides us with both challenges and opportunities. It expands what our learners use to find and share information. So it adds to the list of what we could (should?) teach.

BACK TO BASICS: TEACHING CONCEPTS, NOT MECHANICS

The continuing information and technological explosion makes it more important to ensure we are teaching concepts and strategies rather than "push this button now" mechanics in our ILI. We have no idea what our learners might be using to access and share information down the road. So, while we still have to teach about the here and now, we need to continue to emphasize long-lasting and transferrable skills and strategies so that our learners will develop a metacognitive approach to life. If we are successful, our learners will have learned how to learn, become lifelong learners, and therefore by definition will be information-literate individuals (ALA. Presidential Committee on Information Literacy, 1989).

So, while we want to empower our learners to become evaluative, critical thinkers who can determine the credibility, authenticity, and timeliness of the information they found, we also endeavor to use LCT approaches in order to help our learners develop the "how to figure it out" skills they will need for the future. That is, to develop the capacity to know what to do when they encounter a never-before-seen resource or become intrigued by some new technology. We do this through the inclusion of exercises, activities, and hand-on practice opportunities that help learners discover the way into these resources for themselves. With our guidance and support, our learners determine not only how to use the resource at hand but also how to explore new ones down the road.

FINAL REMARKS

LCT with its emphasis on collaboration, participation, and shared responsibility (CPR) and its reliance on learners doing it for themselves helps learners develop these "how to figure it out" concepts and strategies. If we tell them or even show them how to use what is available to them in the here and now, we have offered them only a quick fix. But if we involve them in the learning process and allow them to work directly with the material to be learned, we give them not only the opportunity to learn about what is in front of them but also the chance to develop their own, unique, and meaningful approaches to figuring out what is yet to be.

I believe that LCT provides a more valuable, long-lasting, and empowering experience for our learners. If we want to do our best for those we teach, we need to prepare them for the world in which they live—one that morphs and changes at what sometimes feels like breakneck speed. LCT approaches can provide this preparation so that we can send our learners out into their unknown futures confident that they can tackle whatever tomorrow may bring. I hope you will join me in my dedication to this worthwhile cause.

Thank you for reading this book and for sharing in my journey. I look forward to seeing where the future takes all of us.

REFERENCES

ALA. Presidential Committee on Information Literacy. 1989. *Final Report.* Chicago: American Library Association.

Brookfield, Stephen. 1995. *Becoming a Critically Reflective Teacher.* 1st ed. *The Jossey-Bass Higher & Adult Education Series.* San Francisco: Jossey-Bass.

Cruickshank, Donald R., Deborah Bainer Jenkins, and Kim K. Metcalf. 2009. *The Act of Teaching.* 5th ed. Boston: McGraw-Hill.

Grassian, Esther, and Joan Kaplowitz. 2009. *Information Literacy Instruction: Theory and Practice.* 2nd ed. New York: Neal-Schuman.

McCombs, Barbara L. 2003. *Defining Tools for Teacher Reflection: The Assessment of Learner-Centered Practices (ALCP).* ERIC Centre for Curriculum, Transfer and Technology. ED478622.

McCombs, Barbara L., and Lynda Miller. 2007. *Learner-Centered Classroom Practices and Assessments: Maximizing Student Motivation, Learning, and Achievement.* Thousand Oaks, CA: Corwin Press.

Index

Page numbers followed by the letter "t" indicate tables; those followed by the letter "f" indicate figures.

About the Author

Joan R. Kaplowitz has a Doctorate in Psychology as well as a Master of Library Science degree. She retired in 2007 after 23 years as a librarian at UCLA. Dr. Kaplowitz worked at UCLA since graduating from UCLA's Library and Information Science program in 1984. She began her career as a reference/instruction librarian and later Educational Services Coordinator and Head of Public Services at the Education and Psychology Library. She ended her UCLA Library career as the Head of the Research, Instruction and Collection Services division at the UCLA Louise M. Darling Biomedical Library in June 2007.

Dr. Kaplowitz was heavily involved in information literacy instruction at the local, state, and national levels for her entire career and continues to be active in this area despite her retirement from the UCLA library system. During her early years at UCLA she taught several sections of UCLA's undergraduate course "Library and Information Resources." In 1989 she collaborated with UCLA's Esther Grassian to propose and develop the UCLA graduate library program's course "Information Literacy Instruction: Theory and Technique." She and Ms. Grassian have alternated presenting this course since 1990, and Dr. Kaplowitz is continuing to teach this course despite her retirement from the library. Dr. Kaplowitz was also part of the faculty development team for Association of College and Research Libraries' Institute for Information Literacy's Immersion Program and taught in six of the programs between 1999 and 2004.

Dr. Kaplowitz was awarded several Librarians' Association of the University of California research grants in support of her research and publication endeavors. She held office in the American Library Association's New Members Round Table and the California Clearinghouse on Library Instruction (now known as SCIL or the Southern California Instruction Librarians group). Dr. Kaplowitz was also involved with the American Library Association's Committee on Accreditation and served on several ad hoc teams reviewing ALA accreditation for several graduate library programs.

From 2001 to 2003, Dr. Kaplowitz was a member of the UCLA Library's Information Literacy Initiative's steering committee and remained on that body when the Initiative became a full-fledged program. She remained involved until her retirement in 2007.

Dr. Kaplowitz has published and made numerous presentations on various topics such as the psychology of learning and cognitive styles, assessment in information literacy, student-centered learning, and mentoring within the profession. She is the coauthor (with Ms. Grassian) of *Information Literacy Instruction: Theory and Practice.* The first edition of this book, which was published in 2001, received the ACRL Instruction Section's Publication of the Year award. The second edition of this book was published in 2009. They also coauthored *Learning to Lead and Manage Information Literacy Instruction* (2005).

Dr. Kaplowitz and Ms. Grassian wrote the Information Literacy Instruction section for the current edition of the *Encyclopedia of Library and Information Science* (2010). In addition, Dr. Kaplowitz contributed the Psychology of Learning chapter to the 2008 *Information Literacy Handbook* published by the Instruction Section of the Association of College and Research Libraries. Since her retirement Dr. Kaplowitz has been offering single-day workshops in the areas of active learning, assessment, expected learning outcomes, instructional planning, and learner-centered teaching at various university and college campuses in California. Most recently she was invited to teach her information literacy instruction course for the University of Texas's distance program for information studies students in southern California and offered her course to the program's first cohort in spring 2011.

Lightning Source UK Ltd.
Milton Keynes UK
UKOW031059110112

185159UK00002B/2/P